190902018

# **THE**RENEWABLE**CITY**

**Peter Droege**

This guide is dedicated to all who work on a more advanced human habitat – as a means of sustaining human life fairly, and without eroding this fragile earth's natural support basis on which it is founded, but in helping nurture it back from the brink. It is written in admiration of all who are committed to see their dreams fulfilled, and fight to keep their nightmares from becoming reality. It pays homage to all those committed to liberating human civilisation from its fossil fuel drip and to defeating the Sword of Damocles that is nuclear power: to the cities, towns and villages embarked on a path to renewable-energy based autonomy. It is written in honour of my family and friends, for nurturing my determination in seeing this work completed.

# THERENEWABLECITY

## A comprehensive guide to an urban revolution

Peter Droege

**WILEY-ACADEMY**

Published in Great Britain in 2006 by Wiley-Academy a division of John Wiley & Sons Ltd

Copyright © 2006    John Wiley & Sons Ltd, The Atrium, Southern Gate, Chichester, West Sussex PO19 8SQ, England

Telephone   (+44) 1243 779777

Email (for orders and customer service enquiries): cs-books@wiley.co.uk
Visit our Home Page on www.wiley.com

***Other Wiley Editorial Offices***

John Wiley & Sons Inc., 111 River Street, Hoboken, NJ 07030, USA

Jossey-Bass, 989 Market Street, San Francisco, CA 94103-1741, USA

Wiley-VCH Verlag GmbH, Boschstr. 12, D-69469 Weinheim, Germany

John Wiley & Sons Australia Ltd, 42 McDougall Street, Milton, Queensland 4064, Australia

John Wiley & Sons (Asia) Pte Ltd, 2 Clementi Loop #02-01, Jin Xing Distripark, Singapore 129809

John Wiley & Sons Canada Ltd, 5353 Dundas Street West, Suite 400, Etobicoke, Ontario M9B 6H8

Wiley also publishes its books in a variety of electronic formats. Some content that appears in print may not be available in electronic books.

ISBN 978-0-470-01925-2 (HB)   978-0-470-01926-9 (PB)

Cover Photograph © Jacqueline M. Koch/Corbis. Image courtesy of Australian Picture Library & Corbis
Cover design by Artmedia Press Ltd, UK

Typeset in 9.5/13pt Melior by Integra Software Services Pvt. Ltd, Pondicherry, India
Printed and bound by TJ International Ltd, UK
This book is printed on acid-free paper responsibly manufactured from sustainable forestry in which at least two trees are planted for each one used for paper production.

# Contents

# Acknowledgements and Photo Credits

Many friends, colleagues and a number of institutions have stimulated the making of this book in both immediate and indirect ways. I am deeply indebted to them for their support over this past half decade. There is room to mention just a few of these. To be thanked in particular, and in largely alphabetical order, are Lex Bosselaar, at the Dutch national environment agency SenterNovem, The Netherlands, for chairing the International Energy Agency's Solar Heating and Cooling Executive Committee, under whose tutelage the Solar City research development effort was embraced and grew, with Fred Morse, Washington, DC, as insightful advisor; John Byrne of the Center for Energy & Environmental Policy (CEEP) at the University of Delaware, for his infectious and open enthusiasm, on behalf of all Solar Citizens; Helen Castle, Louise Porter, Jenny McCall and Calver Lezama at Wiley-Academy for their enthusiastic encouragement, and for patient and repeated reviews of the manuscript; Mike Eckhart, founding chief executive of the American Council on Renewable Energy (ACORE), and Angelina Galiteva, World Council for Renewable Energy, both United States, for contributing valuable leads and insights; Ichinose Toshiaki of the National Institute for Environmental Studies, Japan, for sharing his personal research and other leads in urban heat island formation; Obayashi Corporation and its Technical Research Institute (TRI) and its gifted young researcher, Akagawa Hiroyuki, who so generously gave of his valuable time to work with me at the University of Sydney; Stephen Karekezi, African Energy Policy Network

(AFREPREN), Kenya, for making available his work in transport innovation; Kim Jongdall of Kyungpook University, South Korea on behalf of all active contributors to the IEA Task 30 Solar City concept development; Marco Keiner at the Institute for Spatial and Landscape Planning (IRL), Swiss Federal Institute of Technology (ETH Zürich) for sharing his work on urban networks of urban sustainability; Irm Pontenagel, the engine of Eurosolar, Germany, for generous backing and encouragement; solar ordinance pioneer Josep Puig, of Ecofys and the Autonomous University of Barcelona, Spain, for sharing his work, that marvellous city's statutory innovations; the University of Sydney as a general setting for creative as well as scientific networking; Anis Radzi, urban designer, Sydney, Australia, for volunteering countless hours in creative and diligent research across most topics in this book; and Hermann Scheer, German parliamentarian and father of the German renewable revolution, president of Eurosolar and general chairman, World Council for Renewable Energy, Germany, whose ideas and leadership have supported my work both directly and by proxy. Essential thanks go to JS Thaddeus, of Universal Renewable Systems, for faithful support and general guidance; Christian van Ees, Technical University Delft and City of Amsterdam, The Netherlands, who has not given up on my getting the message right; and all my friends at the International Solar Energy Society, the World Wind Energy Association and other renewable power organisations.

I would like to extend an especially enthusiastic thank you to the Institute for Global Leadership at Tufts University, Boston and its inspired and enthusiastic director Sherman Teichman, who invited me as Fellow, Institute Scholar and Practitioner in Residence (INSPIRE) for the Education for Public Inquiry and International Citizenship (EPIIC) 2004/5 Oil and Water programme. This gratitude is particularly owed to the Lorenz and Laura Reibling Family Foundation, Boston, for the generous sponsorship of this brief but intensive tenure. Last not least, my gratitude is offered to the indefatigable David Wortmann who as assistant to Hermann Scheer contributed immensely to the World Council for Renewable Energy, Germany and particularly the Solar City notion – and who worked with me selflessly during our residence at the Institute for Global Leadership, Tufts University.

All images are courtesy of the Australian Picture Library & Corbis Cover image © Jacqueline M. Koch; p1 © James Leynse; p13 © Henri Bureau/Sygma; p59 © Smiley N. Pool/Dallas Morning News; p87 © Tibor Bognár; p219 © Paul Almasy; p191 © Hulton-Deutsch Collection; p215 © Ashley Cooper; p253 © Australian Picture Library/Corbis.

## Last of the fossil cities?
Pudong, the futuristic new Shanghai city centre built only a few years ago using a firework of international design input, is already a monument to yesterday's technology. Were it to be planned today, it could follow very different principles: those of Renewable City building — an inescapable mandate for China.

# Introduction

Depending on one's viewpoint, there is very little or a great deal that links ancient Babylon and contemporary Houston. But one aspect these great cities do have in common: they are creatures of their energy regimes. From a city perspective, both ancient city and modern metropolis share with all other human settlements that their form, function and future have been and continue to be a direct result of their energy conditions. Early Athens of the 2nd millennium BC; Babylon the Great – flourishing between the 18th and 6th centuries BC; Çatal Hüyük of 7500 BC – the large Anatolian village site euphorically described by the archaeologist James Mellaart as the world's earliest city (Mellaart 1967) – and all settled communities that have existed during the more than nine millennia since this important Neolithic urban centre was formed, were the result of historically specific technological articulations of regional resource and energy frameworks. They were shaped by methods and tools founded on biomass, animal strength and human power augmented by the forces of the wind and the sun, along with climatic response, social organisation, commercial activity and cultural beliefs. They have been as much outcomes of their respective energy conditions as the rise of the modern suburb with its vehicle-friendly and television-suffused form and culture is a by-product of the global fossil fuel economy that holds sway today. But the principles driving fossil-powered urban form and global urbanisation differ vastly from those that guided cities whose economic and socio-cultural regimes relied on local, non-fossil power. The historical energy environment that gave rise to Babylon the Great has long since been transformed – but may yet rise again one day. The contemporary urban power structure, too, is about to change dramatically.

# ABOUT THIS BOOK

This book is a manual for a revolution in the making. It is a guide to the impending move away from fossil and nuclear power and other forms of unsustainable energy generation, to a renewable and sustainable power base for urban communities, whether cities, towns or villages. This book focuses on the most fundamental form of sustainable urban development: the Renewable City, and shows how it can help solve a vexing modern conundrum. As a historical phenomenon the use of oil, gas and coal is extremely short-lived: a mere blink of an eye at a little over 1 per cent of a total history of urban living of under 10,000 years. Yet today's global urban civilisation is almost entirely based on it. As a result, the fossil fuel economy is fragile: not only does our dependency on it pose a massive security risk and endanger our survival, it also lies at the root of the vast majority of urban sustainability problems. Fresh water depletion, air pollution, widespread human fatalities – all can be directly linked to the excessive use of these dirty energy sources. Climate change, triggered predominantly by fossil fuel combustion, only reinforces the profound questions the impending peak of petroleum production raises about the global urban system's ability to survive. The fossil disease is a complex global pandemic.

To many, conquering this pandemic seems like an extraordinary challenge for technology: there is an urgent need to reengineer the way urban civilisation is powered, advancing a future envisioned in numerous studies since the 1970s. But even the most feasible technological plans have not been realised on a global urban scale because, first and foremost, the disease is culturally, psychologically and politically anchored. The global economy is entirely identified with its underlying fossil fuel supply frameworks – it is fossil in nature. It is driven by a literally incendiary illusion: the celebration of petroleum combustion as the source of an abundance achievable by all, determining virtually every aspect of contemporary culture. But the fossil-fuel society is also blighted by enormous pockets of deprivation, by ever increasing voices raised in disbelief, criticism and dissent. The impending battle to overcome the petroleum malaise must vanquish the entrenched forces resisting change, powers both psychological and economic and which together constitute the sheer might of what is an infernal development system, however short-lived that will inevitably have been.

Despite the lip service paid to 'energy savings' and 'environmentally sustainable development' in urban policy documents and brochures across the globe, dominant political and financial interests demand that as much fossil fuel as possible is used, and as quickly as possible, to secure the highest possible profits for the most powerful, and in the shortest period of time. Which is why so many national governments and international bodies find it so difficult to position fossil-fuel replacement high on the global agenda. It is easier to avoid this topic and talk about buffering – mitigating what are little other than subsidiary, knock-on effects and collateral outcomes of an unsolved energy conundrum: air, water and soil pollution, public health problems, deforestation or fresh water depletion. Rarely, if ever, is pandemic petroleum abuse clearly decried as a root cause.

In the face of global and national collusion in putting off the inevitable, some urban communities and city leaders have found it easier to dissent radically, not only with words but in deeds. For limited periods at a time they can remain relatively sheltered from pressure from the main energy interests – but they, too, risk becoming lost in symbolic or therapeutic agendas, surrogates for real action, thereby even delaying necessary change. For example: while 'using less energy' – the vague staple call of most municipal conservation and efficiency drives – is indeed crucial, 'energy use' in itself is not the ultimate challenge, rather it is the destructive incineration of fossil fuels or the unleashing of nuclear power to produce it. This guide is intended to help overcome this brief and dramatic historical phase – and to show how to build the Renewable City.

The book consists of six chapters, each focusing on a particular theme and each capable of being read independently. The text ranges from a broad introduction to the issues to a set of checklist-type instructions on how to transform a community in preparation for the renewable energy revolution. From the fundamental arguments covered in its first half, in the second the book advances to offer increasingly specific advice and guidance, suggestions and data, ending with provision of detailed frameworks for policy and action.

## RENEWABLE ENERGY

*The Renewable City* is written about and for urban communities – cities, towns, villages, neighbourhoods, citizen groups, people – that pin their hopes for greater autonomy and prosperity on a broad, systematic and targeted application of renewable energy and energy efficiency principles. It is devoted to cities that wish to rely increasingly on renewable energy. But this is not a call for institutional, cultural and political change in the interest of technology substitution alone. Renewable Cities are also cities of 'weather lovers': they are designed to respond to and benefit from the local climate: air movement, sunshine and precipitation; they harvest local water and energy resources while wasting little of either.

All forms of renewable energy are placed within a community context: good building design, soporifically known as 'passive solar'; and water, wave, wind, solar-thermal, photovoltaic, biofuel and heat-pumping power. Some people brazenly refer to all of these as *solar*, since they all are based on the action of the sun, whether through direct radiation, or by creating pressure differentials in the atmosphere to generate wind, or in photosynthesis to create all plants – biomass. But such broad definitions have their problems: petroleum, too, is solar energy but embodied in hydrocarbon compounds. Generally subsumed under 'renewables' are also other, related forms of benign and virtually inexhaustible non-solar power generation. *Lunar power* involves generators harnessing the movements of the tides. *Terrestrial power* is harvested by tapping into geothermal energy, derived from shallow or deep underground reservoirs of heat emanating from the earth's molten core. Definitions of renewable, sustainable, green or alternative energy vary, adding to the confusion. For example, landfill gas and waste incineration are frequently subsumed under renewable or sustainable energy categories. But these are instances of sloppy nomenclature or blatant mislabelling. Neither landfill gas nor waste is a renewable because each depends on the finite supply of resources embodied in such urban *cradle-to-crematorium* material streams; and in encouraging more waste and contributing to environmental pollution, many are not sustainable either.

*Efficiency* is the essential planning and performance base on which any Renewable City agenda is founded, while *energy conservation* is basic to civilised civic manners. This guide gives a number of best-practice directions and models for adaptation or adoption. Conservation is largely about managing demand, preserving assets and reducing waste, while efficiency is a broader concept with existential ramifications. Its pursuit at the level of cities and city regions is measured in reduced travel times and greater proximity between activities: as a function of enlightened land use, transport and other policies and regulations. And from the user's perspective, at building scale, at the product base and material level, it is expressed in industry or government controls, and is manifest in the codes that underpin industry efficiency rating tools. But if the bane of fossil fuels and uranium is to be overcome the challenge lies in going beyond efficiency and conservation measures and embarking on paths to achieving community wide renewable energy autonomy. While this book touches on several key urban efficiency measures, its emphasis is mainly on renewable power generation techniques.

A definition from the United Kingdom is quoted here, to illustrate how government policy documents can usefully define and circumscribe renewable energy:

> *Office of the Deputy Prime Minister, Planning Policy Statement 22: Renewable energy*
> ... covers those energy flows that occur naturally and repeatedly in the environment – from the wind, the movement of the oceans, from the sun and also from biomass ... [and] therefore cover technologies such as onshore wind generation, hydro, photovoltaics, passive solar, biomass and energy crops, energy from waste (but not energy from mass incineration of domestic waste), and landfill and sewage gas. (ODPM 2004, p 3)

## THE FOURTH INDUSTRIAL REVOLUTION

The original, first *Industrial Revolution* was an era of profound socio-technological transformation, and took place in the period roughly between 1760 and 1830 (Ashton 1998). The revolutionary application of coal, metals and other primary resources set human civilisation and its habitat on an exploding, extraordinary path of scientific mechanisation. The advent of the Machine Age saw a great technological landmark, the invention of the steam engine. A great collective bargain was struck for unprecedented prosperity, health, technological change and population growth, traded against irreversible alterations to what was the very basis of civilisation. A set of dominant but only broadly so, rudimentarily tool-and-technology dependent civilisations evolved into a global, heavily machine-augmented way of life, nurtured in the brood chamber of ever-increasing and environmentally corrosive fossil-fuel combustion. The culmination of this historical incineration frenzy is yet to be reached: it forms what is termed here the *Incineration Revolution*, the second great wave of industrialisation. The technological changes of the 18th and 19th centuries essentially evolved linearly in terms of logic – but exponentially in terms of resource consumption, pollution and impact on urbanisation and population growth. These processes were marked by great shifts in both the economy and society's energy base and associated breakthroughs in material, machine and cultural engineering – the guided evolution of society, its language, art, science and beliefs.

The *Information Revolution* was the third great revolutionary transformation of industry, marked by the advent of ubiquitous computing and telecommunications, and by related shifts in philosophy, literature, the visual arts and, more recently, discoveries in genetic science. It has its technical roots in the late 19th century and fully emerged in the years following the Second World War, with the industrial use of electricity, the telegraph, telephone, then radio and television, ultimately boosted by the present and ever-present use of globally networked microcomputers. While accelerating the global exploitation of resources and urbanisation, and cementing a collective fantasy about a universal freedom that lies in friction-free globalisation, it is also to be credited with enhancing the efficiency of some resource use, and enabling a global understanding of the biosphere's rapid deterioration, through real-time mapping, modelling, study, the sharing of insights and the use of globally networked computers in the mobilisation of environmental movements, protests and campaigns. (Droege 1997; passim).

This book is about the Renewable Energy Revolution, a central feature of what I have originally termed the *Inversion Revolution*. In this, the fourth of the great industrial shifts technological change is sought to undo the damage caused by earlier transformations and invert the very logic of the growth they unleashed. It commenced in the early 1970s, with a handful of landmark events. In 1972 the Club of Rome report *The Limits to Growth* was published (Meadows et al 1972), shattering confidence in boundless economic growth. And the controlled implosion of the neglected, crime-ridden Pruitt-Igoe housing project in St Louis, by New York World Trade Center designer Minoru Yamazaki, has, rightly or wrongly, come to serve as the central monument to the official end of the age of faith in technologically and hardware determined forms of urban renewal, and machine-age concepts of urbanism. The Munich Olympics of the same year suffered from the infamy of the attack on the Israeli athletic team and the first globally televised act of urban terrorism, hijacking the delirious athletic festival and its worldwide audience for a ride into the brutal reality of the Palestinian conflict and Western complicity. And 1973 was the year both of the official end of the Vietnam War and the deep crisis of ideological Modernism it represented. It was also the year of the first 'Oil Shock' the world experienced, again involving the Palestinian question. It immediately doubled the price of crude oil, leading to an extreme petroleum shortage in the United States, and helped precipitate the global recession to follow. By exposing the fragility of advanced petroleum based civilisation it inflicted a significant psycho-cultural trauma on Western motorists and industries – if only mildly and temporarily when compared to the long roller coaster of dwindling oil supplies that is about to become reality.

The *Inversion Revolution* marks the very beginning of a move away from fossil-fuel incineration and linear resource use and the cataclysmically mounting waste in which both practices have resulted. Recycling, ecological thinking, efficiency, renewable energy, circular-economy or resource re-use, Greenpeace, the antinuclear movement – all these practical and theoretical approaches to the problem are attempts to slow the great industrial race to the environmental abyss, some of them ideas that have been advanced since the mid-19th century but came to prominence as central features of global public discourse and dissent only in the early 1970s. What I have termed originally the Renewable City concept, too, has a few of its roots here – along with its focus on technological, industrial and cultural innovation. It is about the radical transformation of the first three great industrial revolutions into a fourth stage, also referred to as the period of *envelopment*, in contradistinction to conventional forms of development (Droege 1992). Far from being a futile call for the reversal of evolutionary events and errors in historical development, envelopment is the art of creative 'un-developing', or deliberately targeting and undoing the most debilitating of progress's afflictions, and so achieving greater security and autonomy for cities, towns, villages; for human settlements and urban areas around the world.

Both the art of envelopment and the concepts underpinning Renewable Urbanism are about gaining greater autonomy and distance from the misguided fixation on the modern city as the pinnacle of human achievement, while the great global experiment with fossil-fuel urbanism shows signs of fatigue and failure. Urban renewable energy autonomy is about severing the tentacles of fossil fuel dependency and thereby helping undo the damage urbanisation has wreaked on the global ecosystems: it is about reducing urban footprints. This is no distant, noble goal, but an urgent act of self-preservation. Perhaps the greatest immediate risk – and one only possibly still capable of human control – is that the energy transition from a fossil and nuclear powered economy to a global renewable civilisation cannot be accomplished in time to avert precipitous decline.

A call for greater autonomy in these times of globalisation and increased networking around the globe: does this not smack of anachronism, of neo-Luddite anti-industrialism and of anti-urbanism? From a superficial standpoint, such a call may indeed seem to be somewhat out of step with current ideas of globalised urban life: the free flow of the creative classes and universal trade between cities as hallmarks of the contemporary Promised Land. Yet tangible moves towards energy autonomy are not only in keeping with countervailing responses to globalisation – those of *regionalisation* and *localisation* – they are essential elements in all future-minded urban policy. They are essential because they will help safeguard the most valued features of urban living in times of increasing energy and environmental uncertainty, or, put more precisely: we are in a period of increasing certainty that two pivotal features of 21st-century urban life will be the exhaustion of commercial fossil fuel resources and mounting, calamitous environmental change associated with global warming.

## CITIES AS SETTINGS OF HOPE

At a time when change is both diffuse and slow at national and international policy levels, cities can make a great difference by acting quickly and decisively. Renewable energy independence is the call of the times. Cities, city regions and small villages and rural communities everywhere are beginning the journey towards greater energy autonomy through renewable sources. If pursued without delay this would translate into extraordinary prospects by 2050. But can large metropolitan areas be supported by traditional urban agriculture and advanced solar hydroponics, by pervasive power storage, embedded heat pumps, solar parks or ubiquitous small wind installations? Could Shanghai be operated on a vast portfolio of renewable energy systems? The whole of Dubai be powered by huge solar panels steaming in the desert? Might China and India's galaxies of villages and towns be empowered from within, through autonomous, hybrid renewable infrastructures? Could Bangladeshi rural communities come to rely solely on photovoltaic arrays, produced cheaply in local plants? Is there a real prospect of German Autobahns abuzz with ultra-light, biofuelled vehicles, electronically choreographed and advancing at an intelligent pace? Of South Korean cities, towns and villages freed from reliance on uranium, fossil fuel dependence and household waste incineration? Can cities become networked bundles of ubiquitous renewable energy users and producers? Is a global revolution in city architecture and urban design underway, based on an entirely new energy paradigm, one that is triggering the emergence of a new and hybrid infrastructure of facilities and building components with embedded energy features?

The future is unknowable. But visions can sometimes be projected and with great accuracy and impact, and a sign of great leadership is to predict and seize the inevitable. While projections of possible futures are very much limited by present realities, and a technological switch of this magnitude involves a conceptual shift in how cities are defined, how they are managed and whom they benefit, the principles underlying this transformation are not utopian: they frame a plausible, even necessary future. The actual renewable energy systems and technologies deployed can only be an expression of the overall shift towards an autonomous urban future. Social, environmental and broader public infrastructure innovations and investments in the service of equity and access will continue to form an essential plank of urban policy. New Orleans's tragic destruction and inundation by Hurricane Katrina demonstrated the pressing need for this in 2005. While the national government engaged in military intervention abroad to secure dwindling oil resources, it deflected attention from domestic needs and depleted local resources. In New Orleans, levee maintenance had been neglected. The urban poor and the issues they represent were swept under the carpet of aggressively regressive social policies. Urban transport and evacuation procedures were rendered dysfunctional through lack of interest and disinvestment. The city's extensive wetland buffers were drained in a wrong-headed attempt to control river floods: they continue to disappear at a dizzying speed, exposing yet more communities to what looks to be an increasing incidence of ocean storm surges. Ecological, social and public infrastructure investment failures combined to expose the Unsustainable City, the Fossil Fuel City – not at its worst, but in all its cruel normalcy, its deeply flawed, every-day state.

The construction of a Renewable City – a supportive renewable habitat capable of withstanding mounting environmental crises – transcends the comparatively trivial task of installing renewable energy hardware. Solar deprived slums and energy-poor cities and neighbourhoods are anathema to the aims of renewable energy transformation: they are as incompatible with the principles underpinning its technologies as their application in environmentally unsustainable ways. Seen in this context, and rolling out this vision across the world, urban renewable energy policy is community empowering, and a central building block in the drive for global peace, prosperity and security policy. Depicted here, hence, is not a hollow hardware heaven. The moves now in train will bring about momentous change: the celebration of creativity, a new focus on quality of life and delight in sufficiency and sharing.

## THE PRICE OF INACTION

No period in history has seen such dramatic urban expansion as have the past 50 years, and no future period is likely to see it again soon. Yet this recent era, the source of great pride and much hyperbole, is founded on a dirty secret. For much of the 20th century a great illusion has been disseminated, and a vast collective blind spot nurtured in the discourse about cities, urbanism and urbanity. The great majority of current urban development discussions are not only largely disconnected from the true price paid in environmental and ecological damage, but both deaf to and mute on the manner in which cities are powered – the root cause of the massive urban challenge confronting humankind.

The global price paid for the *urban century* has been enormous; a Faustian bargain has been struck. Salvation in cities was traded for the diabolical spectre of rapid climate change. As documented in this guide, 85 per cent of global commercial energy supply is fossil-fuel derived, and hence the major source of total anthropogenic greenhouse gas emissions (USGS 2005). Among Organisation for Economic Co-operation and Development (OECD) member countries, three-quarters of this staggering level of coal, oil and natural gas consumption are urban based, used for transport and urban management (OECD 1995). And the use of both dirty power sources, fossil fuels and uranium, is still rapidly rising. They are dirty since jointly they heavily contribute to the vast majority of global and local environmental crises. global warming; fresh water depletion; soil, water and air pollution – to name but a few.

Nuclear power especially deserves to be relegated to the science museums, as a curious yet frightening engineering antiquity, the 20th century's great dead-end technology. It has long been decried as hugely expensive in terms of power generation; lethal in its massive production, uranium processing, staggering waste storage requirements and weapons proliferation risks; and enormously wasteful of fresh water along its entire processing and generation chain. Yet, given the demise of oil and natural gas as long-term fuel sources, many governments want to see it reintroduced, even if it means serving only short-term interests. Few appreciate that the global uranium supply is as limited as petroleum with reserves stretching ahead barely two human generations, given current rates of use (Scheer 2002).

The continued and accelerated use of dwindling nuclear and fossil energy sources poses massive and mounting military risks. Renewable energy, by contrast, is in infinite supply, and yet, amazingly, much of urban development discourse remains largely oblivious to it. Given these sobering prospects, and the fact that all necessary technologies have long been within reach, it appears startling that a massive, citywide shift to renewable energy has not yet occurred. Renewable energy – clean wind, water, sun and biofuel based power – is capable of replacing fossil fuels and nuclear power within 50 years: this is demonstrated by the recent speed of introduction of renewable power in Germany where current annual capacity growth has been an astonishing 3,000 megawatts in the years leading up to 2005. But Germany is an exception, and a backlash against renewable power may yet be forthcoming. The last great renewable energy roll-back was staged after the first 'Oil Crisis' of 1973, which consequently remained unheeded as a harbinger of the inevitable petroleum peak. The resulting global interest in renewable energy had so frightened conventional generation, oil and nuclear interests that a concerted effort was made to bury any such initiative in the United States. Indeed, a number of studies have demonstrated the technical potential of renewable energy to replace fossil and nuclear power without any difficulties in sheer capacity terms (Scheer 2005).

The price of inaction is far too high: cities are the most advanced, but also the most risky and fragile constructs ever devised by humankind. Humanity has staked its very civilisation on their smooth and ever-rising performance – and has done so increasingly since the mid-20th century. But this commitment to terrestrial urbanity occurs at a time when the very foundation of urban prosperity and survival is being eroded. The vast majority of global financial transactions, trade, command and control and cultural production today takes place in and among cities: and yet, the twin realities of fossil-fuel supply peaking and climate change make large, globally networked and conventionally powered cities the least secure settings imaginable for essential functions. The urban renewable energy revolution is an essential, inevitable component of a secure and prosperous future.

A historic revolution is in progress: the move is a foot from fossil fuels, nuclear power and other forms of unsustainable energy use generation to a renewable and sustainable power base for urban communities, cities, towns and villages. Many examples of positive initiatives encourage, and are testimony to the ability of cities and towns to perform as purposeful communities, and evolve into settings of greater independence from fossil and nuclear power sources. They carry the promise of greater energy autonomy based on renewable energy, of recapturing regional productivity, mobilising local resources and enabling new industries and employment opportunities.

**Infernal city: postcard from the 20th century**
Iranian oil refineries burn in Abadan. The city and its oil installations were a major target in the Iran-Iraq war of 1980–1988: it was annihilated in Iraqi assaults. All modern cities are fossil-fuel constructs and intimately linked to the mounting, global battle for oil, and all are vulnerable in this infernal dependency, directly and indirectly.

# CHAPTER 1

# In the hothouse, beyond the peak: the logic of the urban energy revolution

## 1.1 ENERGY AND URBAN SUSTAINABILITY IN THE 21ST CENTURY

*The secret of great wealth with no obvious source is some forgotten crime, forgotten because it was done neatly.* Balzac (in Manning 2004)

Our time has been declared the age of the city. Urban centres are heralded as the engines of the global economy. A large library of books and articles hails cities as drivers of national prosperity and home of the leaders in creativity and innovation (Castells 2000; Florida 2002; Friedmann and Wulff 1976; Hall 1977; Hall 1998; Jacobs 1985; Mazza 1988; Sassen 1991, 1994/2000). The city-giddy genre has fuelled a worldwide urban marketing frenzy, while sparing not a thought for the most basic and most tenuous of all present growth drivers: cheap and abundant fossil fuel. Among the best researched and most thoughtful of these culprits is Saskia Sassen's *Cities in a World Economy* (Sassen 1994/2000) which attempts to describe the global economic system without reference to its underlying fossil energy economy: it ignores the very engine that propels the much-admired global financial industry. Examined critically, the financial sector is but the froth on the churning, petroleum-rich global resource consumption and value-adding streams. And while Peter Hall's definitive tome on Western *Cities in Civilisation* (Hall 1998) did describe the electrification of Berlin as contributing to its cultural ascent, it misses altogether the larger nexus of the 20th-century fossil fuel revolution and the rise of contemporary urbanity and urbanism. There are, however, several soberer and specialised studies emerging, on cities, energy and greenhouse gas emissions, that provide an insight into broader urban policy and institutional change, such as a policy evaluation study examining urban energy use and greenhouse gas emissions in Tokyo, Seoul, Beijing and Shanghai, produced at the Japan-based Institute for Global Environment Strategies (IGES) (Dakal 2004).

But in general, dreams about attaining city salvation in the nirvana of comparative advantage – the obssession of many city governments with achieving economic superiority – have distracted urban observers from facing the sobering reality that the urban world thrives on a rich Petri dish of only temporarily plentiful petroleum nutrients. Conceptually, both the modern ideal and its postmodern critique drift blindly on the vast, warm ocean of wasteful abundance that has been engendered by the empowering regime of coal, petroleum, natural gas and uranium combustion during the 20th century. The amplifying force of these new power facilitators helped to accelerate dramatically the exploitation of natural resources, feeding the present dogma of massive and conspicuous consumption as the global religion of progress (Sloterdijk 2005). The energy blind spot of current urban literature is understandable, given that fossil fuels have had an overwhelming role in defining and determining virtually all aspects of contemporary social, technological and cultural reality. Ironically the energy question has been largely ignored within disciplines of infrastructure engineering or economics.

Understandable it may be, but not forgivable given the enormously erroneous conclusions that can be drawn from a partial understanding of the world. A favoured soundbite featured in urban policy conferences holds that close to half the earth's population 'lives in cities' or, more accurately, in areas defined as urban or urbanised in one form or another. This reinforces the truism that virtually all of the present global population increase is registered in urban areas. Yet no migrational phenomenon – the impetus of a rural exodus or the massive pull by the electrified metropolises of the developing world – supports the suggestion that higher cultural destinies or basic evolutionary principles are being fulfilled in the urbanisation phenomenon. No new or eternal age of cities is upon us as a preordained crowning of human civilisation. There is also considerable lack of clarity, to say the least, about the root causes of urbanisation: some argue that it is triggered by changes in global and regional economies; others point to structural adjustment policies eroding the viability of rural productivity and places; and quite a few have taken the compelling statistics as cultural epiphany: they sincerely believe that the world's population is waking up to the fact that universal human progress and destiny lie in cities. Some of these and other factors are certainly at work but these alone could not exert a powerful force for urbanisation without the 20th-century's fossil energy regime having performed as the primary architect and driver of urban evolution.

## Modern cities thrive on petroleum

There would be no modern form of globalisation without global, fossil-fuel charged supply chains, trade routes or military hardware. It can be argued – however moot and meaningless such fascinating speculation might be – that had the Industrial Revolution led to a path of renewable technological innovation, there would be no modern cities, no internet, no global shipping industry, no air traffic, no modern weaponry – certainly not in the form that these are known and understood today. Renewable energy optimists would argue that today civilisation would be far more advanced, could expect superior survival prospects, substantially less pollution and exist on a far smaller ecological footprint within a general realm of ecological equilibrium. Pessimistic fossil apologists would insist that humanity would either be stuck in renewably charged quasi-tribal, proto-democratic territorial skirmishes, or have arrived at a solar doomsday machine by now, given its most powerful nations' well-established appetite for and meticulously honed skills in conquest and destruction. Whatever the type of retrospective futurism in which one wishes to indulge, it is difficult to overstate the significance of *black gold* in defining virtually everything that cities are today: spatially, economically and culturally.

It is also important to remember that the fossil fuel regime creates an enormous drag on global and local prosperity. Trillions of dollars in damages are incurred annually – including social and environmental costs – in warfare, village exploitation, oil spills, soil and groundwater pollution, freshwater depletion, and widespread disease and deaths due to cancer and respiratory ailments triggered by toxic gases and airborne particles. The rising insurance and reinsurance claims arising from climate-change prompted weather events alone are staggering. Storm damage cover in the United States grew sixty-fold between the 1950s and 1990s, to US$ 6 billion annually (Mills 2005). World Bank studies show that China's fossil air pollution is responsible for US$ 50 billion in health costs every year: in the European Union these costs are estimated as US$ 70 billion (Geller 2002). This gargantuan cost of doing business is disregarded in planning the energy systems of new urban areas, industries or infrastructure investments. The promising City of Tomorrow is heavily discounted: its intrinsic value substantially diminished by the enormous price to be paid.

In contrast, the prospect of a pervasive global renewable-energy matrix offers the promise of far greater global prosperity, in two ways. First, the enormous environmental, social and economic costs of the fossil and nuclear energy regimes would be avoided. And second, a massive boost would be provided to technological innovation, employment generation and wealth creation opportunities across the socio-economic spectrum. Large parts of the economy would be liberated from the shackles of an antiquated set of industries, freeing innovation potential from the heavy restrictions of the fossil/nuclear power generation and distribution oligopolies. Contemporary cities are caught in the conventional fuel trap, and are therefore best labelled *fossil cities*, while both idea and reality of the Renewable City are firmly focused on shedding the fossil and nuclear shackles, as quickly as possible.

The Fossil City has reached its apex. The simultaneous concentration and expansion of cities since the mid-20th century were realised through massive investment in centralised infrastructure, and especially in power systems, within a heavily subsidised and hence seemingly cheap fossil fuel economy, now at its peak. As a result, the cities in the 30 members states of the elite Organisation for Economic Co-operation and Development (OECD) consume between 60 and 80 per cent of their respective national energy production, including transport within and among urban areas (OECD 1995). This highlights modern cities' powerful role in worldwide, manmade greenhouse gas emissions: in 1998 fossil fuels, the main source of anthropogenic $CO_2$-equivalent emissions, made up a staggering 85.8 per cent of total global commercial energy consumption: 40 per cent from oil; 23.3 per cent from coal and 22.5 per cent from natural gas. Nuclear power plants supplied 6.5 per cent; and 7 per cent were derived from the renewable hydroelectric facilities. A mere 0.7 per cent was captured from biomass, geothermal, solar and wind sources combined (USGS 2005). And since the fossil peak has not quite been reached yet, the zombielike abuse of fossil fuels continues to mount at a rapid rate – along with that of nuclear power – their consumption presently still growing faster than that of all renewable energy systems combined. Between 1990 and 2002 global fossil energy use – of coal, gas and oil – expanded by 44 per cent, while the total renewable-energy share has increased by only 33 per cent (Scheer 2005).

Since the early 1980s, about three-quarters of human-generated or anthropogenic greenhouse gas emissions were attributable to fossil fuel use (EIA 2006). In the wealthier countries fossil fuels are the dominant source by far, and in the developing world land clearing and other forms of deforestation are more significant, but with fossil fuel use on the rise here also (Nakicenovij and Svart 2001). And the carbon-friendly International Energy Agency projects a further 60 per cent increase in world energy demand by 2030, with a steady 85 per cent of this hike attributed to rising oil, gas and coal demand (IEA 2004).

But as fossil fuel use and emissions rise, awareness increases enormously, too – as it has over the past 30 years. As global demand surges to another record high without any prospect of abatement in sight, the nerves of many urban leaders are getting frayed. Significant security, supply and sustainability shortcomings have surfaced. A race to press renewable sources into service has commenced, although the collective public policy consciousness has for the most part still to join it. The looming threat of global environmental collapse, precipitated by greenhouse-emission induced climate change and paired with the inevitable plateauing of global fossil fuel production, have unmasked as pretty pipe dreams the infinite-growth ideologies that swept the late 19th and 20th centuries. Yet despite having been intellectually discredited, these nostalgic doctrines still linger on, out of sheer inertia and popular need for collective comfort blankets. As a consequence, global warming trends continue, unrestrained by the woefully inadequate Kyoto-based carbon management efforts.

## Kyoto: neither far enough nor fast enough

The combined reduction target for $CO_2$ emissions for all Kyoto-subscribing nations was set at a modest 5 per cent below their collective 1990 levels, to be met between the years 2008 and 2012. Yet emissions have increased substantially since this target has been agreed to, while the reductions needed to halt climate change at current risks levels are generally and consistently seen to be closer to 60 per cent, to be reached by 2050 (Byrne et al 2002; IPCC 1996). Given that the United States, responsible for 25 per cent of the world's fossil-fuel consumption, is not a Kyoto subscriber, and China, India and other significant emitters in the developing world are exempt from its provisions, the Kyoto process is unlikely to achieve any reduction at all, let alone one approximating the level required to halt climate change. The terms of the various carbon trading schemes in circulation are not aimed at total overall reductions and, paradoxically, can even work to subvert these (Byrne and Glover 2000). The most recent Conference of the Parties to the United Nations Framework Convention on Climate Change (COP 11), held in Montreal from 28 November to 9 December 2005, has not changed this tragic picture. It has merely highlighted the limitations of an increasingly symbolic process, presenting it as little more than a surrogate for action.

While some argue that a Kyoto-style agreement is not needed since the realities of oil and gas depletion would anyway reduce emissions (supplies are predicted to peak and begin to decline globally in 2010 (Campbell 2005), IPCC (Intergovernmental Panel on Climate Change) experts convincingly predicted that some if not many nations could move to coal and carbon-intensive nuclear energy in their desperation to compensate for the shortfall, maintaining a politically shackled and ideologically blind stance vis à vis renewable power (Coghlan 2003). The general discourse still skirts around the inevitable conclusion, studiously avoided by most decision-makers, that a massive and global turn to renewable sources is both vital and overdue. Fossil peaking and depletion realities are widely accepted even among conservative industry research institutions and have entered the wider discussion. Coal is also widely understood as an evolutionary error even in its 'advanced' state, and carbon sequestration is too limited and distant a prospect to feature seriously. Yet not enough information on the great shortcomings of uranium has been offered to the general public. The generation of electricity through nuclear fission is both significantly greenhouse-gas emitting and faces a firm depletion horizon, besides being fraught with massive and very long-term health and proliferation dangers. Because even 'high-grade' uranium contains only 0.2 per cent uranium oxide it is exceptionally energy-intensive to mine and process: it takes up to a decade for a power station to compensate for the energy embodied in its refined fuel and plant. At current use levels, high-grade uranium ore will have been depleted by 2025. And for low-grade uranium the entire nuclear-fuel cycle generates more greenhouse gas than a natural gas-fired power station (Green 2005).

While Kyoto and the ensuing carbon trading schemes attract much attention yet deliver little action, the rapid changes in the earth's climate cause increasing and irreversible damage to the terrestrial ecosystem. While ever larger environmental conferences are held with decreasingly tangible results, cities' risk-management costs rise dramatically, in social, economic and physical terms. The local consequences of climate change have begun to challenge municipal planning and governance arrangements, and bring their very viability into question. And if the present, free-wheeling global course of mounting energy demand is maintained, the inevitable decrease in oil and gas production levels will wreak havoc on the global, highly urbanised economy, cause steep price rises and destabilise cities, the world's central and insatiable nodes of fossil fuel consumption.

An urban-focused revolution of distributed renewable power systems is the only option to avert a spectacular urban and wider economic cataclysm. To rational minds this change is inevitable – and yet no serious, concerted action centred on the energy transformation of human settlements, and cities in general, can be detected as even under discussion. The current rate of 'normal economic' change – change induced by shifts in market forces and individual actions – is far too slow to avert serious crises. Despite several examples of exceptional local leadership such as that exhibited by Chicago's five-term, 'green' mayor Richard M Daley, general urban energy policy, like all complex institutional challenges, remains an amalgam of entrenched interests, institutional inertia and narrow technical expediencies. Powerful fossil fuel and nuclear industry interests fight a desperate battle for increasing market share despite shrinking resources. Their struggle will grow more desperate as it becomes clear to even the most loyal or stubborn customer that both sets of technologies are hopelessly outdated, offer no longterm prospects, and in the short term only represent a continued and accelerated dash into a technological dead-end. A worldwide backlash against renewable energy, like the one experienced after a short-lived boom of energy sanity in the 1970s, is a significant threat today. Even as I write, worldwide fossil fuel and nuclear industry interests position themselves for a renewed battle for the hearts, minds, policies and wallets of governments around the world, lured by booming prospects of profit.

## Fossil and nuclear industries: fighting to maintain their grip

Despite or because of the sobering prospects for the nuclear and fossil industries in the long term, significant rollback campaigns targeting renewable energy successes are underway. In the very year in which the global Renewables 04 congress was held in Bonn, Germany, two other, darkly ominous events dimmed the hopeful horizons of progress. In Moscow the International Atomic Energy Agency (IAEA) held court, international steward of the nuclear power lobby. Its representatives cheerfully predicted a 400 per cent increase in the number of nuclear power plants worldwide by 2050, in a conference run under the slogan '50 Years of Nuclear Power – and the Next 50 Years'. And at its Sydney congress the staunchly pro-nuclear and pro-carbon World Energy Council (WEC) disseminated its industrial message, declaring that fossil fuel use 'will increase' another

85 per cent of current levels by 2050, while nuclear power is hoped to become more important than renewable energy, seen as providing only 10 per cent of world commercial energy supplies – indeed, a level below its present contribution (Scheer 2005).

The worldwide nuclear lobby has already established its favourite candidate as global waste dump, setting its sights on remote Australia. Bob Hawke, one of the country's former prime ministers, publicly volunteered his nation for this role, as lucrative as it this would be lunatic (Reuters 2005). And as a forum at which to festively proclaim the nation also as major uranium exporter – more than 40 per cent of the world's uranium reserves are found here – the six-nation Asia Pacific Partnership on Clean Development and Climate was convened in Sydney, early in January 2006. It brands itself as a 'beyond Kyoto' alternative to Kyoto, seeking 'technological solutions' to the unfolding climate change disaster. The partnership involves the countries culpable for nearly half of the world's greenhouse emissions: Australia, China, India, Japan, South Korea and the United States. Instead of government commitments to change it prefers to promote 'industry solutions' such as uranium mining and nuclear power proliferation, and the continued use of coal and other fossil fuels under the mantle of a search for carbon sequestration methods: the expensive and unproven notion of pumping carbon dioxide 'back' into the ground (Peatling 2006; Peatling and Frew 2006).

The first infamous backlash against renewable energy demolished the vision of a *solar America* in the wake of the so-called OPEC Oil Crisis of the 1970s. This concerted rollback effort was commenced under President Carter and completed under Ronald Reagan. It sealed the fate of the nation as a *Fossil America* for another generation – wasting 30 years of potential progress (Scheer 2005, pp 17–20) also in other countries, given the United States' leadership role. This tactical delay in reducing fossil dependency in the world's premier pollution producing economy cost countless lives, lost to cancer, respiratory disease and other health damage; pollution incidents and spills; oil wars; and other past, present and future fatalities brought about by the aggregate effects of potentially irreversible climate change. These past omissions could be easily avoided in the future. For example: were readily available greenhouse gas emission reductions techniques adopted in four large cities alone – Santiago, Mexico City, São Paolo and New York – the associated reductions in ozone and particulate air pollution by only 10 per cent would, over the next two decades alone, prevent 64,000 premature deaths and 65,000 cases of chronic bronchitis, and save 34 million person-days in lost work or activity (Cifuentes et al 2001). But even in the face of many of such extensive and well-documented benefits, backlash campaigns against renewable energy use run today again with impunity, within the European Union, the United States, Australia and numerous countries of the developing world. Despite the glaring evidence, Orwellian endeavours to 'bury' scientific information about climate change are reaching new heights, such as the 2006 attempts at censoring statements and public appearances by veteran climate scientist and director of NASA's Goddard Institute for Space Studies, James E Hansen (Revkin 2006). Resistance to inevitable change will mount, as dusk descends, as it must, on the fossil fuel and nuclear power age.

## The global urban explosion: the end?

For more than three decades, urban growth management, growth boundaries, *smart growth* and other means of limiting peri-urban sprawl have been intensively explored not only in many urban centres of the developed world, but also in cities of so-called developing and less developed countries. Numerous conferences have been devoted to managing the explosive, seemingly uncontrollable force of rapid urbanisation and mega-city formation, particularly in countries of the South. A plethora of linear or local trend projections reigns. However, discussions about impending energy scenarios as likely drivers of urban growth do not generally feature in the literature, conferences, policy bodies or universities. The rampant expansion of cities from Beijing to Bogotá – particularly dramatic over the past 20 years – is registered with amazement, and even a sense of jittery pride, as if globalisation, economic strength, market liberalisation and so-called development – in China often defined by narrow and old-fashioned Gross Domestic Product (GDP) accounting applied to even the tiniest local government area – were indeed the sole, or even the prime movers behind this change. The synchronous bulging of cities has been graphically documented in the spectacularly colourful, coffee-table sized atlas of satellite images *One Planet Many People – Atlas of Our Changing Environment*. The book was launched by the United Nations Environment Programme on World Environment Day 2005 – hosted by San Francisco under the inspiring motto 'Green Cities – Plan for the Planet!'

With this singular urban focus, regional and rural development needs and longterm resource self-sufficiency and food security concerns are easily ignored. Ideas about local autonomy and calls for greater levels of safety and sustainability get swiftly swept aside in this dangerously myopic discourse, which harks back to the type of perceptions epitomised in the seminal *Urban World/Global City* (Clark 1996). Such perceptions were prevalent in the 1980s and 1990s when seeing 'the world as an urban place' and 'urbanisation as a global phenomenon' became *de rigueur* among geographers, sociologists, avant-garde designers and city marketeers alike. As a legacy of this era, many still see it as axiomatic that urbanisation will continue unchanged at the precipitous rates known since London's explosion in the 18th and especially the 19th centuries: from 1800 to 1900 the British capital's population expanded nearly seven-fold. But this is not a terribly plausible scenario for the 21st century. Some evidence of a certain degree of energy price insensitivity among consumers at relatively low energy prices aside (IEE 2005, p 6), major structural shifts such as Peak Oil and rising carbon pressure on fossil fuel production costs are bound to put a dampener on urbanisation rates, encourage more autonomous urban – regional constructs and boost the rise of rural self-sufficiency models.

Urbanisation is the process of transforming regions and nations from an agrarian or rural land use and settlement model into a city-based community and its associated cultural forms. This process takes place in economic, geographic, demographic and social dimensions and is focused on manufacturing, cultural production, trade, administration and other services, typically resulting in dense and contiguous patterns of settlement and infrastructure. A highly energy-intensive process, continuous urbanisation requires a permanently increasing resource stream, energy supply chains and economic mechanisms that support both the new urban expansion processes but also maintain existing urban areas – and these represent extraordinarily energy intensive processes themselves. On a global scale, rapid urbanisation and mega-city formation directly flow from and in turn reinforce the conventional energy, primarily fossil-fuel use explosion: both growth dynamics are causally linked. But it is inconceivable to expect exponential or even linear urban growth without an implausible, even fantastic rise in productivity and sheer effort to be delivered by the kind of industrial machinery and relatively cheap supply of combustible liquids and gases that were so readily available during the 20th century.

Will urban growth continue unabated? The people at the United Nations Population Division of the Department of Economic and Social Affairs (UNDESA) still seem to think so. In a recent report the organisation has determined that in 2007 the number of urban dwellers will equal rural population 'for the first time in . . . history', projecting that virtually all population growth over the next three decades will take place in urban areas (UNDESA 2002). But UNDESA does not ask whether growth *can* in fact continue unabated. If it did investigate this question, it would come to the conclusion that the early 21st century is not the best period in history to engage in long-range linear projections of any kind, let alone those involving highly energy-sensitive phenomena such as major metropolitan growth dynamics and global urbanisation rates. As the world's dominant economies rapidly reach the end of the fossil era, the logic of global urban growth is likely to change as significantly as it did with the dawn of the fossil era, albeit in the opposite direction.

Historically speaking, the post-fossil fuel era has already dawned, and it is reasonable to assume that it will be accompanied by a broad and significant decline in urbanisation growth rates, and ultimately their reversal. Renewable urban development relies on internal, embedded and regionally sustained energy streams, while fossil urbanisation depends on external sources and globally secured flows. In a science-fiction sense it is conceivable to envision an autonomous and internally, renewably powered urbanisation process, like the 'grey goo' nightmare of self-replicating 'nanobots' that was the stuff of techno-fears from the 1980s through to the early 2000s (Drexler 1986; Freitas 2001). But fortunately, in part due to the necessarily limited technological and spatial capacity of internally sustained energy sources and in part to a reinforcement of non-urban sectors of the economy, the Renewable City is more likely to exist in a steady state, approaching the levelled growth curve of global development scenarios that underlie the most optimistic and hopeful visions available today – like a well-balanced ecology of ecosystems (Meadows et al 2004).

## Cities are seeds of change

Communities in cities and towns around the world recognise that large-scale efficiency and energy conservation programmes and the introduction of revolutionary renewable energy generation technologies tangibly help to pursue beautiful visions of the future as an alternative to the nightmarish paradox of global doom by development. But in the eyes of these champions of change they also offer highly practical and immediate paths to cost savings, energy security and new economic development impulses through industrial and business innovation. Communities in cities such as Adelaide, Barcelona, Chicago, Curitiba, Freiburg, London or Munich understand that the transformation of transit systems, urban form, human settlement patterns and land management practices presents another side of the renewable city building challenge. Renewable hardware and combustibles – stationary and transport power systems and fuels – represent only a fraction of the urban reengineering challenge. A new paradigm emerges from the smog of 'fossilist' urban discourse, revealing an exhilaratingly refreshing conceptual yet practical framework. It spans all aspects of the urban renewable energy revolution, delineating the cultural and economic shift to local and regional autonomy and sufficiency, manifest in the more sober, drier domains of land use and transport efficiency, finance, regulation, demand management and distributed renewable energy generation technology.

Human settlements emerge as the most visible and tangible staging ground for this global revolution. Here renewable energy technology and other carbon emissions reduction programmes are being introduced most visibly, and at an increasing, ultimately global scale. Sizeable organisational and cultural barriers are waiting to be overcome. Challenges abound and setbacks lie ahead, in planning, legislation, pricing, network architecture and access issues, let alone from the established politics of power and primary resource interests. These last have frustrated the change that has been technically feasible for more than a generation. As a consequence, progress today is still small-scale and piecemeal when compared to the impact of corporate fossil fuel and nuclear power leviathans in their stranglehold on the supply of homes, workplaces and communities.

In light of such odds the growing initiatives to reinvent fossil urban areas as renewable cities deserve to be celebrated. They are great sources of inspiration and insight. Important changes are taking place in towns and regions, large and small, more and less developed, spanning the world from Amsterdam to Cape Town. Communal efforts are reinforced in a web of supporting measures at other levels as well: action groups, industry alliances and individuals push from within these communities. State, provincial and regional policy and legislation programmes are being deployed, such as recent and powerful legislative initiatives by the State of Washington in the United States (Broehl 2005a). National and geo-regional efforts provide further support, such as the German *Energieeinspeisegesetz* (EEG), the energy feed-in law supporting building-integrated photovoltaic systems, wind and other renewable energy production, by requiring that large energy utilities purchase this power at set prices (RE 2006).

International bodies handling humanitarian and development issues – the World Bank, the United Nations Development Programme, the United Nations Environment Programme, disaster relief organisations – are also beginning to embrace renewable settlement policies, however slowly. They face the traditional energy blindness of contemporary town planning practice, ultra-short or nonexistent planning horizons, established supply lines, limited know-how and the influence peddling that is endemic to the global development and aid industry. The major urban policy challenges of the 21st century are situated between the global nature of greenhouse gas effects and fuel depletion dynamics on the one hand, and the local reality that represents both original source and final impact of such global changes on the other. At a local level their resolution is made more challenging by the established energy-blind institutional culture, the technical complexities of emissions accounting techniques and the vagaries of municipal policy development and planning.

Yet here, at the local level, the risks posed by continued inaction are enormous. The nature of contemporary forms of investment in new buildings and infrastructure guarantees their premature obsolescence. Urban developments, infrastructure systems, individual buildings and other facilities based on fossil-fuel construction, maintenance and operation risk being rendered dysfunctional well before the end of their natural life. The very notion of a modern 'end of life cycle' as designated by demolition and disposal, so central to fossil practice, is called into question. Today's connective urban hardware – roads, rail, air and seaports, and telecommunications – is nurtured and maintained in an environment of near-total fossil-fuel reliance. And the city-centred internet relies on conventionally powered processing, routing and transmission systems, too. For electronic communications to be reliably sustained they will have to be supported by autonomous, ubiquitous and networked renewable energy sources. Yet both the technology and implementation tools exist – indeed have long been waiting to be advanced, adapted and applied (Droege 2004).

## Cities at risk

Resistance to change is enormous. The sheer weight and momentum of established investments, institutions and interests, power centres and management cultures constitute one massive and inert force. And denial vanquishes fear. It is safer to subscribe to a warmly glowing illusion of urban permanence than to coldly contemplate the prospect of cities reeling under an energy-induced existential threat; and that to one's own home town in particular. Calling the city's energy stability into question is hardly conducive to strengthening the local sense of comparative superiority that many have fought hard to achieve. The word 'city' itself has a calming effect; it exudes a sense of safety and stability. An entity that can be named with such certainty must exist in perpetuity. Popular urban history reinforces this illusion of certainty and permanence – Tokyo, London, New York, Rome, Athens: do not these cities attest to permanence in the face of change? Much is made of the resilience of cities in the wake of disaster: Tokyo's rise after the 1928 earthquake and the 1944 fire-bombing for example, or the reconstruction of war-devastated Dresden and

Warsaw (Lynch 1981; Popham 1985). Yet permanently perished cities are rather common: Angkor, Babylon and Carthage head the list of a legion of early and recent cities – and untold numbers of villages and townships – that have dramatically declined or vanished forever in the wake of technological, economic and environmental change.

The tragic and possibly permanently damaging destruction of New Orleans and other Gulf of Mexico communities by Hurricane Katrina in early September 2005 has triggered a global wave of disbelief. Few considered that such an instantaneous collapse of a modern urban system was possible, forever unravelling its social fabric. And fewer fathomed the pathetic enormity of a situation in which the poor, the elderly, the sick and even the tourists were abandoned to their fate without warning, support or timely rescue. Urban leaders around the world shuddered, realising how ephemeral the collective construct of the city is. And while the future of any city is fragile, the age of human-driven climate change represents the first time in history that the fate of the urban system may be in doubt: the vast majority of major settlement centres have become dependent on a single set of expiring infrastructure systems: fossil fuels. Urban resilience in the wake of wars and disasters is well documented, but permanence is the exception when cities' overall support structures deteriorate. Not one city, or even the urban culture of one particular nation, but the very future of the entire advanced urban system of modern civilisation is at risk.

## 1.2 FOSSIL AND NUCLEAR ENERGY SYSTEMS AND THE INDUSTRIAL CONSTRUCTION OF REALITY

> '. . . the city is the result of war, at least of preparation for war' (Virilio and Lotringer 1997)

Virilio's view of urban genesis and evolution was shared by Lewis Mumford, expressed in the latter's theories about early cities as phenomena and instruments of war (Mumford 1961). To both, commerce has only come second in spawning sedentary settlement. By the Industrial Revolution the role of cities as seats of government and their organisational affinity to military regimentation also led them to perform well as wider command and control centres, exerting local and global reach under sometimes rapidly changing regimes and political systems. And capital and other important cities continued to serve as centres of national hegemony and war preparations. Identified in this manner, they can serve as both symbolic and militarily significant bombing and terrorist targets, whether Berlin, London, Moscow, Paris, Tokyo or Washington. At the same time, a self-perpetuating and aggressive process began to take root: urbanisation as a momentous, technologically driven social and economic force, fed by cheap fossil fuel supplies. Urbanisation itself had become an industrial process as well as a socio-cultural and economic feature of the industrialisation age. A cultural argument can be advanced that detects in its logic the seeds – or genes – of war. Urbanisation is an aggressive, expansionist process, and urban populations are traditionally susceptible to collective biases and calls to arms, justified or not. And civil urbanity, civic life and urbanisation are linked to global warfare through the medium of petroleum – the main driver of numerous armed conflicts around the world.

Global urbanism – the dominant way of life in cities and towns as increasingly shared throughout the world – has also emerged as an international vehicle for the aggressive promotion of consumption, a path for the multinational corporate warrior, a road to progress for progress's sake, and an end in itself. Marketed as a desirable lifestyle product the concept city grew increasingly removed from other interests and aims, whether communal, spiritual or mercantile. As cultural ideal it had become disseminated and implanted globally, through the fossil powered media of advertising and political propaganda, and sometimes under the guise of national interests and liberation. The instantaneously televised, terrorist destruction of New York's World Trade Center helped trigger the equally spectacular and murderous acts of collective revenge exacted on countless Afghan towns and villages, and the 'shock and awe' style demolition of Baghdad, meted out in a sad and surrogate act of carefully misdirected retribution. Such acts of urban mayhem seem aimed less at routing specific perpetrators of heinous crimes than at destroying the visible, cultural heart of the disobedient – sideshows in the grand narrative of the struggle for oil. Fossil urbanism – the city today – is a form of mass communication, a worldwide advertising medium and, as such, subject to manipulation and abuse in the battle for conventional power dominance.


## Expiring mindsets

The mid-20th-century frame of mind is alive but no longer well. It expresses the industrial realities of the 18th and 19th centuries. It still colours the dominant systems of values and ideas about urban development today. The heroic rise of the steam engine and electricity as fed by coal power, and the spread of oil and advanced petrochemical products, as well as foodstuffs and pharmaceuticals, went hand in hand with the mystical belief in a preordained evolution from solar to fossil to nuclear energy sources as the divine vector of innovation. They also bolstered the unshakeable credo of progress in infinite, continuous, linear growth still adhered to by so many. While these ideas are now generally regarded as historical or discredited as untenable scientifically, spiritually and in terms of common sense, they continue to loom large in the dominant yet archaic power structures and planning chambers of urban infrastructure, energy supply, extractive industries and primary resources, military strategy and global trade. Although most societies like to portray themselves as complex, diverse and open to the free flow of ideas and information, many of their institutions, laws, notions of progress and communal beliefs have been erected on this dominant technological foundation, making a departure from its basic tenets rather challenging. The rule of coal, oil, gas and their darker sibling, uranium, is categorical. The fossil-nuclear fuel regime, and the powerful up- and down-stream interests it represents, also projected its credo through the dawn of the digital age, the information revolution.

But this assessment is perhaps a little too gloomy. Signs of hope-inspiring change abound, manifesting a fourth phase of industrial change: the *Inver sion Revolution* of values, heralding the inevitable turning away from linear resource consumption and fossil fuel incineration. Urban communities provide the most graphic examples of this change: renewable-energy pioneering cities from Barcelona – famous for its Solar Ordinance – to Sacramento, widely admired for replacing nuclear with solar power. Even new corporate initiatives responding to a shift in the mass consumer mindset should be seen as hopeful even if some of these may be shrewdly opportunistic. As an example, retail behemoth Wal-Mart, the world's largest company – 'larger than ExxonMobile, General Motors or General Electric' (FC 2005) – has styled a new Texan big-box retail outlet into a low-carbon shopping machine. It sports a range of advanced renewable energy and efficiency features, ironically in the service of efficiently satisfying fossil-age consumption cravings (Broehl 2005b). But even if many of today's sustainability programmes and features seem little more than lip service paid to assuage public concern or head off the threat of regulatory pressures, they should nevertheless be seen as a positive sign of change, even if in the short term some of these may serve to slow, not hasten progress.

The current era of empty words, green labelling, feigned commitments, postponed action and piecemeal response is bound to reach an end. Even the most conventional retail giant can have no interest in riding the fossil wave until it crashes. Worldwide, new public and private capital investment programmes are being established to help assemble a renewable energy-based economy. The fiscal case for this is increasingly compelling as previously externalised costs are beginning to be accounted for on some national and corporate ledgers. On a practical level the fossil leash is regarded as a massive liability: centralised power systems are unreliable and quickly become a risk factor in uncertain times. The great recent natural disasters – the Indian Ocean tsunami, or the hurricane destruction of New Orleans, both in 2005 – saw social resilience and survival rates lowered by a systemic fossil fuel dependency leading to failing centralised power and water systems. Rescue, relief and subsistence efforts may well have been more effective had distributed, redundant renewable systems been supporting the urban infrastructure, delivering power for medical personnel, to distil drinking water and maintain energy for communications. On a global scale, the same logic applies. The overwhelming dependence of entire cities, regions and national conurbations on central supply systems makes these vulnerable to network decay, overload, sabotage, incidental plant failure and primary resource scarcities and wild price fluctuations in distant, volatile and increasingly embattled markets.

## Expiring oil, natural gas and uranium supplies

The inexorable – and imminent – peaking and subsequent decline of world oil production is well documented and widely accepted as fact. It was first described half a century ago by geophysicist M King Hubbert in a paper designed to propose nuclear energy as the ultimate energy source for the United States (Hubbert 1956, Figures 29 and 30). While his predictions in respect of uranium use proved fundamentally flawed – Hubbert envisioned a nuclear heaven for at least the next 5,000 years, conveniently making up for failing petroleum fields – he projected the great Oil Peak with uncanny precision for the year 2000. Geologist Colin J Campbell of the Association for the Study of Peak Oil and Gas and others have since adjusted this date, if only marginally, to 2010 (1995, 1998, 2003, 2004, Campbell 2005; see also Deffeyes 2003; Goodstein 2004; Heinberg 2003; Klare 2002; Roberts 2004; Smil 2003). The actual, nominal year of the global supply peak is less significant than the underlying reality that maximum production capacity for the most readily usable of toxic fuel sources – oil and natural gas, but also uranium – will soon be reached, given finite reserves, and decline as demand continues to rise, creating an increasing worldwide supply gap.

Of oil-producing countries not belonging to the former Soviet Union (FSU) or the Organisation of Petroleum Exporting Countries (OPEC), 70 per cent are well past their respective supply peaks, including the United States, Canada, China and Oman (Aleklett 2004) as well as the whole of Europe, with Southeast Asia's twin oil and gas peaks following close behind. This global reality is already transforming industrial and community mindsets. To avoid military and economic cataclysms oil should immediately be treated as a precious and endangered resource, and largely replaced as the primary energy commodity by 2050. Coal resources, too, should be phased out as too costly in carbon load. Finally, a global moratorium on new nuclear power plants should be declared, given the risks of catastrophic accidents, the unsolved storage problem and the spectre of weapons proliferation.

Petroleum, natural gas and coal price rises will be the natural consequence of this peak, exacerbated by development booms celebrated in China and India. Significant security threats have already resulted. Four facts underpin this historical phenomenon: (a) most estimates of the world's oil reserves lie at around 2 trillion barrels, a figure that has not changed since the 1960s; (b) discoveries of new oil fields have been steadily declining globally as well as regionally since the 1970s; (c) worst, mean and best case scenarios describe the global peak as occurring sometime between 2000 and 2015; and (d) the vast majority of oil reserves lie in the Middle East (64.5 per cent in 2003), with only 4.8 per cent in Western Europe and North America combined (1998, 2003, Campbell 2004; Campbell and Laherrere 1995; Goodstein 2004; Meadows et al 1972, 2004; Scheer 2002). This means that the leading users of oil rely on a geographically concentrated, highly contested resource. Among their number is the rapidly growing nation of China, the world's largest consumer of coal and second largest importer of oil after the United States.

High-grade, lower-cost uranium ores are estimated to reach depletion levels by 2050 at current levels of consumption, and not taking into account the rapid expansion of nuclear power currently being embarked on (Green 2005). Early depletion would seem to be a godsend, given the massive cost, security, safety, disposal and public acceptance dilemmas that already weigh so profoundly against their use. Yet, despite the risks, and a waning willingness among enlightened governments to pursue nuclear fission further, nuclear energy use rates are on the rise, and not only in developing countries. This carries the risk that low-grade, high-cost ore will eventually be relied on, in a desperate attempt to stretch a fatal resource. Nuclear fusion, more than half a century after its arrival as a great modern dream, continues to struggle with enormous conceptual and technical flaws, and huge financial, environmental and political costs.

The prospects for a breakthrough in the struggle to yield net energy, let alone to do so in a commercially viable and socially acceptable manner, lie as far beyond reach as ever. Yet the mythical search still carries great prestige, as the grand expenditure lavished on European fission research demonstrates. Beyond the glory of multi-billion dollar programmes, widespread public resistance to a new generation of nuclear super-reactors is looming. Still, enormous research and development funds continue to be poured into this futile and wasteful dream, for the past decades conclusively demonstrating only that the establishment and maintenance of fusion plasma indeed require significantly more energy input than it produces. Without specific consent, precious personal tax contributions are being diverted from urgent programmes in tangibly functional and abundant renewable energy, healthcare and education, to be sacrificed on an altar of illusory hopes, in a gargantuan magic ritual.

Securing global oil and other vital resources flows by military means and forms another mounting fiscal burden – not counting the enormous human cost involved. While it is difficult to gauge what portion of United States defence outlays is dedicated to such purposes, they undoubtedly form a significant driver, with over half of today's global conflicts energy-resource related. The official US military budget – without the Afghanistan and Iraq War campaigns – was US$ 399 billion in 2004, at 51 per cent of the national United States budget more than all other governmental expenditures combined (education accounted for US$ 6.4 billion and transport for US$ 1.6 billion). No detailed or comprehensive figures on the financial cost of the oil- and gas-supply targeted Iraq War have been released by the US government, but one projection contrasts an estimated annual cost of *US$ 100 billion* for the Iraq War alone with the following comparative price tags for missing and badly needed services, both in the US and elsewhere: children's educational funding gap, US$ 6 billion; emergency financial aid to states, US$ 9 billion; fighting AIDS worldwide, US$ 11 billion; world safe water and sanitation programmes, US$ 19 billion; and the strengthening of US Social Security, US$ 70 billion (Hartung 2005).

## Age of the fossil fuel city

*Chandigarh is rightly associated with the name of Goddess Chandi – Shakti, or power.* Jawaharlal Nehru, India's first Prime Minister, 4 April 1952 (Chandigarh, 2006)

*. . . a befitting capital, where the mind is without fear and the head is
held high.* K.R Narayanan, President of India, about Chandigarh, 1999

*The sun rises forever in this city that opens itself to tomorrow .*
Juscelino Kubitschek, President of Brasil, about Brasilia, 1984

A critical glance at the history of modern cities reveals the breathtaking
panorama of a grand, delirious detour into a fossil fuel cul-de-sac – an historical
error on an epic scale. Modern cities flourished economically and physically on
fossil-fuel nutrients. They soon evolved into elaborate stage sets for the projec-
tion of widespread illusions about the nature of advanced global civilisation.
The largest, most rapidly growing conurbations are also the most effective in
projecting this collective mirage as cultural backdrop: Tokyo, London, New
York can be seen as global financial centres (Sassen 1991), but they also perform
as great mythological sceneries of human civilisation at its pinnacle. There
is a bitter irony inherent in the contrast between their seeming potency and
their dependence on centralised, networked power and basic supply systems:
these are as fragile as the images of safety, continuity and progress they help
project. The global rise and regional spread of both urban settlements and their
symbols of aspiration flow from a high-risk existential source: powerful, centrally processed and distributed, abundant fuels: coal, petroleum and natural gas.
The logic of the industries and technologies to which they gave rise has established urban settings as increasingly automated, mechanised and monitored
structures, serviced by carbon or nuclear powered construction machinery,
transport structures, industrial processes and manufacturing systems. Intensive
local economies and labour markets cluster around globally networked city
regions, anchored by heavy investment in infrastructure: power, transport and
communications. This evolution has boosted the primacy of cities over – and
ultimately their detachment from – their agrarian hinterlands (Sassen 1991;
Scheer 2002).

Fossil City's rapid contagion-like spread around the globe is an extraordinary
historical phenomenon, fit for this paradoxical age of abundance-in-scarcity.
The cities of the 19th and 20th centuries, and the culture they manufactured,
were a product of the rising combustion economy. London rapidly expanded in
tandem with the development of coal-based power and steam machinery which
made its unprecedented growth possible. Mid-20th-century urban historian
Lewis Mumford referred colourfully to the urban transformation in industrialising countries between 1820 and 1900 as the rise of 'Coketown,' a 'Paleo-
technic Paradise' (Mumford 1961). Early 20th-century urban innovations in the

Soviet Union, United States, United Kingdom, Europe, Australia and across both Asia and Africa were animated by the jolt of the new and exciting energy technologies.

The new urban transformation was driven by mechanised forms of mobility: General Motors' *Futurama* pavilion and ride at the 1939 'Century of Progress' World Exposition in New York, designed by Norman Geddes in a building by Albert Kahn, uncannily anticipated the car-bound urban and regional realities yet to come (Droege 2004). And in the 1940s and 1950s industrial and government-led transport policies revolutionised urban America – and later Australia and other hapless followers of fashion – shifting them away from rail-based modes to technologies promoting petroleum, automobile and tyre consumption (Morris 1982). The rising car dependence in most cities and the parallel spread of electrified suburban households under expanding power grids, began to pose one of the most daunting challenges in the management of urban environments worldwide. The stage was set for the modern city and its expanding suburb as mass consumer haven; a vast, collective machine to live and shop in.

New visions were expressed in a wide range of petroleum-inspired urban form ideas. Many of these early plans and premonitions contained practical concepts: already very early in the 20th-century the great electric inventions of the telephone and the elevator gave rise to skyscraper cities, initially as utopian visions and soon as pervasive reality. In the middle of the 20th-century nuclear power manifested itself in the abject nightmares of Hiroshima and Nagasaki, perceived as landmarks of urban horror and epic atrocities among civilised societies to this day. Yet in its so-called peaceful application nuclear power seemed like a dream come true: the perfection of the naïve Modernist vision; a world humming with an infinite supply of clean energy, allowing human civilisation to evolve freely from reliance on ancient and primitive solar power systems, to graduate to fossil combustion and, finally, find redemption in the eternal bliss of atomic fission and fusion. The nuclear catastrophes of Three Mile Island and Chernobyl, rising energy costs, long-term uranium supply problems, unsolvable issues over disposal and the frightening reality of weapons proliferation helped put an end to this beautiful fantasy. Yet nuclear power is still cherished as the great Faustian utopia of progress, lingering in the hearts and minds of many powerful players today, like the promise of a dangerous, forbidden cult.

The leaders of the great Modern design movements adored industrial innovations as drivers of urban change. From the dawn of the 20th century the new fossil powered civilisation begat a string of ideologically driven and frequently socially motivated iconoclastic design trends: Italian Futurism,

Russian Constructivism, Dutch De Stijl and the groundbreaking creations of Germany's Bauhaus as well as the pronouncements of the International Modern Architecture Congresses (CIAM – Les Congrès Internationaux de l'Architecture Moderne, 1928–56). It was design innovation epitomised by the International Style, the distinctly capitalist, United States brand of socially concerned Bauhaus approach that established its autocratic rule throughout the industrialised world, reaping both glory and devastation. All of these movements are now, in hindsight, unmasked as giddy stooges of the new fossil fuel age. Indeed, the term *Fossilism*, more accurate in denoting the key historical technology driver, is here proposed to supplement or replace the more ideologically grounded term of *Modernism*. Where *Fossilism* describes the causes of a historical shift, *Modernism* denotes merely its effects.

The fossil machine age is founded on earlier Industrial Revolution technologies, such as those based on waterpower for grain and textile mills. The application of coal, electricity and photographically supported methods of scientific workflow analysis helped give rise to the innovations of Frederick Winslow Taylor (1856–1915) and Henry Ford (1863–1947) in the mechanisation of manufacture and industrial production (Gideon 1948). Progressive waves of industrialisation propelled by coal-fired steam, electricity and gasoline combustion engines drove the spread and supremacy of cities. They also stirred visionary yearnings for machine-like urban form. *Technopian* urban design ideas and models proliferated, many as revolutionary politically as they were inspired industrially. Peter Kropotkin's (1842–1921) proposals for ideal communities were a sign of the times, as were Sir Ebenezer Howard's (1850–1928) plans, and the birth of the Garden City movement. The Regional Plan Association of New York and its inaugural plan of 1929 were of this vintage, along with Frank Lloyd Wright's (1869–1959) Broadacre City, described in his 1932 work *The Disappearing City* (Wright 1932). Ludwig Hilbersheimer's (1885–1967) mass housing concepts, Brasilia, Canberra and the British New Towns were the fossil age articulated in city plan and urban form (Droege 2004).

Modern carbon-based civilisation is also epitomised in the work of its architectural titans. Eminent among these were two US-bound German Bauhaus architects Walter Gropius and Mies van der Rohe. In their work building functions and forms were both transformed with the advance of the new fuels and by the economic and social realities they helped engender. Civic settings and built form changed radically in the new fossil age, breaking with all earlier traditions. The Modern Movement shaped and refined the avalanche of applications in electric and petroleum powered machinery, air conditioning, industrial steel products, advances in glass manufacture, mass produced curtain walls, prefabricated building systems and a number of other energy-intensive technologies. The new thinking about buildings, expressed by the International Style, yielded aesthetically rarefied yet brutally honest, ornament-free, skeletal, ephemeral, industrialised and distinctly corporate structures. It was a thinking that evolved into the *aesthetic of the possible*, as the advanced fossil age dawned in cities around the world. Buildings became disconnected from their climatic and cultural context – a logical consequence of the end of local resource dependency. But this visual purity was a beautiful lie: the air-conditioned skeletons merely disguised the building's messy mechanical systems, hidden deep in internal closets, set out of the way on roof-tops, or stashed into cavernous basements. Berlin-based solar architect Astrid Schneider has powerfully documented Mies' National Gallery in the city as an exercise in a surface illusion of perfect clarity and structure – albeit one that profusely bleeds heat in winter and leaks cold air in summer – with huge, messy, intestine-like ventilation machinery and ducts squeezed into the mechanical spaces below (Schneider 1996).

Under the influence of gasoline and dazzled by the seemingly endless possibilities of the shining new machine age, pioneering Swiss architect and *urbaniste par excellence* Charles Edouard Jeanneret (1887–1965) – otherwise known as Le Corbusier – formulated extraordinary and beguiling ideas for a radical remake of traditional cities. His schemes were celebrated for their formal brilliance and yet rejected as cold, naïve and dangerously superficial. Ever the techno-determinist, he was keenly alert to the dreams of a new age in industrial production and the cultural aspirations of mass consumption. He advocated the City of Tomorrow as a clean slate – the razing of pre-fossil urban areas and their wholesale substitution from the template of standardised, pseudo-industrial patterns deployed in parkland settings or parking lots (Le Corbusier 1929/47). Corbusier's formula of social salvation prescribed the suburbanisation of core cities, in keeping with what the new technologies could most easily deliver.

This thinking was exemplified in his powerful *tabula rasa* concepts: the Parisian *Plan voisin*, *La Ville radieuse* or the automobile-inspired viaduct and speed-way shaped city formations introduced in his Obus planning schemes for Algiers, an obsession that was sparked in him in 1931 and hounded him for almost a decade. It led to no planning or design approvals locally but helped secure him worldwide publishing penetration and influence – still a favourite surrogate activity among some architectural leaders today. The plan for the Alsatian city of St Dié (1945) was presented by the Ministry for Reconstruction, but famously united the entire city, every class and faction, in roundly rejecting the scheme. His vision of the City of Tomorrow as a vertical living machine came closest to implementation in the famed, lone pilot project for a mass-housing module, *Unité d'Habitation* (1946–52). A myriad of copycat schemes swamped the world in the following decades, but precious few built projects of authentic Corbusian urbanism resulted, among them the initially ill-fated but subsequently, famously user-adapted mini-garden-city settlement of Pessac in Bordeaux (1924–6) and his contributions to planning India's Chandigarh regional capital, a city which proved a suitable setting for several of his memorable architectural designs. Le Corbusier's crowning urban planning achievement, his mid-20th century's Camelot of liberation-by-Modernism, was indeed Chandigarh (1950–62) whose planning had originally been commenced by American designers Albert Mayer and Matthew Nowicki. The municipal motto today is 'The City Beautiful' but it was named in 1952 by India's first Prime Minister, Jawaharlal Nehru, in honour of the goddess Chandi, or Shakti, meaning power or energy.

This new capital of India's Punjab – its former capital Lahore was sequestered into Pakistan when British India was divided into these two nations – still looms large as a tangible if wistfully forlorn icon among the pioneering fossil-fuel based urban innovations of the world. Today, Chandigarh and that other great contemporary new capital foundation, Brazil's inspired, richly symbolic and delicately geometric national capital Brasilia (1956–64), deliciously lampoon the fossil-fuel era and its dreams, standing as they do as perfect historical artefacts of a bygone era. Appropriately, Oscar Niemayer and Lúcio Costa's oddly toy-like, aeroplane-plan capital has been listed as a UNESCO World Heritage Site, an unwitting landmark of High Fossilism. In these two capitals, one national, one regional, Brasil and India acquired expensive, full-scale fossil-age stage sets, serving as instant, surrogate symbols of a beyond-developed-country status, as life-style theme parks of modernity and as national incubators for new cultural, political and economic developments. Yet despite their ostentatious celebration of the new power systems and technologies in city form, Brasilia and Chandigarh contain some of the 20th century's finest examples of climatic design expressions in Modern architecture, by Oscar Niemeyer and Le Corbusier, affording a visionary remnant of local responsiveness expressed in memorable form.

In his urban work Jeanneret discovered and rearticulated a set of revolutionary yet simple doctrines – reeking of petroleum – with exceptional intelligence, wit and elegance. Unfortunately, others came to adopt and apply the principles: quasi-Corbusian derivations were deployed mercilessly and without humour in cities across the United States, Eastern and Western Europe, the Soviet Union, China and countless countries around the world. *Corbism* also gave built form to ill-conceived policies resulting in urban destruction and blight through wholesale urban renewal of what were identified as inner city slum areas. The neighbourhoods of the poor and disenfranchised, and the pre-fossil urban relics they inhabited, were to be redeemed in so many Pruitt-Igoe-like habitations. Europe's postwar years saw the realisation of massive urban expansion plans, suspended among the spreading webs of electrification that crisscrossed former farmlands. The Greater London plan by Sir Patrick Abercrombie (Abercrombie 1945), Copenhagen's Finger Plan and Stockholm's 'planetary cluster' schemes of the 1960s as well as the myriad of satellite city concepts rising after the Second World War – and especially in the 1960s and 1970s – in Europe and elsewhere, gave bold plan form to the worldwide move to life in cities. Structural shifts and new opportunities brought about by the rise of the fossil fuel economy and its promises drove rail expansion and road network schemes. The dichotomy between public transport provision and individual car-based modes of urban growth is important from an urban design and regional identity viewpoint, but represents a marginal differentiation of functionality and form within the same energy paradigm, since both forms of urban expansionism were and continue to be fossil-fuel dependent.

Meanwhile, the increasingly urban and automated production – consumption system of the advanced industrial age has boosted global power use at an exponential rate. From the outset, the momentous move to shed all renewable-energy based traditions, such as water and wind power, bio-fuel reliance and the emerging discoveries of advanced solar-energy conversion, and stake the future of human civilisation on the massive combustion of the new fossil finds of coal, oil and gas – and, to a lesser degree, on the splitting of the uranium atom – had largely been motivated by the legendary profits to be made in the gold-rush like entrepreneurial frenzy surrounding the discovery and marketing of these new and strategic resources. By the middle of the 20th century global civilisation began to be swept up in these pioneering perspectives on progress. Oil-blessed Texan success stories from Howard Hughes to the Bush dynasty still stir the popular imagination. The iconic highlights in the cultural history of petroleum include two celebrated United States television series promoting hydrocarbon based lifestyles and stimulating the aspirations of a mass consumer audience. One was the 1981–9 American Broadcasting Corporation's (ABC) *Dynasty*, which depicted a Colorado oil clan, the Carringtons. Its working title had been *Oil*. Another blockbuster ABC series, *Dallas*, first aired in 1978, revolved around the feud between two Texan oil families. Its most memorable highlight was the shooting of petroleum magnate JR Ewing and the question of who did it. Both productions celebrated the near-mythical suburban dreams-capes of high fossil culture, set against a backdrop of idealised, heavily panelled downtown offices rife with duplicity and deception; both touted the values of a section of society living it up off a dirty secret: the realities of fossil affluence.

## The rise of the suburb

The modern suburb is a logical corollary of this fossil fuel powered narrative and expresses it in holographic detail. And its ascendancy continues: suburbs and their appurtenances mushroom at and between the fringes of the world's metropolitan cores, following Doxiadess' *ecumenopolitan* premonitions with the precision of a large oil spill (Doxiades and Papaioannou 1974), oozing across the land in patterns that may well follow the rules of chaos theory's fractal geometry (Mandelbrot 1982). Early subdivisions blossomed as shiny and hopeful new communities along train lines, beside the tracks of what were initially horse-drawn but soon became electric tramways, to form the streetcar serviced suburbs of many American, European and Australian cities. Once it became readily affordable, the combustion-engine powered personal vehicle allowed for the creation of a radically new urban reality: new suburbs predicated on car-owning residents, expanded along and between motorways, extending as a two-dimensional field. Television, radio and print helped promote the new gasoline based lifestyle on advertising hoardings, in TV commercials and soap operas. The mass media had already firmly established the automobile and petrochemical-product based industrial civilisation, prior to but especially in the years directly after the Second World War. The suburb emerged as a powerful urban vision to which everyone around the globe aspired.

The suburb did not simply embody the technological legacy of the fossil fuel age in human settlement form: it quickly evolved into a media-projected, mass-produced yet highly individuated and networked urban phenomenon, seemingly capable of penetrating everywhere, including the collective subconscious. Emanating from the large exurban retail complexes – themselves masquerading as new town centres – the suburban stage surroundings emerge as the true shopping malls. Suburbia as this more recent urbanisation phenomenon has mutated from placeless exurb and choice-deprived consumption machine into the rich and vibrant aisles in the lifestyle section of a global and open-air mega-mall. It has obliterated much of natural and traditional local space subsuming it under the rubber stamp of stereotypical places – and their props for localised, particular versions of the *Truman Show*. As a mass-produced space for consumption

suburbia is as honest and real as any of the landmarks of High Modernism –
yet it is also richly saturated with escapist irony in the profoundly anti-modern
pretence of the aspirations it expresses.

Both anti-urban ideologies and romantic urban design ideals were current
from the very outset of the suburban story in the early 19th century. These
promised a paradise far from the perceived corrupting moral and physical
dangers of the industrialised city cores. The early North American suburb
epitomised these, and served as the founding inspiration of equally unattain-
able utopias in many other countries today, from Australia to China. It was an
escapist pastoral dream, Jeffersonian, Emersonian, *Elysian*: the very idea of a
suburb enticed with the allure of both communal connection and individual
autonomy, as expressed by Thoreau (1817–62) in his famous political work of
1854, *Walden* (Fender 1997). It was a work tinged with imported social ideals
such as had found expression in the initiatives of horticulturist and architect
Andrew Jackson Downing (1815–52), proponent of New York's Central Park
and a firm believer in the civilising force of simple accommodation and public
spaces (Downing 1974). It was an ideal that found its application in America's
extraordinary garden suburbs of the 19th century, such as Riverside, west of
Chicago (1868/70). Riverside was the creation of the famous Central Park architects and superintendents Frederick Law Olmsted (1822–1902) and Calvert
Vaux (1824–95), design partners for a number of public space and master-
planned community projects. The historical genre it represented contained
the seeds of the Garden City and Garden Suburb movements, leading to the
simultaneously utopian and pragmatic yet deeply fossilist form of urbanity we
identify with suburbs today.

By the late 1980s *New Urbanism* advocates began to offer their own critique
and alternatives, decrying modern suburbias as constructs with the cultural
depth and intensity of cow pastures. The idea of the early Garden Suburb
turned out to be still alive, albeit in the rather contrived settings of commercial
master-planned communities. In the United States, the suburban vernacular has
evolved from early townships such as Colonial-era Hadley and Northampton,
Massachusetts, to pre-Civil War Shaker Heights, Ohio, to post-Second World
War modern Levittown, New York, and has been reconstructed with the genetic
material derived from early settlements into the Post-modern *New Urbanist*
landmarks of the 1980s and 1990s, such as the earlier, sparser Seaside and the
later, more opulent Celebration or the Kentlands, Maryland, all three in Florida.
Here neo-traditional townscapes offer a new and rational framework for the
housing needs of the affluent. Their iconography denies their fossil logic while
being deeply steeped in it. Yet today, whatever its formal, local articulation,

the suburban realm, in its 21st century incarnation and fossil legacy, is best thought of as a great, amorphously networked, city-regional megalopolitan web (Droege 2006).

## Renewable energy and sprawl

Since the 1970s, calls for more densely concentrated and public transport-based forms of urban development have signalled the declining stage of the fossil-fuel economy, when advances in energy conservation and fuel efficiency began to be identified as the cheapest and most immediately useful means of emissions reduction. Denser cities were thought to be more fuel-efficient, while car dependent, low-density urban forms, such as suburbs, incapable of sustaining public transport infrastructure have come to be understood as major obstacles to achieving a sustainable urban way of life (Newman and Kenworthy 1987, 1992, 1999). Yet, barring economic cataclysms, urban consolidation, efficiency, conservation and transportation reforms will not suffice to halt the global rise in $CO_2$-equivalent emissions, let alone to reverse the trend and reduce them. The replacement of conventional energy technologies with renewable systems is essential. In order for these new technologies to be in place in time to be of use in an inexorably warming, increasingly petroleum-deprived world, they must be introduced without delay, on a global scale. Transit-oriented development, smart-growth initiatives and attempts to recreate pre-industrial urban patterns in forms of *neo-traditional design* can serve as important interim measures, but are more effective as communication devices, symbolic of larger aspirations. Some see them as counterproductive, merely lulling planners, politicians and other people into a false belief that sustainable development is nigh. Yet if urban consolidation and efficiency measures are designed to constrain fossil energy use, will their substitution with renewable power sources not remove this limitation?

Indeed, the history of modern suburbanisation is marked by technological innovations that have served to remove spatial constraints on both the range and form of urban development. Up until and including the age of coal, both location and size of urban settlements were considerably more constrained than in the current high age of fossil urbanisation, within the limits imposed by the key technologies of energy, resources, transport and communications. Modern suburbanisation, by contrast, is a petroleum-charged, information-technology augmented articulation of a much older phenomenon: the growth of cities and urban settlements.

Archaeologist Roland Fletcher's remarkable discourse *The Limits of Settle-ment Growth* aside (Fletcher 1996), little useful research has been conducted into cultural, political and technological constraints on the phenomenon of city expansion. Yet while Fletcher's valiant volume focuses on *material-as-behaviour*, or socio-cultural modes of interaction and communications, it disregards the dimension of energy altogether. Indeed, pronounced and wide-spread cases of energy blindness were rampant among urban scholars during the all-encompassing age of High Fossilism, and certainly before the 1970s. Then, after a very brief period of OPEC-induced energy enlightenment during that decade, this pathological condition spread again from the early 1980s into the first decade of the 2000s, when the approaching Oil Peak, mounting hurricane damage and petroleum-inspired geo-regional military meddling whipped up shortages once again. During the interim periods it was as if fossil fuel dependency was seen as too ubiquitous to be studied as a specific driver of urban change.

How will the renewable energy revolution affect the logic of what, broadly, is called urban sprawl today: the allied forces of residential, industrial and commercial expansion? A historical correlation exists between the lowering of resource, infrastructure and other technological constraints and the lifting of urban size limits, synonymous with peri- or sub-urban growth. Throughout the 19th century, the development of the steam engine – powering locomotives and rolling out continental rail networks – and the invention of telegraph and telephony supported a process of simultaneous urban concentration and expan-sion in Europe, the United States and other urban regions around the world. In the 20th century, the combined effects of the proliferation of the motor car, massive road construction programmes, electric power grids and the advent of distributed computing and advanced telecommunications – even the steep rise in intercontinental air travel – carried this process onto a global scale, at ever greater heights of intensity. Since the 1980s metropolitan regions from Beijing to Sydney have experienced a 'lily on the pond' phenomenon: runaway, low-density suburban growth has spread at an exponential rate, filling all regional open space in a flash, up to 30, even 50 kilometres from the respective main epicentre. Blasting its way across the urban plains along transport corridors, between ring roads, around main intersections and other nodal points, such creeping suburban encroachment has crystallised on the polycentric of old village cores, mere specks in the fog of the new and expansive, uniformly urbanised metro-space. A textbook case is the rapid chewing up of farms and forestlands under suburban carpet growth around Washington, DC, quickly relegating an earlier 'green wedges' plan for regional radial open space networks to a mere memory in urban planning: the new suburban subway web combined with proliferating highway orbitals to provide the very armature for instant suburbanisation and commercial sub-centre formation.

Is it plausible, were it spatially even possible, that a further reduction in growth constraints could add momentum to the great suburban urge apparent in current urbanisation processes, by replacing conventional, ie long-distance, contested and polluting power supply lines and grids with autonomously powered, quasi-self-sufficient urban units? Leon van Schaik describes the work of bio-climatic designers Hamzah and Yeang in a pocket volume celebrating the 'simultaneity' of 'ecocells,' ie the multi-functional and parallel autonomy of intensively conceived and integrated, virtually self-contained environments (van Schaik 2003). In his tropical design work Ken Yeang expressly rejects renewable energy technology as promising salvation. Instead, he proposes to augment conventional power with efficient and plant-suffused, 'bio-climatic' design. Still, while this pre-renewable vision owes its *raison d'être* to the preservation, not replacement of fossil fuel, it is only one step removed from crossing a critical threshold and severing the petroleum tether. It exudes the thrilling yet unnerving vision of highly integrated urban systems that also tantalise in their bio-energetic thinking; raising the unnerving spectre of an autonomous, runaway process of urban metastasis, with each cell unit being less dependent on external resource supply and hence more capable of unrestrained spatial replication.

But it would be a mistake to apply traditional carbon-spatial development logic here. In principle and in the long run renewable energy systems do not seem capable of further accelerating uncontrolled urban growth, so unleashing a new force working against restraints on expansion. Rather, these new and decentralised energy sources represent the only option to sustainably augment the power infrastructure of urban environments; they promise to define a new set of internal constraints by virtue of their limits to spatial and technological power generation at a time when fossil fuel and nuclear alternatives become more risky and less affordable, and coal is increasingly ostracised. Global fossil power supply lines have engendered the phenomenon of contemporary globalisation: as these decline present modes of globalisation will of necessity give way to more regional and increasingly autonomous forms of subsistence and prosperity. While limiting demographic pressure for further urban expansion, this model of urban development also offers little in the way of available resources to service urban sprawl and conventional forms of suburbanisation; as an example, the limit of sun exposed surfaces combined with climatic criteria form two simple constraints on a city's theoretical internal solar power generation capacity (see Chapter 4 'Building the Renewable City' below). Once the global chains of oil and uranium distribution deteriorate and are eventually severed, regional land and water resources will become too precious to waste on inefficient, low-density and other high-carbon urbanisation and settlement patterns.

This is only a longer-term, merely speculative outlook. Theoretically and in the short term, distributed power systems could indeed contribute marginally to the continued unfettering and decentralisation of urban development. During the impending transitional decades the fossil-based suburban world may well maintain its precipitous ascendance, temporarily continuing to run rampant even as it disconnects from power grids and global fuel supplies, and is served by solar-hydrogen and bio-diesel vehicles (Lovins and Cramer 2004). In the short run, as a mere augmentation of conventional power systems and combined with wireless telecommunications and renewably powered information systems, stand-alone hybrid or single-mode renewable energy supplies are not likely to serve to reinstate historical constraints on spatial agglomerations. They may reduce the relative infrastructure costs of sprawl and, in their association with 'green' or 'sustainable' development values, in fact help mitigate the effects of some growth boundaries set around cities and communities with growth management legislation such as those in the northwest United States.

Eventually, new forces will impose firm new constraints on urban sprawl and settlement growth. Internal and regional energy generation capacity and resource access will form a formidable technical limitation. Resource price increases and restricted fossil fuel access plus regional and wider economic restructuring will take place, in a move away from globalised trade and flows to regionalised and localised dynamics, curtailing demographic and investment pressures on large urban nodes, and supporting smaller rural and quasi-urban production centres. Land development, servicing, insurance and construction costs will rise in response to climate change impacts, as described in the next chapter. Family homes constructed to withstand increasingly severe weather events will become more costly: a prospect that would seem to favour denser and more defensive multi-unit dwellings. In existing conurbations there will be increasing competition for land to meet rising demands for local fuel and food production, and for open space reserves required for heat island mitigation – the basic method of cooling urban regions (see Chapter 4 below). Without such likely constraints and the planning measures needed to take advantage of these as opportunities, a *Renewable Age* in itself – while offering massive benefits in terms of autonomy, innovation, security and greenhouse gas emission mitigation – would not contain many solutions to today's urbanisation dilemmas. Cities embarking on a renewable energy conversion path will have to pay the price of the fossil fuel momentum – for the energy, expectations and excesses of that age – for some time to come, in economic, political and policy terms. In the short term, it is healthy to be cautious, and not regard the renewable revolution as an all-embracing technological panacea for urban and even wider environmental ills.

For a very long time to come, the renewable revolution will have to cope with the most damaging features of fossil urbanisation, the unintended side effects of progress past. Many earlier and technologically inspired visions were also well intentioned, and some have been pursued with an equally unequivocal faith in techno-salvation. But the early *fossilist* vision of renewed and more orderly, healthier and socially more equitable cities quickly became mired in the nightmarish environmental cost dilemma of advanced industrialisation. The mass incineration of fossil fuels at once fostered and fumigated cities. City dwellers gagged on a lethal cocktail of sulphur dioxide, nitrous oxide and airborne carcinogenic particles. In London in particular, thousands choked to death during the infamous smogs of the 1950s prior to legislation in the early 1960s. And the air of the Faustian city continues to be implicated in the deaths of millions annually in cities around the world – not to speak of the massive water and soil pollution issues flowing from the fossil fuel economy. While the most extreme levels of toxicity may seem to have been curbed and so are no longer seen as immediately lethal hazards in many cities of the industrialised world, air pollution continues to represent a terrible urban scourge in Europe, the United States and other countries of the so-called developed world, but especially and increasingly plaguing developing metropolises. And with progress and rising living standards the massive escalation of greenhouse gas emissions supplants or augments the bane of local pollution, which itself may be experienced locally as colourless, odourless or non-toxic and therefore harmless; but such pollution is incomparably more damaging and fatal at a terrestrial scale, in its time-delayed, flow-on and distant impacts (McGranahan et al 1999).

## Fossil war, renewable peace?

It is wise to be cautious, and embrace change with a sense of realism. The sheer momentum of the old industrial regime poses a daunting challenge. Its end may be in sight, but the old energy systems have defined all aspects of modern society, from personal and family life and its transformed role in the new mass production and consumption cycles, to the structure of the global economy. And these energy systems have, too, revolutionised a central domain rarely addressed in studies on cities, yet of central significance to them, both in terms of competing funding priorities and in their economic and physical vulnerability: the very waging of war, its tools, strategies and tactics in supply, battle and occupation – and the rapid evolution of new killing machines and officially sanctioned weapons of mass destruction. These range from coal and later oil-fired battle ships, petroleum and nuclear submarines, the long rise of the tank to the fossil-fuelled tools of air supremacy – featuring such industrial marvels of mayhem as fighter planes, long-range bombers, Cruise Missiles, and that apocalyptic Cold War innovation, the intercontinental ballistic missile (ICBM).

Intuitively, the idea of a solar tank or biogas bomber seems less menacing, even absurd. The reason may in part lie in the tragic irony that the most advanced fossil-fuel weapons today are largely and increasingly deployed to safeguard the very oil resources that power them: they have become their own end. The 140,000 US troops stationed in Iraq during 2005 consumed a staggering 1.4 million barrels of oil a day, all imported. The United States has engaged in 150 oil-related armed interventions since the early 1990s and, as outcome of its national energy policy, begun to militarise and permanently occupy the major global oil flow chokepoints, moving from the Persian Gulf to West Africa and the Caspian Sea (WDR 2005). While these figures suggest that significant present causes for conflict are – needlessly – energy related, the reduction in national oil dependence does not in itself promise peace on earth. The history of human civilisation has been deeply steeped in conquest, conflict and warfare – and, indeed, there is nothing inherently peace-loving about renewable energy. As one example, the United States Army has long been interested in solar thin-film development, as tent cover material or uniform fabric, to enhance communications power (Gartner 2004). The current preoccupation with securing global petroleum supply lines militarily highlights how national priorities have hitherto been defined and met, and how globalisation has been structured over the past 50 years. But new developments such as the United States President's January 2006 call for a move away from fossil fuel serve as reminders of the greatest present promise of global peace and equitable development: the defusing and ultimate removal of perhaps the largest risk for triggering a Third World War – global and rising fossil and nuclear dependence. Unfortunately, the subtext of Mr Bush's call was enhanced support for atomic power, increasingly fashionable again around the world.

## Fossil and renewable forms of globalisation

The global chains of petroleum-product supply and processing support even drive the modern phenomenon of globalisation. This is the logical conclusion to be drawn from Hermann Scheer's seminal treatise on the global aspects of the fossil fuel economy, and his argument for a broad shift to solar – renewable – sources (Scheer 2002). Indeed, modern forms of globalisation would not exist without worldwide fossil energy trade and market protection measures, supported by military policy and practices of safeguarding both markets and supply lines. *Global urbanisation*, too, is a central plank of the fossil fuel economy, characterised by an abundance of fossil power available for urban infrastructure: telecommunications, freight and transport systems, on land, sea and in the air. Modern infrastructures and relatively reliable, abundant, low-cost fossil fuel sources combined with globalised trade arrangements have served to link cities to one another globally while bypassing their local regions. Globally interdependent urban systems are more vulnerable to the decline of global fossil fuel supplies and other systemic disruptions than those that rely more on their local and regional human and land resources. The deployment of renewable energy technologies on a large scale has the potential to support an era of *differentiated globalisation* (Droege 1999b, 2004), broadly distinguishing between local provision of food and basic goods, and the comparably more global, footloose trade in financial and other advanced services.

Rising regional economies are likely to be marked by a search for resources capable of supporting local urban centres: this may well inaugurate an era of large-scale food, solar, bio- and wind energy production farms. Some forms of a rudimentary reconnection of central cities with their regional economies and associated spatial structures can already be observed in a number of communities. Examples include Swedish and UK *ecocycling* programmes building regional and local material flow cycles; the growing interest in regional energy farming, such as Melbourne's early investment in regional wind fields; Germany's agricultural renaissance based on biofuel markets; Copenhagen's municipal offshore wind energy generators; or Australia's early carbon-trade geared afforestation efforts of the 1990s, financed by the Tokyo Electric Power Company (TEPCO) in the eastern state of New South Wales. Initiatives of this nature can be used to help revive the resilient mechanism of rural–urban support economies, reinvigorating old and boosting new forms of agriculture and forestry. In short: cities, regions and states around the world have already begun to link their renewable energy needs to regional resources capable of meeting those needs. This is bound to spawn new local manufacturing and advanced industry sectors in renewable energy generation, supply and services (Droege 2004).

While a few local urban centres and regions may seem sheltered from the shock of the inevitable fossil-fuel peak – or, in a few decades, uranium stock depletion – through their local reliance on hydro-electric, or biomass power, no non-fossil energy source is sufficiently deployable on its own to maintain the vast majority of cities. The degree of wider market and supply interdependence and global resource networking makes the isolated prospering of regional pockets of self-sufficiency rather difficult to imagine, certainly in the short term. The only viable long-term option for securing the continuity of urban civilisation is a systematic and system-wide move to broad portfolios of renewable energy sources, based on the overwhelming availability of solar, wind, wave, and other renewable forms of energy generation. A global shift will engage international, national and local institutions; focus more sharply on long-established conservation and efficiency innovations; and increasingly deploy the autonomy-enhancing production, consumption and trade principles of differentiated globalisation.

For cities, massive shifts are in the making. The old industrial paradigm is fading quickly, although it may seem still frustratingly pervasive and unquestioned in many developed and developing countries alike, compounded by energy-blind local governance structures and planning frameworks. Many countries are still trapped in a set of self-fulfilling assumptions about the nature of technology and the trajectory of progress – and hence the nature and role of their cities and urban networks. It is difficult to face today's basic strategic urban planning paradox: cities are an outcome of the dominant global energy regime – yet the fossil world no longer holds out any promise for the future. However, while urban power change is necessary it is fraught with institutional difficulties. Due to structural changes in power industry and public administration concepts since the early 1980s, many cities in the developed world have been deprived of their municipal power companies and now are at the mercy of an anonymous and distant energy industry: state, national, corporate or transnational dominated. As a result of what seemed like measures of efficiency and rationalisation in the past, these communities now find themselves disconnected from energy policy and practice. In some countries such detachment is still seen as the essence of modernity and progress, and held onto with increasing desperation, at the very point in time when its fate is sealed. The struggle of Sacramento to establish its own power institutions is a good example of how these illusions can be overcome and powerful benefits reaped (see Chapter 4 below).

## Myths and denials

The international chains of natural gas and petroleum supply are the focus of mounting energy security concerns, particularly for cities and city regions. Russian energy monopoly Gazprom's short-term termination of natural gas supplies to the Ukraine during the 2006 price dispute precipitated instant short-falls of up to 40 per cent in a number of European countries as far west as France (BBC 2006; Finn 2006). This incident served to recall the more significant and sustained production reductions marking the so-called OPEC 'Oil Crisis' of 1972. Yet neither the evidence of such immediate risks nor the looming twin background threats of inexorable supply declines and climate change impacts helped to sway mainstream energy policy: it shifts only slowly, and almost imperceptibly so, in a world where individual and national stakes and riches are tied to the dominant power regime.

The psychological response mechanism of denial is powerful and only slowly weakening. As evidence of risks mounts and awareness of the problem spreads, efforts at reinforcing a wider state of denial increase in their isolation and absurdity – akin to the famed small orchestra hastily gathered on the deck of the *Titanic* after the iceberg had struck, an empty measure that neverthe-less served to convey a sense of security and normalcy as the doomed ship begun to take in water. To help understand the world of obstinate disbelief, German renewable energy champion and veteran parliamentarian Hermann Scheer has mapped the means required to maintain a disastrous course. He lists the questionable technological and economic premises frequently advanced to justify the prevailing interpretation of reality, and the manufactured consent to it, allegedly in the direction of human civilisation. Nuclear and fossil fuel resources and systems are presented as necessary due to a number of alleged conditions: the insufficient capacity of renewable energy; the extensive time frame required for its implementation; its high price; the immaturity of the technology; the fossil energy embodied in renewable supply; the bird kills from wind mills – and so on. It matters little to the purveyors of these myths that all have been repeatedly debunked, and evidence to the contrary has long been widely available (Scheer 2005).

A popular but untested assumption holds that the intensity and magnitude of urban activities require high-intensity and single-source systems based on large generation plants capable of meeting massive volumes of energy demand. Most conventional infrastructure planners prefer to see cities as large factories or machines, akin to ocean liners, requiring a finely tuned, centrally controlled and limited set of large-scale systems: road and rail, water and sewage systems, reliable and copious forms of centralised, one-way energy supply. This thinking recalls the predictions of early electronics pioneers that the entire worldwide market for computers could only ever be tiny, given the that these were then massive, expensive machines quite beyond the reach of individual users. The current domestic and workplace ecology of desktop, laptop and handheld computers presents a direct analogy for the likely future of urban energy systems based on ubiquitous and embedded devices and means, within a framework of marketable efficiency measures and demand management. The new vision of the city is that of a *virtual power plant*, an open energy market in which everyone can participate as producers, consumers and traders. This is not a dream about a technical fix but a plan for emancipation and empowerment, a weaning from the confining and dangerous fantasies embodied in cities' current power structures. And, fortunately, cities increasingly embrace this reality.

## 1.3 SUMMARY AND OUTLOOK: FOR URBAN EVOLUTION THERE IS NO ALTERNATIVE TO RENEWABLE ENERGY

### Three axioms of urban change

The new reality will not gain acceptance for altruistic reasons or as an ethical effort to 'save the environment'. Urban eyes begin to open because three axioms of global change are now widely accepted. What will be described here loosely as *axioms* are so either because the vast majority of scientists, leaders and people endowed with common sense have come to embrace them as sufficiently researched to be true, and calls to await further study results can safely be interpreted as blatant attempts at further delays, or because a final scientific resolution would be impossible to achieve, while further inaction would perpetuate destructive practice or create or add new and overwhelming risks. The three energy development axioms are: (a) the fact of rapid climate change as triggered by humans through carbon emissions, and the corollary that a dramatic reduction in manmade greenhouse gas emissions will help to positively address its fundamental, long-term dynamics; (b) the impending peaking of oil and gas supplies, and equally finite availability of uranium; and (c) that petroleum and nuclear power chains are a root cause of worldwide environmental damage and constitute a threat to urban health.

**Climate change** is the leading driving factor behind establishing equity-based emission reduction targets and methods, and it has been demonstrated that neither Kyoto targets and process, nor the various carbon trading and implementation schemes (Joint Implementation (JI), Clean Development Mechanism (CDM) and variations) are capable of fundamentally addressing the emissions conundrum in ways that can meet Intergovernmental Panel on Climate Change (IPCC) identified targets of a 60 per cent global emissions reduction over 1990 levels (Byrne et al 1998, 2000, 2002, 2004). The imminent production peak of oil and gas may well help reduce emissions, but it is quite likely that coal incineration would make up for the shortfall – a calamitous response that would be tantamount to policy failure. More constructive, focused and direct means are needed, marked by an unwavering focus on renewable energy implementation, rather than the indirect, complex and difficult-to-verify and cumbersome emissions baselines and targets.

**Peak oil** – The evaporating physical resource base of the fossil fuel economy not only threatens to create a historical bottleneck in energy prices, with dire consequences for economic prospects, but will also lead to deteriorating national, regional and global security conditions, given the general lack of planning. At the same time, a number of industrialising countries face a mounting dependence on oil and natural gas imports. Most of the very poorest of developing countries are caught in a vexing energy debt trap: their foreign aid is often to an overwhelming extent dedicated to paying off fossil fuel, uranium and other conventional energy technology imports. This creates a massive economic and military security problem. In the absence of a long-term and broad-based switch to renewable energy, intensifying military conflicts and campaigns of resource adventurism are inevitable. They threaten global prosperity and directly impinge on major cities which, in their role of national command and control centres, would also become directly involved in these conflicts.

Nuclear power use, like that of fossil fuel, is steeply on the increase, yet it offers no long-term solution either. Fusion is not working, wastefully absorbing massive amounts of research funds for decades to come, while fission reactors are an anachronistic and needless burden on society. The nuclear industry has to contend with mounting costs due to a finite uranium supply, staggering technical, security and weapons proliferation risks, and insoluble waste disposal requirements.

The third axiom holds that **there can be no sustainable development while fossil and atomic power sources prevail**. Petroleum and nuclear power prospecting, production, refining, transportation, processing, combustion, fission and disposal chains are the world's most potent single cause of environmental destruction, water, soil and air pollution, global warming, fresh water depletion whether in least-developed, developing or so-called developed nations (Scheer 2002). Fossil fuels are also involved in what McGranahan and colleagues have termed the *environmental transition*. While in poorer cities of the developing world immediate health problems are due to transmitted diseases and poor nutrition, such concerns have mostly been alleviated in less impoverished urban centres and regions, although here, too, health is compromised by air and water pollution due to mounting fossil-fuel combustion. This problem is said to have been largely overcome in cities of the advanced world – a relative gain in that as of 2005 the number of Europeans dying from the consequences of air pollution exceeded 300,000 – but is now superseded by the equally complex problem of unsustainable levels of greenhouse-gas emissions (McGranahan et al 1999). The costs are stratospheric yet almost entirely disregarded in fossil-fuel prices. They range from widespread damage to human health to massive and mounting asset destruction due to catastrophic weather patterns. These burdens can only mount, due to the increased costs of dealing with pollution and its consequences, including attempts to manage the damage wreaked by greenhouse gas emissions. These costs are bound to neutralise and surpass any economic gain generated (Gleick 1994, 1998; Meadows et al 1972, 2004; Rees and Wackernagel 1996; Scheer 2002).

These three axioms of urban change are founded on basic truths about environmental damage, security risk and resource flows. They inevitably drive the current global energy regime towards renewable power sources. The key question is whether this transformation will be fast and sweeping enough to avoid cataclysmic change brought about by holding on to the declining fossil fuel era for too long. Despite this urgency, some leaders in certain coal and uranium-rich countries ignore these facts, or perpetuate the comforting myth that their countries could turn inwards, and act as fortresses defending independent resources. They hope that the broader decline of regional and global economic and political conditions could be magically screened out: a dangerous illusion in today's interconnected world. It would spell disaster for the economy and viability of the cities involved. All of them depend on healthy geo-regional and global economic conditions, even under circumstances of heightened urban autonomy.

Fortunately, renewable energy technologies are affordable and infinite in supply – in stark contrast to fossil and nuclear sources. And they are not only competitive but also become wildly profitable once fossil-fuel subsidies are discounted and external costs taken into account. Production costs continually fall and comparably few environmental, social, political and security risks arise. Increased renewable energy technology uptake, mass production and systems innovations prompt further cost reductions. Prices generally become more affordable as markets gain confidence under improved legislative conditions and through the introduction of policies designed to reduce the enormous international and global subsidies and other, hidden advantages enjoyed by large fossil and nuclear power conglomerates.

## The urban energy transformation: both possible and necessary

Transformation from the current, archaic urban power regime to a renewable energy urbanism is both possible and necessary. Its technical feasibility has long been demonstrated at national levels, in numerous studies ranging from the classic 100 per cent renewable France study in 1978 (ALTER 1978); the 1980 call by the US Federal Emergency Management Agency for a 'renewable America' to enhance national security (FEMA 1980); to the Greenpeace-commissioned study for a 100 per cent renewable, energy-rich Japan (Lehmann 2003). For Germany, a recent, Eurosolar-commissioned project showed that 40 gigawatt in conventional electricity generation can be replaced through renewable energy systems, meaning that the combined application of wind, sun, bio-fuel and geothermal capacity would make it unnecessary to replace expiring conventional generation capacity with fossil-fuel technology in that country (Peter and Lehmann 2004). In short, gradual yet determined replacement of fossil and nuclear generation capacity by renewable sources is a practical reality.

Germany is a leading model in the determined drive to convert to renewable energy: nationally, and in the practice of its regions, cities and towns. The country has introduced the political, statutory and technological conditions that have created a robust new industry with a turnover of €11 billion in 2004, and delivered more than 130,000 new jobs. Some 14 gigawatt electrical power capacity from sun, wind and other renewable sources have been newly created since 2000, at a rate of 3,000 megawatt each year. And this has been an affordable change: the additional cost for end-users amounts to less than that arising from decommissioning German nuclear power plants (Pontenagel 2005). There is an important longterm aspect to this change: if current trends and change rates continue, the German economy and its communities will be entirely renewable-energy based by 2070. And several cities were pioneers in this change – converting their energy systems well before such changes were embraced nationally. This should come as no surprise – it matters in cities and local communities first.

## Local change is underway

Indeed, more and more cities refuse to engage in defeatist energy illusions any longer. They look at pioneering fellow communities such as Palermo in Italy, Freiburg in Germany or Sacramento in California – and see the benefits of municipally owned control over the urban power regime. And entirely new institutions emerge to meet a pressing need: in the United Kingdom, community focused, low-cost regeneration bodies such as SEA/RENUE firmly focus on advancing social equity and community empowerment by eliminating fuel poverty and building wider urban sustainability in mobility improvements. Merged from two separate organisations, Sustainable Energy Action (SEA) and Renewable Energy in the Urban Environment (RENUE), the charity begin to show excellent results, in this case in the revolutionary assistance rendered to the London Boroughs of Southwark, Merton and Wandsworth. Starting in 2005, the charity reported some thirty-three local and international public and private partnerships that both contributed to and benefited from the expanding 'Solar for London' hot-water heater promotion effort; built a biogas plant, as well as a bio-diesel factory for transport fuel; developed urban wind power projects; studied the introduction of solar power to the Palace of Westminster; and in 2006 received a £6m grant from the European Union and United Kingdom governments to develop a combined renewable energy and efficiency project. The charity has been designated an Energy Action Area by London mayor Ken Livingstone, in recognition of its services in advancing local regeneration, community development and prosperity objectives (SEA/RENUE 2006).

The linkage of renewable energy autonomy to socio-economic and cultural development is an essential ingredient in transcending old mindsets. Constructed culturally, the traditional, fossil frame of mind is politically and economically driven. It consists of a complex, partially shared and partially conflicted landscape of beliefs, shaped and maintained to serve old industrial interests. But refreshing initiatives such as SEA/RENUE demonstrate that enlightened industrial and business leaders have come to recognise that the old premises underlying these interests have fallen apart: fossil energy resources are peaking, and the capacity of the biosphere to assimilate the staggering amount of waste – solid, liquid and airborne – has exceeded its limit. New growth opportunities have coalesced a trillion-dollar global industry: in demand management, in efficient production based on circular resource chains, in renewable energy, in industries focusing on quality over quantity, in new finance products aimed at real and sustained development needs – and in investments that support local autonomy. Herein lie solutions that serve local interests and can be locally sourced. New, regionally based renewable-energy policy in the United States, Europe and elsewhere reflects this understanding, prompting legislation that builds healthy cycles of environmental innovation and market development.

There are refreshing signs of change in two broad domains: one, institutional and the other, related to urban planning. Institutionally, energy transformation aims and traditional urban management and planning realms are slowly beginning to merge: renewable energy and energy efficiency aims are incorporated squarely into mainstream urban administration and design. To date, urban energy supply has been very much a highly segregated concern, and renewable urbanism a marginal concern at best. The transformation of the solar-energy hardware-focused Million Solar Roofs Partnership Initiative in the United States (MSR 2006) into Solar Powers America (SPA) programme was ostensibly motivated by a concern to move from add-on systems solutions to ensuring that renewable energy deployment and efficiency will become integrated into community and infrastructure programming, development and delivery processes. And the second area of change concerns a significant shift in planning and design culture, in the urban landscape of ideas: local geographies become important, again, in the renewable energy regime: local climate, watercourses, vegetation, soil conditions, topography, land use practices and pressures – and local economic, financial and resource policy conditions. The transformation of globalised thinking into local attentiveness and inventiveness will require significantly less effort than most critics of change believe. This resurrection of the local will open up new dimensions, and is already reflected in a still marginal if burgeoning, worldwide call for local and regional economic autonomy.

## The global context: rise of the renewable energy economy

When working in the urban development, design and policy arena, one can easily miss a dramatic change in the global energy profile and policy environment. Cities can filter and mask many trends – as can the professional frameworks active in their management. One significant feature still very much absent from the discourse surrounding urban communities is the dramatic shift in wider energy policy and paradigms. The Renewables 2005 Global Status Report is optimistic about strong growth trends and mounting importance for renewable supplies relative to conventional energy. It found that an equivalent of

US$30 billion were invested in renewable energy worldwide in 2004, excluding large hydropower plants. In comparison, conventional power investment was US$150 billion in the same year. Large investment accounted for US $20 to $25 billion, largely assigned to projects in developing countries (REN21 2005).

The 2005 Status Report summarises global renewable power as having reached 4 per cent of global power sector capacity, or 160 gigawatts, without counting large hydropower installations, which themselves supply 16 per cent of the world's electricity. Of this capacity, 44 per cent, or 70 gigawatts, is realised in the developing world. This equals one-fifth of the world's nuclear power. Grid-connected solar photovoltaic power is the fastest growing sector, rising by 60 per cent annually in the five years to 2004, covering close to half a million rooftops across Germany, Japan and the United States. Wind power's growth rate is second, at 28 per cent, led by Germany's installed capacity of 17 gigawatts.

Solar collectors supply 40 million households worldwide with hot water, most of them in China. More than 2 million heat pumps are deployed across 30 countries for the cooling and heating of buildings. Today biomass powered heating – predominantly wood burning, broadly renewable, but in the long term unsustainable and a contributor to carbon emission and indoor pollution generates five times more heat than solar and heat pumping combined. Ethanol and biodiesel production stood at more than 33 billion litres in 2004, accounting for 3 per cent of the 1,200 billion litres of petrol consumed globally. Ethanol constituted 44 per cent of all fuel combusted in Brazilian cars during 2004, and was blended into nearly one third of all gasoline sold at United States pumps.

Immediate new jobs created surpassed 1.7 million worldwide in 2004, with almost one million in the biofuel industry. Over 4.5 million electricity consumers chose green power across the United States, Canada, Europe, Japan and Australia, buying power retail or via renewable energy certificates. Sixteen million households lit their homes and cooked with biogas, and 2 million used solar lighting systems. At least 48 countries have a renewable energy policy, including 14 in the developing world. By 2005, at least 32 countries and 5 states/provinces had adopted feed-in policies; half of these since 2002. Almost 40 countries, states or provinces have adopted renewable portfolio standards since 2001. Renewable energy subsidies, grants or rebates are offered in more than 30 countries. Most US states and over 30 nations provide tax incentives and credits. Renewable energy targets are pursued in at least 45 countries, ten of them developing nations, including all 25 European Union members, and many states or provinces in the United States and Canada. Most targets aim at electricity production shares of, between 5 and 30 per cent by 2010–12. An

EU-wide target of 21 per cent of electricity production by 2010 is set. China's target of 10 per cent of total power capacity by 2010 excludes large hydropower installations and implies 60 gigawatts of renewable energy capacity by 2010, an increase of 23 gigawatts in five years. Cities also set targets for government or total city consumption in the 10–20 per cent range; some cities have established $CO_2$-reduction aims and many promote solar hot water and photovoltaics, and structure urban planning policies in ways that incorporate renewable energy.

Solar and wind power costs have halved in 15 years. Many renewable technologies are beginning to compete successfully with conventional energy, even as conventional technology costs also decline – while fossil fuel costs fluctuate and broadly rise. Large commercial banks are beginning to invest in green technologies, and several embrace renewable energy in their lending portfolios. Venture capital investors and investment banks like Babcock & Brown, Goldman Sachs and Morgan Stanley have begun to understand the renewable opportunity. Multinationals like British Petroleum, General Electric, Sanyo, Sharp and Siemens are investing heavily in renewable energy. German solar giant, SolarWorld AG, acquired the entire solar division of Shell in early 2006, doubling its workforce. Five of China's largest electrical and aerospace corporations have entered the wind energy industry. The 60 leading public renewable energy companies or divisions are underwritten at a combined $25 billion.

Total government support for renewable energy was $10 billion in 2004 for Europe and the United States, including direct funds and equivalent value leveraged through policy, including over $700 million in research and development expenditures annually. But only half a billion dollars are assigned each year to developing countries as development assistance for renewable energy projects, training, and market support, even if one includes the contributions of the German Development Finance Group, the World Bank Group and the Global Environment Facility as well as dozens of other donors and programmes. At least 150 market facilitation organisations (MFOs) help foster renewable energy markets, investments and businesses through information exchange, market studies, education, facilitation, consulting, finance, policy support and technical assistance. These are comprised of a rich and growing ecology of governments, non-governmental organisations, industry associations, development institutions, networks and partnerships, all focused on the worldwide and local proliferation of renewable energy (REN21 2005).

**Urban response to climate change**
Weather damage to cities and coastal communities has dramatically increased over the past decades; changes attributed to global climate change induced by fossil fuel combustion. This post-hurricane view looks east towards central New Orleans on the morning of Tuesday, 30 August 2005: urban life altered by a climate-change boosted agent of destruction: Katrina.

CHAPTER 2

# How to cope with Peak Oil by
# preparing for climate change

*'a city constantly moves between uncertainty and incomplete knowledge.'* Saskia Sassen (in van Dalm 2005).

## 2.1 CONFRONTING THE RISKS TO CITIES

A coal and oil combustion frenzy of epic proportions has powered urban growth for almost a century. This carries two immediate risks: the imminent peaking of the prime fuels feeding this infernal ritual; and dangerously shifting, largely warming, global climate patterns. Of the two, Peak Oil poses decidedly more imminent risks to cities and human settlement and, some argue, may well serve to help mitigate climate change, albeit in economically disastrous ways – unless coal burning is massively increased. The opportunities for cities in bracing themselves for Peak Oil are in many ways similar to the measures required to avert climate change risks. They consist of two policy and action realms described in detail in this chapter: *mitigation* – the massive reduction of fossil fuel use; and *adaptation*: the preparation of strategies to reduce the impact of hazards.

When Peak Oil occurs, probably by 2010 (Campbell 2004), and if no global actions have been taken to slow the consumption of fossil fuels within the next half decade, these hazards will consist of numerous unpleasant prospects. These may well include regional and global warfare; disruptions to the food supply (food production and distribution being highly fossil-fuel intensive activities (Manning 2004)); a breakdown in local power supplies and regional communication systems; and the temporary or permanent collapse of water and sewage systems, highly fossil-fuel dependent for pumping and processing (up to half a city's electricity supply can be taken up in maintaining its municipal or metropolitan water and sewage network (Gleick 1994)). But these would merely be the short-term impacts of power supply problems; the longer-term issues would include price rises and reduced urban competitiveness, depending on the locally applied fuel mix; global and regional economic decline and depression affecting many or all cities. With the exception of specific climate change impacts such as severe weather events, temperature increases or drops, a rise in sea levels or fresh water shortages, Oil Peak risks to many if not most cities would be similar, if not identical.

In a nutshell: immediate preparations to free cities and regions from their fossil fuel dependency, and determined moves to strengthen regional and urban economic and energy autonomy, are the most sensible strategies to prepare for both Peak Oil and climate change. Because of the difficulty in ascertaining the precise political, economic and military consequences of the admittedly more immediate Peak Oil scenario, the focus in this chapter is on urban climate change preparations, in the knowledge that the core efforts aimed at managing its risks are also useful to confront the historical twin Peak Oil calamity and opportunity. The prospect of Peak Oil adds a powerful measure of urgency to the call for action against greenhouse emissions.

Among many other enormous environmental costs of global and unbridled coal, oil and gas incineration, the fumes from their combustion increasingly trap solar radiation in the earth's atmosphere, warming the world – and are so extensive that they even overcome the marked global dimming and cooling effect air pollution has on sunlight. Cities play a central role in fossil-fuel consumption, and at the same time have significant capacities to introduce important energy policy changes. Hence, to a great extent global climate change is related to the local actions of urban communities, to how they build and manage their infrastructures, facilities and urban settings, what they consume, and how they dispose of their waste. And due to their collectively constructed and highly managed nature, cities are also the most sensitive elements of the national and global economy. It is critical that urban communities are both ready for the changes these global environmental impacts will bring, and aware of their power and responsibility to be prepared for discontinuous change – and to help slow and ultimately halt further global, fossil-fuel driven environmental deterioration.

The known effects of climate change include extreme and erratic weather patterns featuring cyclones, drought, hailstorms and storm surges; arise in sea levels; temperature drops and rises as well as spreading disease vectors – to name but a few. These are significant in themselves, even before any feedback and flow-on effects are taken into account. This chapter focuses on which hazards these climate change features represent, how exposed cities are to these hazards, and how vulnerable they are to these exposures – namely, how resilient their physical, social and economic systems will be in the face of impending changes. Given rising popular support and calls for change, city governments and community leaders must move swiftly into both mitigation and adaptation modes to help forestall a global urban cataclysm.

This chapter is designed to help cities manage climate change risk by gauging the issues, and constructing a realistic and robust urban planning and action framework, driven by mitigation and adaptation aims. Among all possible strategies to counter climate shift, a fundamental energy transformation is the most important goal to adopt. It is the very core element in any meaningful portfolio of measures. This topic forms the central aspect of the grand urban change narrative that has begun to unravel in front of everyone's eyes. Utterly dependent on local or distant fossil fuel reserves, cities are extremely sensitive to any change in their energy environment, particularly as it impacts their economies in this highly interconnected world. Climate change renders this dependency dramatic and, unless the fossil fuel combustion–carbon emissions cycle is broken, leads to a senseless flight into fossil-powered adaptation strategies – such as coal-fired desalination plants to cope with fresh water depletion.

Cities can act to avoid such absurdities, and at the same time assist in preparations to counter the complex threats emanating from the fast-approaching peak in global oil and natural gas production capacity – without resorting to a self-destructive reach for either the coal or nuclear power option. This chapter offers guidance for such efforts.

## Serial surprises

Cyclones are regular, seasonal visitors to the Mexican Gulf and southern Florida, the Bay of Bengal and other warm ocean stretches of the world. Many are lined with dense cities. Yet each large-scale rampage across populated areas takes on the significance of a shocking new catastrophe. Before the disastrous cyclone and subsequent inundation of New Orleans, the United States Federal Emergency Management Agency (FEMA) and the city government had completed a disaster simulation of the very event that struck in September 2005. The simulation declared the event as virtually certain to occur yet, with no particular date forecast, no action had been taken to guard against it, or to prepare the hapless citizenry for it.

Large cyclones recur and strike cities serially, yet urban group psychology, always betting on the odds of a lucky reprieve, ensures that each is treated as a surprise, an isolated calamity. But what if they become more frequent, or more intense and damaging, as some projections and observations over the past generation have suggested (Emanuel 2005; Knutson and Tuleya 2004; Webster et al 2005)? The prospect of previously isolated disasters becoming accepted as regular features of city living lies very much at the heart of this chapter. Indeed, all cities will have to cope with the major, energy-related transformations of fuel depletion and climate change that are the background to this book. There is hope that the shock of New Orleans' destruction by Hurricane Katrina will not only yield long-overdue investment to prepare for inevitable and intensifying cyclone damages locally, but also be translated globally into the urgent study and preparation for climate change shifts in general, and the inevitable decline in petroleum and natural gas reserves.

## Three birds with one stone

Indeed, a keen interest in urban *climate change adaptation* is on the rise, a quest to understand what urban communities can possibly do to prepare themselves for the inevitable climate shifts and their consequences: unavoidable given the massive carbon pollution that has already been vented into the skies. In also stressing the fundamental need of *climate change mitigation* in any adaptation strategies this guide focuses squarely on putting the brakes on fossil fuel use, thereby at once (a) limiting fossil fuel dependence in case of terminal depletion shock; (b) helping stretch fossil fuel supplies to buy precious energy conversion time; and (c) stemming climate-destabilising anthropogenic greenhouse gas emissions.

## Canary islands

Small island nations and their cities and towns, act as the 'coalmine canaries' of global climate change. They stand to lose the most in an earliest shift of climate patterns and sea levels, and in the least ambiguous way: they vanish like Atlantis. The Republic of the Maldives called for global action two decades ago, during the United Nations General Assembly's Special Debate on Environment and Development in 1987 (Gayoom 1987). The Maldives' representatives could not know that the UN process would become notorious for delaying urgent action on climate change, eventually resulting in another ineffectual policy cul-de-sac in 1994, the Kyoto Protocol. Adaptation through urban planning is a course that may first have been discussed in an article published by the American Planning Association (APA) over 15 years ago (Titus 1991). Given the time lag, to describe urban adaptation as an urgent challenge is hence very much an understatement. Yet it is only legitimate if it is not used to deflect attention from the overwhelming need to reduce fossil fuel use through mitigating action: energy conversion to renewable power.

## 2.2  MITIGATING ADAPTATION

Unfortunately, the call for adaptation to the effects of impending climate change is often and falsely pitted against pleas for mitigation measures that could help remove the causes of such change and thus prevent it from occurring. At the current rate of climate change both are essential and operate in synergy. Mitigation is the most powerful and essential form of adaptation. And many effective and meaningful, enduring forms of adaptation tend also to be important measures for climate change mitigation. No serious urban study or plan for adaptation will ignore the focus on mitigation through unequivocal carbon emissions reductions while steering clear of nuclear power. Adaptation can be a way of attempting a reduction in vulnerability. But it is a hopeless undertaking at best and an irresponsible slogan at worst without firm commitments to a specific extent and time frame for a fossil fuel phase-out, synchronised with the most likely oil and gas peak year: 2010 (Campbell 2005).

The marketing staff of some petroleum industry groups have lavished considerable funds on scientific-sounding arguments designed to ridicule the very idea of mitigation, and to focus attention on adaptation instead. This recommendation is tantamount to advising the proverbial frog in the pot of boiling water to stay put and don an asbestos swimsuit, instead of leaping out, or turning down the flame. Among the most remarkable of these is Okonski's infamous compendium, *Adapt or Die*, featuring a chorus of climate change sceptics (Okonski 2004). Other documents purport to be more balanced, gingerly describing adaptation efforts as being 'complementary' to mitigation measures (Easterling et al 2004, p iii) – like assets in a well-balanced, bet-hedging investment portfolio. In a June 2004 pamphlet, *Coping with Global Climate Change – the Role of Adaptation in the United States*, the Pew Centre on Global Climate Change projects an almost cheerful degree of optimism about the United States' ability to adapt to gradual change, as opposed to that of hapless developing nations (Easterling et al 2004, pp 18 and 19). While it extols the virtues of pro-active over reactive adaptation, warns against the errors of 'maladaptation' and expounds on the great promises of technological innovation, the Pew document manages to stay entirely clear of the very idea of mitigation as adaptation response, and even strenuously avoids *energy* – as word, concept, culprit or solution. Its central flaw lies in an artificial and dangerous separation of mitigation from adaptation. To mitigate is to adapt; and good forms of adaptation help mitigate climate change – especially for practice in the United States, the undisputed world champion in causing climate change, and precipitating Peak Oil.

The seeming ease of semantically contrasting mitigation and adaptation is misleading and artificial: to urban policymakers and planners the two concepts are not even comparable. Pragmatic forms of adaptation come naturally to cities, while general mitigation is seen as a more altruistic concept, feasible only with substantial voter pressure and state or national level support. Seen in this superficial light, adaptation fits more comfortably into the realms of conventional urban planning, infrastructure works and emergency management, misleadingly focused on the self-interest and narrow survival of a city. By contrast, mitigation is a more indirect, abstract and noble cause, aimed at attempting to heal the global commons: the atmosphere, oceans or forests. But, mitigation, too, is adaptation: it is aimed at future, seemingly distant, anonymous and uncertain goals of self-preservation and hence not easily introduced into, and maintained in mainstream and generally short-lived urban planning agendas. In arguing for mitigation, therefore, it is important for cities also to focus on renewable energy autonomy and fossil-fuel technology substitution rather than greenhouse gas emissions reductions alone, and emphasise the more specific incentives and benefits inherent in increasingly urgent measures of Oil-Peak risk management, energy security, technological innovation and employment generation.

## The long race to the brink

Climate change mechanisms and scenarios have been studied for more than a century, since Swedish physicist Svante Arrhenius (1859–1927) formulated the concept of the greenhouse effect (Arrhenius 1896). Arrhenius, having experienced the expanding fossil-fuel reality around him, also warned of the tragic damage that would be caused by excessive petroleum combustion and coming warfare over fossil fuel resources (Arrhenius 1922, quoted in Scheer 2005). But as in Arrhenius's time, successful *mitigation* action is today as challenging to frame as is *adaptation*, if for different reasons. The *tragedy of the commons* is that all benefit from, but none feel responsible for, preserving the collective assets of clean air, healthy forests and unpolluted oceans (Hardin 1968). To do so would not serve any particular individual interest. In a world in which self-interest is rewarded, no one wants to be first in altruism. Even when concerted action is finally organised because of a calamitous decline of shared assets such as the atmosphere, being last is still seen as advantageous by the most shrewd and selfish: one's own cost is minimised while everyone else works and pays to rescue the commons for all.

This strategy keeps a few countries from agreeing to even such modest mitigation mandates as those promoted in the Kyoto process. Identified here as *climate brinkmanship* or, more graphically, the *New Orleans Syndrome* it also keeps individual cities from adopting effective adaptation strategies. Communities and their leaders often count on local resilience in the face of adversity, or heroic capacity to endure and spring back, and confuse this with adaptation (Easterling et al 2004, p 5). These empirical principles mean that effective collective change or adaptation is all too frequently forthcoming only when people are confronted with the incontrovertible evidence that it is too late, or that considerable cost has already been incurred, never to be recouped. Urban planning policy is only seemingly conservative: administrations are decidedly risk-friendly in times that require course-deviating decisions in the interest of avoiding probable damage. Today, the greenhouse phenomenon is widely accepted as a scientific and popular fact, and understood as a proven outcome of the global combustion of coal, oil and natural gas. And yet, a state of paralysis has arrived in which neither mitigation nor adaptation has been fully embraced. When will the brink arrive? What form will it take? Or is it already behind us?

## Beyond the brink: beyond adaptation

Once civilisation moves beyond the brink in a undeniable, publicly acknowledged sense, a desperate scramble for action will commence on a large scale. How well will modern cities adapt to what are likely to be massive and possibly rapid transformations, even if further atmospheric greenhouse-gas concentrations could be ceased at once? Many pre-fossil fuel age cities – the traditional urban centres before the 19th century – are testimony to high levels of adaptability: adaptation has defined urban innovation and framed the dynamics of urban prosperity and decline. Countless adaptive inventions have been developed in and for cities: techniques of defence and attack, writing and information exchange, temporal regimentation and financial management, and those of rural and regional exploitation. Advanced agriculture, infrastructure and built-form concepts were introduced by travellers and traders, and soon adjusted to meet regional and local climates and resource regimes.

The range of adaptation responses developed by earlier urban dwellers is what defines much of the world's urban cultural heritage today. But among these there are also many remnants of community failures – abandoned cities, collapsed urban regions and ruined settlements, outposts, farmsteads and mining towns. Some are the result of political, communication and technological breakdowns, some suffered from water and resource depletion, and others became uninhabitable due to shifts in weather patterns. All experienced change too rapid or severe to be countered by either resilience or deliberate adaptation efforts. Many of these urban relics are popular tourist destinations today: the ruins of Minoan civilisation, its decline thought to have been triggered by the eruption of the super-volcano Thera three millennia ago; Angkor's mystery-shrouded decline and fall from the 13th century on; Mayan drought and famine-weakened urban culture of the 9th century; or South Australia's 19th-century parched pioneer ghost towns. Yet few disaster heritage visitors pause to ponder the possible future of many of today's urban communities.

Even polymath Jared Diamond's definitive guide to historical adaptation failures, *Collapse – How Societies Choose to Fail or Survive*, has its readers wade through almost five hundred pages of meticulously documented accounts of collapse, only to be denied the most important conclusion in the remaining 10 per cent of the volume: the analogy of past civilisations calamities to today's energy predicament. Diamond devotes a dismissive 20 lines to the potential of renewable power, energy sources that have driven human civilisation exclusively through the entire span of the book's narrative. He ends his tome by declaring renewable energy solutions as unfeasible technically since, to his mind, they consist largely of 'solar and wind' power and are available only at too slow a pace. He does correctly stress the need for a dramatic curtailment of fossil fuel use, but without straining to provide much insight into how this could best be accomplished (Diamond 2005).

Global climate change makes past adaptation challenges seem like minor logistical hiccups in comparison. Even the worldwide impact of the eruption of Krakatoa in 1883 has been more short-lived than the effect of the great global carbon flatulence of the 20th century promises to be. Since the fossil-fuel age arrived with a vengeance in the late 19th century, and virtually exploded into the global petroleum-burning orgy that all industrial states were engaged in by and since the 1950s, local climate and resource constraints ceased to be seen as a problem. All such barriers and constraints became mere challenges, to be overcome in a paradise of coal and oil powered innovations: electricity, water and sewerage for all; universal healthcare; national or continental surface transport routes; expanding air traffic; great dams, irrigation schemes and power stations; modern metropolitan infrastructures: pipes, pumps, levees and enabling machinery of all kinds, synchronised by increasing sophistication in logistics. Central cities were transformed into thinly glazed and air-conditioned hubs of global economic activity. Due to the abundance, low cost and seeming harmlessness of carbon energy resources, the age-old principles of adaptation seemed no longer to be an issue. Urban history had ended: an energy-rich technology cocoon could be spun around the city of yore. The most memorable image of this era was Buckminster Fuller's famed Manhattan dome proposal of 1965. Fuller suggested that it should be constructed as an urban-scale weather protection bubble above mid-town New York just south of Central Park. Indeed, Fuller depicted it as a futuristic, indoor extension of the park – anticipating city life as air-conditioned mall. He compared it in its functional elegance with 'a good air-cooled gasoline engine', capable of being encased with one-way mirrored glass or earth-covered to serve as a nuclear fall-out shelter (Fuller 1965).

A seemingly never-ending supply of technical solutions became available to deal with every urban problem. Urban man felt entitled to an infinite stream of technological innovation, solving each and every malaise. Such was the very essence of Modernity, modern democracy and the culture of abundance. But a mounting revulsion against the symptoms of *affluenza* is a hopeful sign that change is afoot (De Graaf et al 2005; Hamilton and Denniss 2005). Some cities, too, become messengers of sufficiency, advocating less consumption-driven lifestyles, like Italy's *Slow City* movement, or the longstanding and successful efforts to stem the rise in automobile traffic by Berlin's and other German cities governments. The end of an era is in sight in which city governance and administrative institutions have been shaped around the Modern illusion of the great urban *techno-fix* and its variegated solutions in energy supply, water and sewage utilities, roads, transit and ports – all deployed to be managed efficiently, but in isolation from one another. Today, cities seek to shed the yoke of narrowly defined, sectoral thinking – a central feature of the fossil-fired era – in a search for adaptation in efficiency and conservation. This has begun to be evident in attempts to find more integrated solutions to deal with the environmental and economic costs of this culture, to find whole-of-government approaches, embrace smart-growth and slow-growth partnerships, and to enter into agreements of regional and catchment management, or regionally coordinated, sound settlement policies – a dream advanced since the 1970s.

The coming decades will be dominated by this new spirit, in an increasingly luminous light. The climatic basis on which cities were founded will shift and, for many, dramatically so, straining, perhaps exceeding their adaptive capacity. It is likely that historical energy-based shifts will occur in ways that go beyond the capacity of individual urban support systems to cope with in sustainable or affordable ways. The process leading to this situation has long been under way. New is the growing degree of popular awareness, and mounting government and industry willingness to submit to the increasingly glaring evidence on the nightly news channels, reporting heatwaves, hurricanes, soggy permafrost and melting glaciers. The very future of cities is in doubt; in its extended consolidation of its fossil dependence urbanising civilisation has been a main contributor to the very climate changes confronting it now. There is no directly useful historical analogy or lesson available for an adaptation challenge of this magnitude, geographic reach and duration.

## Adapting while mitigating

Current temperature change fluctuations projected over the 21st century range from 2 to nearly 6 degrees Celsius and, some argue, even up to 9 (IPCC 2001a). The precise effect of global warming is uncertain, due to complex flow-on and feedback dynamics. But one increasingly probable scenario is strongly supported by recent observations: change may well be at the more extreme end of the spectrum, occur faster than anticipated, and be of millennial proportions in the time scale of its duration. There are strong indications that its full impact is already present but masked and delayed by the temporary cooling effect – *global dimming* – of combustion pollutants and increased amounts of water vapour, floating suspended in the upper atmosphere, creating the paradoxical and vexing effect of enhanced warming as soon as fossil emissions are curtailed (Stanhill and Cohen 2001). In sum, while the ranges of possible climate futures are typically projected within the time horizon of the 21st century, it is important to recognise that this is no distant possibility. Anthropogenic change dynamics are with us, and have been for some considerable time, demonstrably so for the past 50 years.

The currently changing global climate has already substantially transformed the very conditions under which cities evolve. Over at least the past half-century it has begun to modify precipitation patterns, increase pressures on urban water supplies, alter the size and nature of city and village markets, and modify their hinterlands, ultimately also affecting food production. It has set the stage for further reductions in regional bio-diversity levels and more virulent disease vector regimes. It has changed flooding patterns and the frequency and intensity of cyclonic events. Very few of these changes have been, or will be perceived as positive – and virtually all of them are predicted to become more extreme with time. And they will be the more extreme – and possibly abrupt – the fewer, and the more slowly, mitigating adaptation measures are taken.

## Mounting prospects of discontinuous urban change

Present climate change may appear to be slow to some, but many of its effects are felt increasingly directly. Global-warming triggered events have become more violent and prevalent. Local, state or national leadership can no longer afford to wait for so-called *threshold events* to change policy in a crisis response (Glantz 2005). Cities and their communities are critical and integral elements of global and national economic systems: everything is at stake. Leading decision-makers and communities alike must not harbour any illusions about an easily projected, linear future, nor about being able to successfully adapt increment-ally or in an *ad hoc*, unplanned fashion. Climate change has progressed to such an extent that urban futures are likely to be discontinuous. This risk is clear, present and sizeable, creating powerful incentives to secure sustainable means of urban adaptation and mitigation. But while both coordinated and autonomous action at global, national, state and local level is called for, it is only slowly forthcoming, and insufficiently proclaimed as a global imperative.

Two factors may drive a coming boom in combined urban mitigation and adaptation programmes, here called *mitigating adaptation*, or conflated to *mitaptation*. One is a hoped-for and indeed likely, sharp increase in interna-tional greenhouse mitigation requirements within this, the first decade of the Second Millennium; and the other the fundamental need for cities to continue to flourish as communities and economies, even in the face of climate change adversities. Mitaptation will be costly but carries the promise of important innovation and high returns, beyond basic protection from climate calam-ities. Mitaptation is marked by tightly streamlined urban land use and trans-port policies; and more effective building energy performance regulations. The former yield benefits in more efficient urban systems and markets, and a return to rejuvenated urban centres, new and old. And the latter are already proving to be a welcome stimulus in innovative circles of the commercial, residential and industrial building industry. Other strategies include: (a) regional land use regimes dedicated to energy farming and forestry in wind, solar and biomass based power and fuel production; (b) decentralised renewable energy supply systems; (c) locally and regionally embedded and self-contained fresh water collection, recycling, reticulation and conservation methods; (d) a climate-sensitive industrial innovation strategy, aimed at securing new employment in the new and booming renewable energy, climate mitigation, adaptation and risk management industries; and (e) highly articulated, poly-nucleic networks of revitalised and intensive urban nodes structured around all these changes, and focused on enhanced forms of regional autonomy.

Mitaptation is difficult: cities are not merely larger versions of buildings. Greenhouse mitigating forms of adaptation are not achieved through a few and easily identified physical measures, systems adjustments, political levers or financial drivers. Rather, cities as collective and hence not singularly controllable constructs respond to broader shifts, to transformations of their physical, business and political climate – fundamental changes in the climate of ideas as much as in meteorological conditions. Successful urban strategies must prove their effectiveness in a messy world: in notoriously complex, uncertain and open systems. Four decades of progress in systems analysis and modelling has not succeeded in aiding in their understanding. Cities are socio-economic, cultural and political entities first – and physical systems only second: they do not respond well to shortterm, simple-minded or rigidly defined efforts. Unexpected outcomes result when these are attempted.

Urban sociologist Saskia Sassen suggests that cities cope with uncertainty through creativity and resourceful responsiveness (van Dalm 2005). Cities have an innate capacity to respond and adapt, a built-in resilience by virtue of the imagination and inventiveness of their population. Yet in order to muster a city's innovative energy in this historical challenge, it does not suffice to await or nurture a vaguely defined shift in the climate of ideas alone. Rigorous and detailed local and regional planning efforts have to be embarked on, and without further delay. Cities, their governments and communities must visualise how their environment is likely to change, and assess what corresponding actions promise success.

But the mere building of models, scenarios and case studies to inform policy does not suffice either to ensure timely action, however compelling these constructs may be. The carefully simulated and well-predicted 2005 New Orleans disaster has shown this. Effort also has to be endowed with decisive, action-oriented capabilities. Cities must be able to identify and mobilise policy and programme resources that can work within the local institutional, behavioural and cultural environment – that are relevant and supported in these terms. Specifically: in order to reliably generate intelligent and purposeful community preparedness and responses, cities will have to be supported in assembling scenario-responsive decision-making models that are relevant in at least five ways. They must be relevant in terms of (a) *policy*, ie their capacity to be carried out; (b) *behavioural response*, ie their ability to trigger social change; (c) *spatial detail*, ie their ability to be mapped; (d) *decision-making*, ie a capacity to inform choice; and (e) *output*, ie the ability to be meaningful to stakeholders (after Hensher 2003).

## 2.3 URBAN RISKS

The risks human-induced climate changes pose to advanced civilisation in general and modern cities in particular are a global concern. While the precise future impacts on any particular city or region are uncertain, change is incontrovertibly underway across the global urban system. Its nature and degree will depend on the unfolding dynamics of this calamity but also on the swiftness and extent of mitigating action taken globally, the degree to which the global urban system as whole can manage to adapt as network, and on what particular adaptation tactics are articulated locally. The immediate halt, even dramatic voluntary slowing, of further anthropogenic greenhouse gas (GHG) emissions is a utopian call – but mitigating action must be radical and extensive if only to postpone the decline of fossil-fuel resources while dependence is so overwhelming. Given the current level of GHG pollution alone many of the substantial changes now underway are irreversible, and may already be inevitable.

Degree and speed of change are also determined by both flow-on and feedback effects, factors even less accessible to precise predictions than primary shifts. These can range widely and may not necessarily spell temperature increases or droughts for many cities, but rather a drastic drop in temperature for some, and inundation for others. The salt-rich Gulf Stream, or *thermohaline conveyor*, appears to be slowing, possibly to the brink of collapse, diluted by massive fresh-water run-off from Greenland's melting ice cover and rain-swelled Siberian rivers. The evaporation of this source of ambient warmth could spell the sudden conversion of the United Kingdom and Northern Europe's weather patterns into more arctic conditions, while the equatorial region and its massive population could be starved of vital monsoons for hundreds of years to come (NRC 2002; Schwartz and Randall 2003).

But even discounting the more catastrophic scenarios of abrupt cataclysms, a strong consensus has formed among leading scientists on the desperately urgent need for *global mitigating* action in curtailing emissions in order not to further increase the numerous annual fatalities already attributed to climate change – many urban – and to buffer impacts to the most affected, typically the poorest and least able to cope. Global urban adaptation will be climbing the global agenda as a valid concern, too: governments – international, national and local alike – will soon be called upon to invest in finding ways of adjusting to climate change as a system of settlements. Key means will be urban defossilisation efforts; new trading policies that move away from exhorting global interconnectivity as an overarching principle; the development of enhanced support mechanisms for local autonomy; more focused environmental programmes; scenario modelling and planning capacities and institutional change as an adaptation-driven development principle. Climate impact risks span every aspect of urban concerns, highlighting the limits of sectoral divisions: the urban economy; social environment; physical and natural environment; urban structure; infrastructure and land use planning policy – and urban governance.

## Gauging and managing urban risks

The Intergovernmental Panel on Climate Change (IPCC) has defined vulnerability as a function of 'exposure, sensitivity and adaptive capacity' (IPCC 2001b). With its 2001 assessment of *Impacts, Adaptation and Vulnerability* it has helped frame the global focus on these issues, guiding other, regional versions of interpreting the issues involved (Allen 2005, p ix). For the purpose of this guide it seems to be more practical, and useful to city planning, to modify the IPCC structure, and adopt a conceptual frame that is more in line with the insurance industry's approach to calamitous events (Roaf et al 2005a). Here the important notion of *risk* is introduced squarely, and defined as a function of *hazard, exposure* and *vulnerability*. *Hazard* denotes the very nature of climate change threats: sea level rise, temperature fluctuations, droughts or hurricanes; *exposure* is measured by the degree to which a hazard can wreak havoc on a city, its population, infrastructure and regional setting; and *vulnerability* is the degree to which the city or urban system – its people, natural systems, built environment, economy and institutions – are able to cope with its exposure to a particular hazard. Together, these factors establish climate change risk factors for cities.

Risk can be managed by improving on any or all of the three factors. In practice, very different mechanisms and actors have to be mobilised for each. National and international government institutions must unfold persuasive strategies to minimise losses, and reform their energy households, preparing them for changing climatic conditions and flow-on effects. Climate change risk assessment is an essential part of enlightened strategic urban planning: it involves understanding the general risks faced by cities, and even specific areas within a city or city region. It is essential in order to rally institutions and communities to implement both mitigation and locally relevant adaptation strategies. A first step in an assessment is to compile current and emerging urban impacts of climate change hazards, using the readily available atmospheric carbon concentration scenarios, followed by an analysis of their significance and level of threat, and the comparative effectiveness of available alternative responses. This approach meshes well with the way in which industries – other than the insurance sector – define risk, framing it as the *likelihood* of events (AS 2004).

In summary, strategies for managing climate change risk depend on being able to clearly define and articulate: (a) climate change hazards in terms of degree of exposure and vulnerability to these; (b) risk criteria specific to a city, city region or cluster of cities or city regions; and (c) a combination of mitigation and adaptation methods. This guidebook contains model references and templates, useful as part of urban climate change mitigation efforts. As a reminder, the same approach is useful to analyse and communicate Peak Oil risks, by specifying oil and gas peak hazards, specific risk criteria and relevant mitaptation approaches.

## Hazards and exposure

Among the most visible and damaging urban effects – combinations of hazard and exposure – of climate change are (a) temperature change itself, manifest in greater heat levels and a rise in the number of days of extreme temperatures – but also to be expressed in lowered temperatures for some cities; (b) decreased rainfall and a higher incidence of droughts, or, elsewhere, increased rainfall and flooding; and (c) other extreme weather events: cyclones, hailstorms, thunderstorms and lightning, resulting locally in storm surges, floods or forest fires.

Sea level change is an important, longer-term hazard, a result of both the thermal expansion of the oceans and land-based icecap and glacial melts. Global rises amounted to at least 10 centimetres over the past 50 years. They are likely to approach 1 metre over the 21st century, but could amount to up to 7 metres in a longer timeframe, particularly if the recent evidence of a melting Greenland icecap signals a calamitous process of global significance. As an average rule, local damage amounts to 50 metres of foreshore inundation for each metre of sea level rise, not taking into account any land, sand and soil loss incurred through higher current action and wave erosion. For low-lying cities this hazard will yield devastating consequences. In one of the world's first urban adaptation responses, the city of Malé, Maldives, has erected a new sea wall. A new settlement plan has been completed for a relocation area to be founded on an artificial shelf created atop a natural reef formation. The Maldives hosted the Small States Conference on Sea Level Rise as early as 1989, resulting in the much reported but little heeded *Malé Declaration on Global Warming and Sea Level Rise* (Titus 1989).

Exposure to hazards is manifest in urban effects: dangers need to be mapped against specific locations of varying exposure levels to model impacts. As an example of localised exposure to one particular hazard – temperature rise – Australia as a whole will experience between 0.4 and 2 degrees Celsius in average temperature rise by 2030, and between 1 and 6 degrees by 2070, with significant larger regional variations (Allen 2005). Urban dwellers will encounter more days at peak temperatures, and a reduction in the amplitude of temperature changes between day and night – the diurnal swing. Northern regions are likely to see monsoonal rain increases, while the rest of the continent faces a decrease – overall, rainfall will be reduced by an estimated 5 to 20 per cent. Extreme weather events will become more frequent and severe. Sea level rise is expected to be slow and gradual over the next one or two genera-tions, but will eventually impact nearly all of the country's major population centres because national development patterns favour coastal zones.

## Carbon hazards

So-called *carbon hazards* emerge as central features in the new urban planning agenda, too. Although not all are climate-related, they do fit well into a compre-hensive and future-minded mitigation and adaptation strategy. These include the nearing peak in global oil production, rising oil and natural gas prices, and carbon levies. Sooner or later, limits on the commercial use of fossil fuels are likely to be introduced, even beyond the oil peak: restrictions on coal, for example, as a way of making up for any petroleum and gas shortfall that cannot be compensated for by a desired increase in efficiency, or an undesired decline in global economic activity. Carbon-use based hazards pose a dramatic risk to settlements. Cities depend on massive primary energy supply flows and other energy-dependent infrastructure systems such as water and waste systems; in a sum, their role as national and global foci for production and consumption depends on energy in ways that are highly price dependent. Only locally and regionally sourced renewable power systems can help overcome this risk.

## 2.4 URBAN EXPOSURE AND IMPACTS

### Gauging exposure

The risk presented by a hazard increases with the degree of exposure, defined by the actual capability of a hazard to affect urban areas and assets. Urban exposure assessments estimate the likelihood of a given hazard to impact a city's life, viability and function. They look into such questions as: what level of damage will be exerted by which hazard? How, when and where? And how frequently is a particular hazard likely to strike, impair or destroy a particular place? Local urban exposure assessments can gauge direct exposure – by, for instance, recording cyclone paths, sea level rises or disease vector spread – or indirect exposure, by, for example, tracking disturbances in the markets or supply lines of a city or town. Assessments can be carried out as system-wide, citywide or district focused exercises. Assessments produced by national or regional governments will generally be systemic: designed to provide a broader urban perspective. Citywide assessments focus on the exposure of a particular city and its region as a whole; while district studies examine the degree of exposure individual neighbourhoods are subject to. Exposure studies deploy a range of tools: (a) climate models; (b) hazard impact models; (c) case studies of earlier events; and (d) planning scenarios for future events.

Once climate hazards unfold, exposure becomes a fixed feature in a city's life and risk profile. While cities cannot reduce their actual *exposure* to hazards, they can manage and substantially reduce risk through ways of limiting their *vulnerability*, as described in the next section. Individual citizens, companies and industries, on the other hand, can – and often will – seek to reduce their exposure by relocating, and join the growing numbers of climate refugees.

Several variables determine the level of a city's exposure:

**Time**: frequency, duration and horizon. Temporal hazard assessments determine: (a) the number of events per given time period, such as heat waves per year; (b) event duration; for example: heat spikes or extended hot periods; and (c) the point in time when the events are likely to occur – are they imminent, or not likely to take place for another ten years?

**Geography**: hazard zones require mapping. This can be done for storm surge areas, for example; by publishing thermal exposure maps; or producing diagrams depicting regional cyclone zones. *Hazard theatre maps* can be coded according to their time risks.

**Sensitive areas**: ecologically fragile or agriculturally productive open spaces. Forests can dry out, fragile costal vegetation succumbs to heat and precious farmland can be washed away in floods and downpours. These hazard exposure risks, too, can be mapped, and form a sub-set of urban and regional evaluations.

**Vital assets**: core infrastructure and other key facilities. The massive capital expenditure vested in built assets, and in the activities supported and sheltered by these, demand special mapping to determine exposure profiles. For example, urban and metropolitan fire-prone natural areas, such as bush or forest lands, represent a loss risk in terms of the value of the primary incendiary zones themselves, but, in addition, they may place at risk adjacent primary installations and assets such as water supply facilities, power plants, health institutions and concentrations of economic activity such as industrial and business parks.

**Population**: The demographics of exposure are central to this assessment. For example, estimated and recorded should be the number of individuals in heat-wave sensitive groups, such as infants and the elderly; or, in terms of cyclone and flood exposure, the disabled, poor, homeless, tourists, or informal-sector or floating-population workers. For major anticipated events or risks evacuation plans are required. Population impacts are both specific to local geographic conditions and time sensitive: when do they occur, how will they unfold as days and months go by?

## Anticipating impacts: physical, social and economic

Extreme weather events like cyclones are capable of delivering the most visibly dramatic and immediately costly urban punishment of all climate-change related phenomena. Less dramatic but equally vexing changes – decreased precipitation, for example – will weaken and undermine the viability of many cities. The fossil fuel city's structural design flaws reveal themselves now with bleak starkness: for example, the nexus between fresh water consumption and fossil-fuel and nuclear based power generation becomes obvious. These wasteful energy production systems are especially thirsty, for cooling, as well as for process requirements during the entire fuel supply chain from mining to energy conversion.

The viability of urban open space systems can deteriorate, whether due to warming, drying, drenching or freezing. As this occurs, urban environmental management requirements would probably soar. Indeed, the internal fabric of cities may alter – along with the structure and dynamics defining the national and global urban system. Mobility costs may rise, and land values change due to altered weather patterns. The revaluation of new land uses – such as for sun, wind or bio-energy crops – may affect development patterns. The relation between urban centres may be affected; and, due to more complex and competing demands on land use and proximity, the dynamics in peri-urban realms could be rendered more complex. Especially adversely affected may be the fragile, frequently fossil, ecology of existing suburban and *country-city* or *desakota* space: the Indonesian term used by Terry McGee in the early 1990s to describe the quasi-urban, quasi-rural hybrid urban spaces characteristic of many cities today, and not only those of the developing world (McGee 1991). A new *super-desakota*, a quasi-autonomous environmental quilt made up of built, open, agricultural and abandoned zones could well become the paradigmatic urban form of the greenhouse era.

Massive personal and community health risks arise: the incidence of heat-related accidents and deaths is on the increase, and other negative quality of life impacts are almost certain to eventuate. Climate refugees may soon begin seriously to distort inter-urban migration statistics. Economic costs may be incurred as direct and indirect infrastructure expenditures, borne by the community as a whole. Changes in both micro- and macro-economic dynamics could create massive financial losses, given the increasing level of worldwide urbanisation, and the still-rising urban contribution to national economic outputs. The traditional ability to leverage comparative advantage by attracting talents, businesses and the social and cultural institutions that support them will be impaired, but to varying degrees in different cities. The very equation determining the comparative advantage of competing cities will be recast. There will be relative winners and losers, but overall, broadly failing and more costly urban systems are likely to render everyone less well off.

More specifically, **physical impacts** of urban climate change affect: (a) *energy infrastructure*, as power generation efficiency declines at higher ambient temperatures, and generation machinery and transmission lines become more exposed to weather damage; (b) *water supply and sewage systems*, as many cities experience drying and water depletion, and pipes and conduits become damaged; (c) *transport infrastructures*, roads, rail, sea and airports etc, as these fall victim to assault by storm surges, floods and swells, severe storms and heat; (d) *agriculture*, food production and a stream of other basic resources in terms of quantity produced, quality and price; and (f) *the quality of the urban environment* in general as this is threatened by the effects of climate change hazards, compounded by the urban heat island syndrome and the flow-on results of other physical, economic and social impacts.

**Urban economic effects** include rising costs in (a) energy, water and waste management industry and services; (b) impaired mobility, including less cost-efficient freight forwarding and goods transport; (c) greater construction, management, operation and repair costs for built facilities; (d) a greater cost of business for location-dependent services and supply-reliant manufacturing; (e) decreased agricultural productivity; and (f) diminishing tourism and recreation values of many urban destinations and features. Many hazard impacts may be felt across all of these categories, creating feedback loops.

**Social effects** include a diminution of the broader quality of life; greater emergency management burden such as evacuation and relocation, effects on migration; and community health impacts. The human cost of climate change hazards is already staggering today: the World Health Organisation (WHO) estimates 150,000 deaths to occur annually from hazard-related causes ranging from heat-related cardiovascular and respiratory ailments to infectious diseases and malnutrition due to crop failure as a result of drought (Patz et al 2005).

## Characterising impacts

Urban risk analysts would identify, characterise and then rank impacts according to their significance. The following checklist of urban effects is useful for developing a matrix of likely physical, social and economic consequences.

**Can the impacts be quantified?** Impacts on built assets need to be determined, as does the damage to natural environments. And it is important carefully to describe the impacts on the economy, communities, individuals and government.

**Can they be priced?** Financial, human, institutional and environmental costs await determination, as measured in the provision of infrastructure; health, community and settlement services; migration pressures; or the restructuring of government.

**Can they be mapped?** Physical changes are rarely isolated and typically impact others, or have social and economic side effects. Investigating impacts in one area will lead to consequences in other domains.

**Are they understood as part of a dynamic system?** Urban impacts affect complex environments – and they set off flow-on effects and impacts in other areas. To more accurately gauge these effects will require an understanding of the city as dynamic system internally, and as part of other dynamic systems externally. Cities have undefined boundaries and are open systems, interrelated with and defined by their regional, national and international settings. Every city dweller and his/her local economy, environment and culture is very much connected and subject to regional, national as well as global events. Thanks to the fossil-fuel regime entire countries and international regions have evolved into quasi-urban systems – major portions of their populations reside in urban areas. To a certain extent, urban vulnerability is synonymous with national and global vulnerability.

**In sum: can impacts be ranked?** To understand sets of impacts in the context of an urban strategic planning exercise it is important to be able to prioritise them. Five rating criteria will assist in ranking the relative significance of climate impacts. *Imminence* asks: how soon will it strike? *Intersectoriality* raises the question: how pervasive will it be? The degrees of *severity* and *persistence* determine: how serious will it be, and how long will it last? And a determination of *cost* prompts the allocation of a specific financial burden. These and other criteria can then be assessed to produce a relative value for each urban climate impact.


## 2.5 URBAN VULNERABILITY

While exposure describes the potential climate hazard impact on urban dwellers, their shelter, infrastructure and environments, vulnerability is here defined as the degree to which an urban system – 'the city' as composed of its communities, infrastructure, economy and institutions – is capable, or incapable, of managing its specific level of exposure to a particular hazard. It connotes its adaptive capacity, the responsiveness and robustness of the physical, economic, psychological, social, political and institutional resources a city can mobilise and sustain to cope with climate hazard exposure (Allen 2005, *passim*; Easterling et al 2004, *passim*). A simple example: cyclone warning systems, combined with well-resourced and carefully rehearsed evacuation programmes, can render urban populations less vulnerable to cyclones and storm surges, even if the physical and ecological damage threatens to be severe. Flood resistant urban and building design, seawalls, mangrove forests, wetlands and nature zones can all reduce the overall vulnerability of an urban area – and in turn limit the need for evacuation procedures.

## Lowering vulnerability

Vulnerability can be managed, but only if it is admitted to, accepted and confronted. Good management capacity, the degree of community alertness, response capability and disaster readiness all lower vulnerability to short-term hazards. New Orleans was obliterated physically, socially and as a viable community because it was not only highly exposed to Hurricane Katrina, but also vulnerable in a number of other ways. Its position below sea level combined with neglected levee systems to render it vulnerable. The draining and eradication of marshes and wetland buffers – some of it ironically carried out in order to protect the city from flooding by the Mississippi River – compounded its vulnerability dramatically (Grunwald and Glasser 2005). In addition, the city was rendered vulnerable to the point of helplessness in its paralysed disaster response mechanisms, in the way the Federal government failed to act, and in the manner in which old racial and class divisions opened up in ugly ways, slowing the delivery of aid to those most in need.

## Vulnerability: 10 coping strategies

Vulnerability can be confronted and managed in actions responding to a specific calamity or in risk management and planning by preparing for future risks, whether these are powerful cyclones or increased prices for energy and water supplies. At least ten success factors can be applied to reduce a city's level of vulnerability.

- **Urban and regional autonomy** To combat vulnerability, a high degree of diversification in energy systems, food sources, water supply and places of production and employment should be a paramount planning aim. Systems that are most vulnerable to rising temperatures and water scarcities should be upgraded or superseded as a matter of priority. Decentralised, diversified and regionally endogenous energy systems – those based on solar, wind, water and biomass sources – are less vulnerable than those that rely on a highly long and central supply-chain dependent fuel source, and on fresh water for cooling in generation. Also, a broadly diversified regional economy is less vulnerable to exogenous shifts in demand, supply or labour market conditions.

- **Perceived relevance** The degree to which a city's policy, planning, design, project and capital investment programmes are marked by climate change adaptation and mitigation priorities in part determines its vulnerability. To bolster and garner support, studies and related information should be disseminated to decision-makers, stakeholder and communities in order to build broad understanding and consensus on the issues and the measures to be taken.

- **Financial resources** Wealthy countries contribute a disproportionate and excessive amount of greenhouse gas emissions responsible for the disruption of the climate balance. Indeed, they are responsible for most of the urban carbon debit share, especially when measured globally on a per capita basis (Byrne et al 1998). And cities and urban dwellers typically account for the lion's share of their respective national contribution. At the same time, wealthy cities are thought to be more able to absorb the costs of adaptation: the urban poor – just as poor populations in general – are expected to fare far worse when compared to their rich urban peers. Therein lies a double injustice – those who pollute the most are also less susceptible to the cost of the damage caused. But reality is more complex: private wealth does not necessarily translate into municipal wealth – sometimes, especially in countries subscribing to lean-government and other so-called conservative fiscal policies, the opposite is the case. Many larger urban centres in a number of so-called wealthy countries often teeter on the brink of financial crises, and may have difficulty in mustering additional resources beyond those required for everyday management. Also, richer communities have more to lose, and their sophisticated economies may be less able to adjust to disruptions. And as a rather bleak perspective, some comment that cities and urban populations accustomed to blackouts, floods and cyclones may be more able to adapt, cope and survive at already low levels of subsistence than those that depend on very high levels of technological support, sophistication and precision in service delivery.

- **Technical resources** The capability to map, monitor, inform and alert populations assists greatly in limiting vulnerability, as does access to a growing number of popular yet mostly shortterm climate change adaptation technologies, from urban flood gates against storm surges to solar-powered desalination plants.
- **Physical resources** The physical ability of built urban environments to withstand extreme and shifting weather patterns, sea level rises and other change is a classic determinant of vulnerability. An assessment of this aspect will need to examine the state of current buildings, ports and other facilities, as well as the adequacy of design and building standards, to ensure that the next generation of structures is robust. Enhanced standards would range from increased wind resistance in office building to a greater level of energy and water resource independence through greater efficiency, and stand-alone, hybrid or redundantly networked renewable energy generation capabilities.
- **Ability to manage countervailing influences** Resource and industrial interests with a stake in the status quo can act as a significant drag on climate change preparedness, and hence increase vulnerability. Some members of the automobile industry, motorist organisations and the fossil fuel industry and its investors, for example, tend to deny climate change impacts, or fear that even pure adaptation efforts translate into bad publicity for emission-rich features of a city or sectors of the economy. An ability to mobilise industry leaders sympathetic to the need for mitigating adaptation measures as business champions will be invaluable in managing this threat.
- **Organisational capability, accountability and decision-making** Especially critical are the adequacy and capacity of government institutions charged with mobilising and coordinating climate change response strategies. Most failures in this area can be attributed to ill-defined accountabilities and inabilities to frame, resource, manage and implement new strategies. Institutional capacity also relates to *information management*: the collection, processing and sharing of decision-sensitive data and the *monitoring* of hazard exposures, shifts in hazards, action progress or setbacks, population responses and environmental indicators, including the level of food quality and fresh water supplies. The establishment of dedicated and adequately resourced organisations is a key success element.
- **Protection of vulnerable populations** In any given city, the poor, ill, elderly, disabled, infants and homeless will be more vulnerable to climate

change exposure than the wealthy, healthy and those in their prime. For example, periods of elevated temperatures that result in heat related illnesses in a city present a greater hazard to the very young and very old due to their inherent health and physiological status. But psychosocial factors are also involved. The psychological reserves of a city's community or population, which are needed for successful adaptation to change, are especially critical. They are related to age, personal reserves, kinship networks and the prospect of recurrence of catastrophic events. The availability of infrastructure to cope with vulnerable groups is a central variable in determining the overall level of urban vulnerability.

- **Social capital** Local values and traditions of civic engagement and leadership, communities of skilled practitioners and thinkers, universities with engaged departments, media intent on developing a narrative of positive action, outspoken leaders and visionary, positive thinkers – all can help reduce the vulnerability of communities significantly. Strong community ties and social networks can shore up citywide resilience. A desire to show charitable care to the needy after traumatic events is an indication as well – but this is likely to be tested in recurring conditions, unless dramatic changes to the energy, environmental and resource regime of cities take place. Important, therefore, are substantial and ongoing efforts taken by city governments and industrial leaders to make major and tangible commitments to both mitigation and adaptation.

- **Environmental capital** The resilience of natural environments or urban ecosystems is another important factor. Dying marshlands and wetland buffers, or urban open space vegetation, park plants and street trees unable to thrive due to gradual temperature rises or changes in water regimes or precipitation patterns, can increase urban vulnerability dramatically. The urban support service provided by trees and wetlands disappear, such as ambient cooling, local shade, emissions absorption, storm water infiltration or visual amenity and relief, and other psychological benefits. By the same token, the presence and even active boosting of natural resources and species – flora and fauna – can play a supportive role in the urban areas potentially affected by climate change hazards and their consequences. For example, coastal areas that harbour or are shielded by healthy reefs, extensive *casuarina* or mangrove zones, or intact freshwater wetlands, are less exposed to the effect of storm surges and inundation by salty seawater than areas without. Urban waterways, parklands, green belts and nature reserves can significantly counteract several climate change hazards.

# The means of adaptation: planning for change

The steps taken to adapt are typically reactive, and often come too late. Meaningful adaptation policies must anticipate future events while seeking to influence these through mitigation, primarily the curtailment of fossil fuel use. Also, reconstructing lost buildings in the same location, or restoring natural realms can demonstrate a certain degree of resilience in the short term, and provide public reassurance of normalcy. But is not the most useful choice if these measures do not also confront high degrees of exposure and vulnerability. Instead, they can lull the public into a false sense of security, delay critical action and set the stage for future disappointment and frustration.

By contrast, authentic and planned forms of adaptation will involve a reform of urban development processes. New economic thinking, improved technological outlooks and administrative restructuring are key to anticipating climate change. Basic examples include revised building codes and land use laws, the absorption of disaster response into normal management practice, transformed land use practices and a fundamental search for new forms of livelihood. In the United States, a case in point is the state response to the precipitation-induced rising of the Great Salt Lake during the 1980s: short term pumping took place in lieu of more promising but logistically more difficult – and land-value threatening – changes in the lakeside land management regime. More effective, but ultimately ignored, measures would have included the nurturing of wetlands and the permanent exclusion of some sites from development, as recommended by the Federal Emergency Management Agency (FEMA) (Easterling et al 2004, pp 11 and 12).

# Institutional perspectives

In a world facing uncertainty and even threatening change, inherited institutions can make effective adaptation difficult. While we watch our televisions and see Arctic ice and Siberian tundras melting around the world, climate change is still seen as a marginal issue among most local government institutions. There is an irrational search for certainty in terms of local consequences, and even more so when uncertainty increases. Many local officials charged with guiding diverse group decision-making processes are more trained to administer in a reactive mode than to plan ahead. The ability to overcome this intrinsic local institutional challenge lies at the core of a global test: whether cities will prevail or wither in an age of accelerating climate change and Peak Oil.

The management of urban climate and petroleum supply risks through adaptation and mitigation does not necessarily require new municipal, regional or national institutions, but, as a minimum, demands new models of engagement, decision-making and accountability among established ones. Three typical responses stand out, from short term to more substantial approaches.

- **Crisis response** This is a strategy to mobilise and allocate exceptional efforts and resources following a surprise event. It works best for narrowly focused emergencies, but is likely to falter during long-term challenges.
- **Strategic planning** This cross-disciplinary approach emphasises outcome over process. The aim is for the agencies involved to collaborate and share resources accountably against agreed and planned outcomes. This approach often relies on special coordination processes and scenario studies to set targets and outcomes. It is strong in informing agenda and action, but often lacks links to day-to-day decision-making institutions.
- **Institutional reform** This approach pursues sustained institutional change based on concrete analyses leading to consensus, a strong mandate, performance measures and assigned accountabilities. Given adequate resources to gauge hazards, exposure and vulnerability, this model is most useful in gradually introducing climate risk assessment and management ideas while promoting wider institutional reform geared at restructuring governance so that both mitigation and adaptation are addressed in order to respond appropriately to both climate change and Peak Oil risks in the long term.

### Sana'a - ancient renewable city

The historical city core of Sana'a is a living monument to ancient thermal design principles guiding building and urban form alike. A centre of trade, the desert community also contained numerous gardens and small farms, contributing to its relative self-sufficiency in energy and food supply. Today, the old centre struggles to maintain its meaning in a spreading sea of air-conditioned suburbs, to a large extent financed by Yemenis working in Saudi cities, industries and oil fields.

CHAPTER 3

# Renewable geography

Optimistic urban energy visionaries see neighbourhoods, cities and city regions as evolving into autonomous and renewable-energy empowered, efficient environments: the city as renewable power station is a compelling concept (Pontenagel 2001). The idea of distributed solar, wind, water and biomass derived fuel sources driving entire cities is no utopian dream: it is inevitable. Practical visionaries work in many developing countries to see villages and rural communities become energy independent, supplying the micro-loans to finance the acquisition of renewable energy for lighting, cooking, heating and to power computing (IT) systems.

## 3.1 OTHER DRIVERS OF CHANGE

Powerful forces will transform the fossil-fuel dependent and energy deprived urban settlements of yesteryear into tomorrow's renewable-energy based communities. Chapter 2 described how both urban climate change mitigation and adaptation strategies must focus unwaveringly on renewable energy conversion. It explained the great power of a distributed renewable energy supply to assist with disaster readiness and emergency management, medical rescue, recovery through purified water supply and food preparation and the creation of structures of subsistence capable of surviving such disasters. But the cost of deliberately caused mayhem – war, sabotage and other assaults on and in cities and their infrastructures – too, can be buffered. Damage to central power and relay stations can lead to grid collapse and communications failure, and disable security and rescue teams, but distributed power sources are less prone to black-outs and collapse. And looked at more broadly, a renewable-energy based economy is incomparably less vulnerable and susceptible to attacks, failures, blackmail and the risks of foreign adventures to secure oil, natural gas, or uranium, once global supplies begin to dwindle. As discussed, the spectre of Russia's Gazprom shutting off natural gas supplies to Western Europe – even if only as an attempt to force the Ukraine into accepting higher fuel charges – destabilised supplies in a series of countries and unnerved the entire region, utterly dependent as it is on stable gas flows. And a generation ago, a historical United States Federal Emergency Management Agency (FEMA) study made a powerful case for nation-wide renewable energy reliance in the interest of national security (FEMA 1980). But given its call to reduce reliance on the powerful political and economic force of US petroleum interests, the report was shelved almost as soon as it was submitted. President Bush's proclamations of 26 September 2005, in the wake a series of disastrous cyclones that wrecked oil installations across the Gulf of Mexico, were faintly reminiscent of the 1980 FEMA report, but pitched largely and erroneously in support of nuclear power (Bush 2005). After all, and apparently unbeknown to Mr Bush, uranium is as limited in supply as oil and natural gas, and infinitely more risky to use, capable as it is of feeding weapons of mass destruction, and in its transport, power generation and waste processing modes extremely difficult to shield against major man-made and serious natural calamities:

> *It is clear that when you're dependent upon natural gas and/or hydrocarbons to fuel your economy and that supply gets disrupted, we need alternative sources of energy. And that's why I believe so strongly in nuclear power.* President George W Bush, 26 September 2005

A renewable and distributed power geography offers immense and immediate advantages during the ordinary, peaceful and undisturbed lives of cities, too. In fast-growing urban areas the annual cost of expanding, upgrading and maintaining electric power grids can easily exceed that of power generation itself. Therefore investment in distributed generation can be an initial expenditure thus quickly amortised. Grid reliance can be reduced, needed expansions minimised, and transmission system and distribution capacity margins increased. The risk of power outages induced by grid failures is dramatically buffered through supplemental power generation capacity installed on countless rooftops, along with considerable cogeneration capacity for industry,

institutions and mixed-use commercial complexes. These are important benefits available immediately, while the necessary *supply balancing and dispatch
provisions* are made, as described in Section 3.4, Space, time and energy. For
individual consumers, cogeneration in particular, but also certain other renewable forms of hybrid and autonomous energy supply systems described below,
can be a highly economical and competitive way of achieving energy security,
carbon neutrality and broad sustainability in resource use. Finally, distributed
generation boosts overall energy efficiency, eliminating much of the approximately 7 per cent in loss that are typically incurred when carrying electricity
through long powerlines (Perlman 2005).

## Innovation

A determined detachment from the fossil-fuel umbilical cord can unlock
massive innovative opportunities in building technology and design, energy
technology and public as well as private infrastructure technology. Physical
energy transformations take place mostly at a local level: in industries, on
farms, in production and consumption – and in cities and human settlements,
whether these changes to distributed and networked renewable-power generation models are supply- or demand-side based. The wider energy environment
of cities is shifting, making dramatic changes to urban energy regimes inevitable. National policy frameworks are established at a rapid pace. Across the
countries of the European Union, for example, the average of all national targets
in renewable energy generation is 21 per cent of electricity production, to be
reached by 2010. While targets rarely translate into reality, they signal a certain
willingness to contemplate action, and are a prerequisite for shoring up the
nascent European carbon market. Nationally declared commitments range from
targets as low as 3.5 per cent in Hungary, starting from a very low baseline;
to Sweden at 60 per cent and 78 per cent in Austria with its pioneering solar
village network tradition (Martinot 2005, p 21). Today, while the commercial
energy share of non-hydropower based renewable energy is still in the low
single-digit percentile, these systems are set on a rapid growth trajectory. Worldwide, in the decade preceding 2004, wind power supply grew by 30 per cent
annually, photovoltaics (PV) by nearly 25 per cent and ethanol production by
7 per cent. The consumption of all other sources, fossil and nuclear, grew far
less in comparison: in single digits. When expressed as share of growth in
renewable capacity over the period 2000 to 2004, grid-connected PV was the

leader by far, at over 60 per cent, followed by wind and biodiesel (Martinot 2005, p 8).

There are challenges to innovation, particularly at the interface between technological change and the political, institutional and regulatory environment needed to embrace it. Distinctive gaps exist between technological imperatives and both international and local institutional capacity to manage these. The stalling of large solar-thermal concentrator initiatives in Egypt, Morocco and India is explained by a failure of conventional technological, finance and project management frameworks. These can hamper the progress or even success of systems that do not fit conventional institutional expectations (Sklar 2005). These may prove to be growing pains, or errors in application, scale or expectations. If adequately focused upon, they can become a source of collective learning, and overcome. To succeed it will be useful to move away from isolated technology experiments and invite the engagement of cities and urban communities in the design, development and procurement of renewable power plants. This can both test and help create a firm market, help establish meaningful regulatory and accountability environments, and avoid other typical risks in narrowly technology- and supply-side driven, speculative or other heroically pioneering initiatives.

## A rich source of new employment

By definition, advanced urban infrastructure policies rely on renewable energy. Future-minded cities are increasingly focusing on limiting their dependence on large, centralised coal, oil and nuclear power supply systems. Once embarked on this path, the local business and industrial environments begin to unfold in more diverse and innovative ways, trade imbalances are corrected and new jobs created. From a promotional viewpoint, the southern Australian cities of Adelaide and Melbourne have for a number of years proudly published growing sustainable business directories, featuring also renewable products and services (City of Adelaide 2005; City of Melbourne 2005). But beyond mere aspirations, there has been mounting interest in understanding the impact a move away from fossil fuel combustion would have – and does have – on employment (McEvoy et al 2000).

Past shifts into more carbon efficient stages of industrialisation in Europe and Japan have been marked by shifts in labour employment patterns into higher quality jobs, and not overall reductions, yet this shift did not affect the fundamental nature of the energy economy at the time. And where a low level of carbon emissions has been recorded due to economic downturns, as in Eastern Europe in the 1980s and 1990s, this has naturally been marked by high unemployment. But in comparing a fully engaged fossil with a renewable economy very different patterns emerge. Centralised, fossil power generation is labour-extensive: it generates little employment opportunity per energy unit generated. It offers few dynamic or newly evolving job opportunities when compared to the strength that lies in renewable-energy based job creation, individual prosperity and mobility. A full-fledged renewable power economy will demand an extraordinary range of goods and service providers, researchers, innovators, technologists, economists and planners – and it contributes directly to the income of surplus end-use generators: individual households. The flow-on benefits in new income and employment opportunities are striking, because much of the new employment will take place within the city – in the form of efficiency and conservation measures, building- and city-integrated renewable power systems, new demands on materials, design and management.

Employment in the German photovoltaic and solar thermal industry alone has risen from 5,500 direct jobs in 1998 to 22,000 in 2003, and is projected to reach 93,000 in 2010 (Langen 2005). And a recent University of Berkeley study found that 'the renewable energy sector generates more jobs per megawatt of power installed, per unit of energy produced, and per dollar of investment, than the fossil fuel-based energy sector' (Kammen et al 2004, p 3). Basing its findings on more than a dozen other recent studies, by the year 2020 it projects a jobs loss in US fossil fuel industries – coal, oil and gas mining, gas refining and electric and gas utilities – of 152,900, contrasted with an all-sectors gain of 1,314,000 jobs over the same period (Kammen et al 2004, p 15).

These figures reflect only direct jobs gains. Not considered are likely revolutionary transformations due to wider structural shifts resulting from the coming *great energy switch*, and the spawning of entirely new industries, new products and business sectors. As the energy source base shifts into a new industrial revolution, new opportunities and needs for goods and services arise, in bio-fuel, sun, wind and water power generation, and based on the development of revolutionary non-petroleum based fabrics, materials, paints, machines, pharmaceuticals, fertilisers, pest management systems, transport methods, construction and facility reuse techniques, planning and design services and energy systems design, development, marketing, installation and maintenance services. Finally, a significant industry is bound to be created to meet the challenge of dismantling and restructuring fossil corporate and physical infrastructures, finance mechanisms and institutions and adaptive reuse of the gargantuan global apparatus of fossil flow and energy conveyance, from drilling rigs to refineries to the web of pipelines and ports, the global oil, coal and natural gas fleet, not to mention the micro-conversion and adaptation of petrol stations, power stations and distribution networks.

Technological innovation can spawn dramatic new job growth in flow-on businesses and industries. A key driver is convergence, an industrial phenomenon familiar from the revolution that has transformed the information, communications and mass media industries since the 1980s. Image, voice and electronic data systems merged into new forms conveyed in fibre-optics, integrated services digital networks and web-streamed media. Digital technology and ubiquitous micro-computing devices allowed cameras, telephones and music systems to converge into a new generation of devices that also allow the paying of bills, networked computations, personal data management and internet exchange. In energy related sectors we begin to sense the power of convergence, too. We can begin to grasp intuitively the feasibility and potential of networking diverse and spatially distributed power devices into a single power environment. The principle of linking numerous operational and systems functions into one responsive sensing and computing environment was achieved within so-called smart or intelligent homes and office buildings and building groups as early as the 1980s. These early stages of development were confined to a limited range of energy systems and control functions, and to single structures or limited clusters of these. But the deployment of ubiquitous and personally controlled energy technology on a city- region- or nation-wide scale – from grid-connected solar panels to hydrogen fuel cells – helps blur the distinction between producer and consumer, inaugurating the age of a new and hybrid player: the *prosumer*. General examples include the distributed and growing supply of personally generated power to public or private utilities; renewable hydrogen fuel cells in vehicles, capable of the off-grid powering of homes and appliances. The citizen development cooperatives that have built most of Denmark's extensive national wind power capacity are good examples both of the age of the prosumer, and of models of collective or community ownership of power assets.

The flow-on effects felt in the urban, regional and wider economy can be dramatic, as demonstrated by one renewable energy system alone: photovoltaics (PV). Many national and urban solar integration programmes have led to rapid expansion especially in that sector of the photovoltaic industry geared to the residential market, a dramatic start from an admittedly tiny supply base. This has helped trigger growth in other areas of application. Photovoltaic systems are being installed not only on suburban homes but also in offices, industrial buildings, hospitals, churches, laboratories, transport hubs, bus stops, retail centres, storage buildings and petrol stations. Numerous types of modules are applied, and hybrid systems emerge at a significant pace. For example, PV can be combined with wind power, or embedded into hybrid-power lights, whereby PV cells are integrated with light emitting diodes. Design, engineering and certification services emerge, and chains of other industries begin to be positively impacted, such as the prefabricated housing, construction, materials, roofing and cladding industries, not to mention the power equipment and appliances industries (Tanaka 2004).

## Community ownership of power; control over real and virtual utilities

Distributed forms of energy generation imply distributed ownership of the assets involved, by both individuals and communities. They carry the potential for decentralised decision-making, and more widely shared control of energy markets. Regional, national or transnational utilities, be they public or private, are generally distant and anonymous, supply-focused and quasi-monopolistic entities. Like the system operators and energy traders with which they are associated, they offer little choice, control or level of accountability to end users and even local and state governments. Even municipally owned energy companies can display such shortcomings, if they are not appropriately chartered, structured and made accountable. Enron's single-minded accumulation of control over energy generation and its manipulation of gas supplies, energy trades and even utility operations in California would have been difficult to conceive in an advanced renewable-energy economy. The Enron conundrum was an outcome of the very manner in which fossil-fuel power generation and distribution were organised in California and other regions of the United States. But even in a renewable-energy based trading environment it will be necessary to ensure corporate accountability, and manage distributed and diverse energy market players in ways that bar monopolies from forming, and capturing or trading controlling portions of shared production rights.

## Accountability: user sees, user pays, user gains

A powerful and personal argument for distributed renewable power generation is sometimes given as 'the light in people's eyes' when they see their metres run in reverse, as electricity captured on their rooftops flows into the grid. Long straitjacketed as passive consumers, they respond emotionally to their ability to make energy savings, and to seeing their own homes display such productivity, translating into direct income: being empowered as producers. Yet despite great improvements and even breakthroughs in many states in the United States, in parts of Europe, Asia and across the Pacific, conventional utilities continue to struggle with the need to advance demand-side management and other consumption reduction, efficiency and conservation efforts, let alone accelerate the enactment of renewable electricity feed-in legislation and technologies. It goes against their very nature and incentives to curtail and even reduce conventional production. The tendency to measure success in annual fossil generation and consumption increases, new plant construction and grid expansion is still enshrined in specialised energy supply providers in most parts of the world – despite all incentives, accountability measures, and innovations in deriving productivity from the savings incurred by not having to construct new generation plant capacity that have been promoted over the last two decades. Many of these semi-autonomous giants also enjoy close and comfortable links to policy makers, regulators and funding agencies. A decentralised, diverse and dynamic renewable energy environment sidesteps the pitfalls of self-perpetuating energy empires.

## Public policy response

Internationally and locally, policies are inoxorably shifting as new evidence of disturbing climate change impacts mounts, and the ominous year of Peak Oil, 2010, approaches (Campbell 2005). An escalating need to shore up regional carbon markets and lower the risks stemming from petroleum bottleneck scenarios means that the emissions management procedures envisioned under today's timid Kyoto-style arrangements will inevitably be superseded by more direct and effective measures. Industrial and urban greenhouse gas emissions are likely to be monitored in terms of their link to primary pollution source, taxed more directly, and increasingly heavily penalised. So far there has been a consensus in favour of enlightened, voluntary forms of transition, but in the absence of progress and given rapidly deteriorating global ecological conditions, it is only a matter of time before leaders and institutional actors and international organisations, trade agreements and alliances – including the International Court of Justice – will set and enforce firmer penalties for carbon transgressions. Unless early and more effective change mechanisms are adopted, personal, corporate and national carbon credit accounts may be established to control emission cost at the point and level of consumption: the individual, family, business, government department, city or nation.

Numerous public policy frameworks and renewable energy introduction programmes are being explored, but most are still rudimentary, vague, overly bureaucratic or riddled with loopholes. Few have been developed or imple-mented to a satisfactory extent, in ways that promise real and necessary emis-sions reductions. The most effective can be found in Europe and the United States, and especially in Germany at a national, California at a state and at the local level in a number of settlements in countries from Austria to Zambia. The simultaneous sharpening, simplification and expansion of controls will be an inevitable response to the climate destabilisation and fossil fuel depletion conundrum the world has woken up to. Cities embracing renewable energy strategies and plans to pursue carbon emissions reduction campaigns will operate in tandem with national and global environments that are increas-ingly – and inevitably – rich in carbon reduction requirements, policies and incentives.

Many countries – including China, the world's fastest growing economy – have begun to adopt a more progressive stance on renewable energy, but to date most of these have done so at an excruciatingly slow pace, while the challenges have been glaringly obvious for at least a generation. Like heavy smokers or alcoholics in the early stages of recovery, they contemplate the path to abstinence with pronounced reticence. They always find time and reason for another delay, another pack of cigarettes, another drink. In China this has meant the hasty construction of another 30 nuclear power plants, another generation of uranium, gas and coal purchasing contracts with Australia and, virtually inevitably, another decade of secure oil imports, albeit increas-ingly shored up by military, trade and diplomatic efforts around the world. However, in the face of massive environmental and devastating, pollution caused public health problems and mounting resource constraints, the tide is changing in China, too. In the second half of 2005 Shi Lishan, the director of the National Reform and Development Commission's (NRDC) renewable energy division first announced high level government discussions about raising the national renewable energy supply target by 50–15 per cent by 2020 (Graham-Harrison 2005). This was formally confirmed as government policy during the landmark Beijing International Renewable Energy Conference (BIREC), 7–9 November 2005.

This Beijing conference was both a sign of and vehicle for Chinese determination, not an attempt at delays – unlike so many international sustainability conferences. This government event flowed directly from the German-government-hosted Renewables 2004 held in Bonn 17 months earlier, and served to inform the implementation framework of the country's new renewable energy law internally and externally. Yet in themselves, like targets, conferences do not generally translate into action. These need to be backed up by concrete legislative and effective market mechanisms, and the creation of international bodies charged with the global proliferation of renewable energy technology. An International Renewable Energy Agency (IRENA), has been created capable of competing with the powerful representation enjoyed by the nuclear and fossil fuel lobby and its major mentors, the International Atomic Energy Agency (IAEA) and the International Energy Agency (IEA). This policy platform has been consistently supported by the World Council for Renewable Energy (WCRE) and its annual international parliamentary forums, initiated and chaired by German parliamentarian, Hermann Scheer (WCRE 2006).

Meanwhile, oil, coal and nuclear industry interests work assiduously to postpone the inevitable. This tactic serves to secure short-term profits, but national government representatives who feel compelled to do so gamble with the fate of millions, even billions of people. Many cities and states feel themselves hamstrung by such activities. This is expressed at the US state and local jurisdictions, where many have reacted to a lack of progress, even action, at federal level. Some local governments have begun to focus their wrath on power utilities: officials in eight states have taken legal action against a group of utilities responsible for the largest share in greenhouse gas emissions (Smith 2004). In a different response, many Australian state capitals and smaller communities have long been compelled to develop their own climate action and energy agendas, given a national industry policy and regulatory regime that is unsympathetic towards creating any semblance of competition with the coal industry, and expanding the country's minuscule non-hydropower renewable energy base. Perhaps in reaction to a national policy vacuum, Australian cities have long been known for ranking among the world's highest proportion of subscribers to the Cities for Climate Protection™ (CCP) campaign, a trademark programme of the International Council for Local Environmental Initiatives (ICLEI) – ironically with the support of the federal government. These and many other communities hope to overcome national policy limitations through developing local renewable energy autonomy or, at least, the establishment of a firm local policy platform to that end.

## Regional regeneration and revalorisation impulses in the global urban regime

The present urban system is frequently described as articulated into a few and dominant so-called global cities, in which commercial, command and control power are concentrated and which are at the apex of a hierarchy of more and less central, peripheral, marginal and edge cities, smaller centres and core nodes within cities and their regions. Increasingly, this urban system has come to be structured around imperatives of lubricating transnational financial flows and facilitating direct foreign investment (Sassen 1994). These extraordinary flows are the very culmination of the fossil-fuel economy's dizzying rise over its final 50 years, marked by IT advances, regional and global trading regimes, and spreading corporate *transnationalism*. The colossal regional inequities resulting from the articulation of this hierarchy are further expressions of these conditions. The end of the fossil era is likely to result in a dramatic *revalorisation* of the global urban hierarchy – to borrow Sassen's elegant term for value changes in the urban hierarchy – by virtue of inexorable and substantial shifts in the financial and structural frameworks governing commercial energy. Particular features of these will be the imposition of increasing carbon costs; globally steeply declining fossil fuel flows; and regionally and locally emergent, indigenously produced renewable energy flows.

These shifts will manifest themselves with increasing drama as the final petroleum crisis unfolds, ringing in a post-Peak Oil world. The changes are quietly visible as positive innovations, in new but minor trends, still masked by the conventional mechanisms of urban change. Solar-thermal, photovoltaic, wind and bio-fuel energy production represent land uses akin to multi-crop farming and, although these have not yet been carefully studied, it is safe to consider them as ranking among the fastest-growing land use changes today. As the conversion chains of energy become regionalised and locally internalised, some urban and regional land assets will gain in value, and help transform the nature of intra- and inter-urban economic interactions. Many forms of energy farming can be combined with traditional agriculture, grazing and other forms of food production, strengthening rural land values. Local and regional agriculture and silviculture can experience a powerful boost, as it has already across several European countries or South America – Brazil, Germany, Italy and Sweden, to name but a few – with the rise of bio-fuel generation. Large-scale electric power farms using wind or sun resources are a form of industrial land use, albeit in a quasi-agricultural mode. They can also be assigned to and so raise the value of previously unproductive terrains of little ecological or cultural value. Cities and their regional hinterlands may well become reconnected in this way, fostering greater degrees of city–regional autonomy.

At the local and regional levels new fiscal models evolve in keeping with this realignment. A nascent quest to liberate regional economies from the fossil fuel shackles is aimed at money and its flows as carrier of fossil content. Money links regions and cities to the national and global economy; it drives and coordinates local aspirations, and regulates information flow, mobility and energy. The very nature of modern currency and the manner it is managed place tight constraints on the extent and rate to which sustainable development can be achieved, since income, wealth and money in the bank represent a stake in, an entitlement to the global flows of goods and services – the vast majority of which are produced in unsustainable ways, given the global economy's underlying petroleum nature. In response, regional currencies may spread, tied to the value of real solar energy generated locally. Already raising the eyebrows of some central banks that are perhaps needlessly worried about 'parallel money' undermining general monetary stability and liquidity, regional, energy and environmental-services based monetary valuations are again being explored around the world. So-called regional or community currencies linked to the value of electricity produced by renewable energy will not substitute for traditional currency but can nevertheless provide a stable value reference for it. One example is the REGIOenergie initiative that was developed in Weimar, Germany (REGIOprojekt 2005). These concepts are related to, among others, Stephen deMeulenaere's Strohalm Foundation for Integrated Economics (Strohalm Foundation 2006), and have their spiritual genesis in the ideas of the late Howard T Odum (1924–2002), ecology and energy pioneer. In the early 1970s Odum introduced and advanced the concept of the biosphere, and of the ecosystem, using the very paradigm of energy; and warned of the dangers of the poorly understood, high-energy, ie petroleum charged economy, food supply and resource exploitation (Odum 1971). A more specifically pioneering figure in this field is Sydney-based economist and entrepreneurial intellect, Shann Turnbull, who has argued for renewable-energy related currency thinking since the 1970s (Bennello et al; 1989; Turnbull 1975, 1992).


## A new urban reality

The idea of ubiquitous, distributed urban power generation, paired with a comprehensive, citywide framework of emissions accountability, is ambitious and compelling and has, of course, been spelled out in various settings and publications (Droege 1999). For ambitious ideas to be realised, firm policies and powerful market frameworks must be established with conviction and speed. Cities and urban communities are key to this: a number of energy efficiency frameworks and emissions regulations have emerged or are aimed at the local level (CCP 2005; DoE 2006.1; E-C 2005). Austria's famed quasi-autonomous energy townships and regional networks of renewable-energy based villages feature bio-fuel and solar electricity, and have prospered and inspired others for decades. And to signal Austria's solar tradition globally as a beacon of romantic futurism, it welcomes the Jules Verne-like use of mirroring heliostats to send sunlight into a dark valley hamlet: a symbolic installation deploying a second sun (Chapman 2005). Scandinavian renewable energy cooperatives, notably in Denmark, are of a similar, early vintage. In China, small-town and village-level methane bio-digesters, small-hydropower based mini-grids and collectively managed solar water heaters, too, have a long and proud history, if somewhat unsung. And new urban neighbourhoods throughout Europe, such as in the Netherlands, Germany, France, the United Kingdom or Italy, have benefited from sophisticated thermal design thinking and been augmented with solar installations since the 1970s, and increasingly since the 1990s. Italy, in particular, has had the befit of urban scale ideas, thanks to the work of local pioneers, reformed nuclear scientist, Federico Butera, a professor of Applied Physics working in Palermo and Milan (Butera 2004), and Francesca Sartogo, active in and around Rome (Sartogo et al 1999). This long-standing, village-scale ingenuity and commitment now promise to make inroads into larger cities and settlements. Some are linked to state and regional renewable power portfolios, and others based on national government support, such as Germany's celebrated renewable energy feed-in law.

Many cities have begun to embrace this new reality, and deploy a range of programmes and initiatives. These range from Berlin's pioneering solar regulations, to Greater London's wide-ranging renewable energy initiatives, or Oxford's nascent solar urban policy efforts in England; Munich's broad-based innovations in Germany; Spanish solar city ordinances, introduced first in Barcelona, later in Madrid and more than three dozen other cities in Spain; Cape Town's budding solar aspirations in South Africa; Shanghai, Shenzhen and Hangzhou's new energy regulations in China; Australia's federally supported Solar Cities programme commencing slowly in Adelaide and elsewhere; Melbourne's home-grown and wide-ranging renewable energy tactics; South Korea's friendly Solar City rivals of Daegu and Gwangju, and their combined grass-roots, industry and national support efforts; and both San

Francisco and Sacramento's long-standing commitment to distributed photo-voltaic power generation in California. State and urban governments, industries and communities expand their efficiency programmes, industry support efforts and renewable energy implementation schemes, individually and in partnerships. And some invest in regional renewable energy producers such as wind or bio-fuel farms, partner in large-scale solar-thermal and photovoltaic farms, augmenting or replacing stretched or ageing fossil fuel plants or, through state government endorsement, help experiment with Herculean solar towers (EnviroMission 2005).

This change occurs in cities – for numerous reasons that either act to *pull* by virtue of compelling benefits of prestige, innovation and economic improvement or to *push* by the fear of the dire security and development risks of inaction, or both. Shared by all is a desire to overcome fossil-fuel dependency, strengthen local autonomy and secure sustainable forms of prosperity through technology conversion and advancement, and by nurturing advanced industries capable of competing nationally and globally. Many cities are boosted in their efforts by national requirements and provincial legislation. And even a few of the most reluctant national governments begin to rise to the challenge. Some were chastened and hastened into action by the devastating urban impacts of hurricanes in the United States in September and October 2005. After decades of resistance and policy vacuum, voices championing renewable energy have reawakened in both US House and Senate – amid hope that they will not go to sleep again as the disaster scenes fade from the collective memory. Even the Australian government, tireless and wily coal and uranium export advocate, has briefly blinked in the wake of the 2005 Mexican Gulf hurricanes series: Katrina, Rita and Wilma. The oil price spikes triggered by these cyclones prompted the government openly albeit briefly to promote what was for the coal continent a stunning 'unlabelled 5-per cent ethanol content' commitment for motor vehicle fuel, dumbfounding long-misinformed motorists and the local petrol distribution industry alike. The local automobile industry, too, abruptly dropped its earlier, long and solemnly held objections to ethanol as alleged engine killer, as petrol prices soared, threatening to eat into monthly car sales targets.

And elite building and urban designers lead in this new world as well. Numerous veteran and city-focused architects across the globe, from twin design Lords Foster of Thames Bank and Rogers of Riverside, to Thomas Herzog in Germany, Ken Yeang in Kuala Lumpur, to William McDonough in the United States, have challenged and led their peers and clients in technology and design innovation for a generation. And as if to globally signal this shift as a collective change of heart, Brazilian urban sustainability pioneer and architect-mayor

Jaime Lerner was elected to preside over the architects' premier international organisation, the UNESCO-supported International Union of Architects (UIA), assuming this role in 2002, and presiding until 2005.

## 3.2  THE DESIGN OF THE RENEWABLE CITY

### The coming *energy web*

Energy, information and telecommunications infrastructures (IIT) are converging, as distributed renewable sources become poised to play the leading part in this new fusion. Energy-IIT convergence can take two basic forms: supply-led and control-driven. On the supply-led side of systems, hybrid and single-mode stand-alone systems are increasingly deployed to power both central and remote computing and telecommunication facilities, both in advanced industrial countries and in poor rural villages or remote settlements. And in the control-driven world of hybrids, the distributed generation, dispatching and sharing among a universe of different sources and users requires advanced sensing and networking environments and intelligent protocols for data management, monitoring, evaluation and integrated control. Energy systems will be ubiquitous, and are varied across sun, wind, water and biological technologies. Advanced information technology allows them to be woven into synchronised power architectures – virtual power plants via advanced information and communication networks. Generators of all modes, capacities and sizes, both grid-linked and wirelessly communicating stand-alone can be connected into an intelligent energy network, affording powerful market and management functions. This will spell the transformation of what is also termed here the *plain old grid* (POG) to *web energy*, or the *energy web* (e-web). The e-web will be a key element in an advanced renewable energy economy, given the enormous range of suppliers and users, the need to maintain mature markets and the growing need for an open, reliable and intelligent energy framework.

The emergence of more horizontal power markets based on very large numbers of two-way transactions is an exciting prospect for cities, enabling them to perform as virtual power houses comprised of manifold, embedded suppliers no longer supplied from outside, but empowered from within. In an advanced renewable-power economy many small and medium sized providers supplement, and can eventually assimilate or replace the comparably few large and central plants and suppliers currently operating to supply national and international economies and their urban centres. This process can engender a form of *energy democracy* in action, and challenge the power behemoths that have thrived in a carefully managed hothouse of protective policies and regulations. The quasi-marketplace of conventional fossil and nuclear power is notoriously rife with monopolistic manipulation and political intervention. For some this will spell the end of a comfortable era sooner than for others, but eventually all will have to restructure, and transform from fossil power generators and distributors to positive players and energy brokers or clearinghouses in the ubiquitous world of renewable energy management. For far too long many distant and amorphous power utilities have been rewarded for suppressing new ideas and industries – even while their destructive nature has become increasingly difficult to ignore. The e-web, manifesting the new web energy market, will be a platform for the long but inexorable transition from predominantly conventional fossil, nuclear and large hydropower schemes, to distributed webs of renewable power sources, many linked in grids, and some standing alone as autonomous islands.

## Changing the culture

Emerging at the high end of the urban renewable power systems range, how do *embedded applications* work? As distributed, in-built and modular devices they can augment everything with self-sufficient power streams, from pace-makers and watches to cars and buildings. They will soon be as universal and common as microchips, small computers and electric motors are today. At the lower end of the technology spectrum, small hydropower, biogas and solar power systems help deliver light, pumping power, refrigeration, televi-sion, as well as electricity to access the internet and wireless telephony systems, benefiting remote and poor communities by giving access to education and income. Unlike conventional energy sources – coal and uranium mines, large dams, municipal waste incinerators and massive deforestation for firewood – these new systems tend to be incomparably more benign environmentally. They vary greatly from small to medium size in scale, and in their nature, purpose, technology, cost and finance mechanisms. They have one set of general charac-teristics in common: production costs and consumer prices decrease, demand is on the rise and levels of sophistication and efficiency improve. A great time of transition has commenced, irrespective of the fact that some conventional regulatory and financial institutions still struggle with such simple back-up, stand-alone or grid-supplying systems as cogeneration plants, domestic solar-photovoltaic or industrial solar-thermal power generators. But it is increasingly apparent that communities too slow to introduce enabling legislative and partnership frameworks are being left behind. Each day, around the globe, new urban renewable energy applications and programmes are introduced, advancing technology and policy, and serving as models for other cities and smaller communities.

The immediate impetus behind much of this change is increasingly economic, given shifting national and global policy environments, reinforced by the enlightened leadership of pioneering cities and businesses. A comprehensive renewable energy framework offers greater prosperity for developing and advanced economies, and attractive development prospects for the vast majority of cities. When taken seriously, this task goes to the heart of a city's political economy, its very culture of values and ecology of vested interests. To be able to overcome these dependencies, dedicated civic leadership and a creative vision about the future of urban prosperity are essential, of the kind that has made Brazil's Curitiba so well regarded, and its two consecutive mayors so richly credited with the city's miraculous transformation: architect Jaime Lerner and engineer Cassio Taniguchi. The city attained world fame through its revolutionary and affordable public transit systems and traffic improvement successes, armies of recyclers and other employment programmes and, last but not least, ambitious regional park networks favouring local people, pedestrians and cyclists. As demonstrated in Curitiba, Barcelona, Berlin and other settings of sophisticated and inspired urban change, enduring progress requires the integration of social equity, cultural development and economic prosperity into a larger strategic framework. This vision transcends narrow municipal boundaries, too: regional in scale, it engages urban communities in their larger, peri-urban settings.

Authentic urban renewable energy strategies emerge when founded on deep cultural engagement. They are introduced most successfully in cities and communities focused on mobilising all of their psychological, environmental, economic and cultural resources. A good example of this phenomenon was Berlin in the years before and immediately following the fall of the Wall. The city's drive to innovate was extraordinary. It was first energised by its specially supported status as walled city, and after unification became electrified by the regeneration task ahead, combined with the prospect of regaining capital city status. But its successes were in part informed by early successful and socially motivated experiments with a renewably powered urban autonomy, based on 'sustainable blocks' advanced by 1970s' activists and local residents in the working-class district of Kreuzberg and elsewhere. Berlin experimented with far-reaching renewable energy legislation and has advanced, yet so far not adopted, a municipal *solar ordinance*. Continuing the tradition of earlier model innovations such as the International Building Exhibition (IBA) programme of specially commissioned high-quality, high-density inner-city residential demonstration projects in the 1980s, a new capital-city district was developed, in model pursuit of sophisticated renewable energy strategies. Its flagship was the renewable transformation of old Berlin's Reichstag ruin into the nation's new federal parliamentary plenary meeting facility. The refurbished building, endowed with an energy-minded architectural plan by Norman Foster, operates entirely on bio-fuel powered combined heat and power generators, photovoltaic arrays, aquifer thermal storage, heat pumping techniques – and as the *pièce de résistance*, hovering above the assembly in the very centre of the structure, a motorised, mirror-studded, day-light guiding turret, swinging with the sun to illuminate the people's humble representatives.

Berlin's dogged yet incomplete search for municipal solar power legislation motivated Barcelona to become Spain's first city to introduce a *solar ordinance*. Nor was Barcelona's role as renewable pioneer an accident. The city had long been engaged in a drive to self-empowerment, flourishing after the Franco oppression, and bolstered by its potential to regenerate broadly for the 1992 Olympic Games. Yet too much of the wider, fossil-fuel drenched urban reality is unconducive to sustaining such great civic aspirations, in Spain and the rest of the world – as is evident from the internationally standardised apartment and office complexes that mushroom in the forecourt of the Global City like killer weeds. All major cities are plagued by this speculative, showy affliction: uninspired assemblies of commercial-grade, cheaply powered property products that serve to degenerate homes into shallow commodities, are traded as overpriced mass-consumer items, and quickly disposed of like any other class of mass-marketable goods and their associated services. Unfit as meaningful expressions of community, place and belonging, as wasteful as cars in their production, maintenance and upkeep, and threatening to depreciate just as quickly in post-fossil times, modern apartments especially have become single-minded scripts for the staging of neatly defined lifestyles, work styles, short-lived industrial production processes and nervously shifting business settings.

The vast majority of contemporary buildings, facilities and infrastructures are predicated on the destructive rapid consumption paradigm that was shaped by the logic of the fossil-fuel economy, its materials and its products. Sensitive architects and city planners acting on behalf of increasingly alert clients and constituents have long been frustrated with the fallow fruit of their labour, searching for 'sustainable', 'smart-growth' or 'green' paths forward. A new formal honesty seems to beckon, in resource rationality, combining the clarity of industrial Modernism with the energy intelligence of pre-Modern thinking. And increasingly, many see that much of the sustainable-city response smorgasbord can be replaced by a fundamental focus on fossil energy substitution. They believe that high degrees of efficiency – good design and construction – and renewable energy infrastructures can help cities become stronger and more autonomous political entities. *Energy renewability* is fundamental to the design and development of any new and expanding urban areas and communities that claim to be 'sustainable'. With attention shifted to good design, longevity and capacity for reuse much of the cynicism expressed in the modern real estate culture of quasi-disposable, mass-produced units may well evaporate.

## Beyond efficiency

Building efficiency standards, energy conservation programmes and demand management policies have become enshrined as basic elements of urban regulatory practice since the 1970s. This was part of a general lowering in the *energy intensity* of economies, measured by gross inland energy consumption divided by the gross domestic product, both in the industrial states and industrialising countries such as China. The 2001/02 energy intensity of the most efficient – Denmark and Japan, and the least efficient – Estonia and Lithuania, among a selection of industrialised countries differs by a factor of 10, indicating the enormous gains that can be made as economies advance (SCB 2005). Yet reports from the United States show the limits of efficiency drives: for the decade 1985 to 1995 energy intensity studies across a number of sectors – residential, commercial, industrial, transport and economy-wide – indicated inconclusive results, little change or actual increase (EIA 1995). Industry figures were similarly discouraging for Australian trends in technical efficiency for the period 1994–2001 (Saddlerundated).

Regardless of the important efficiency gains that can and must be achieved, the world and its fossil cities are still haunted by an overall and massive rise in conventional urban fuel consumption over the same period, as illustrated in Chapter 1. With energy pressures rising unabated, traditional building and city design measures have taken on a special meaning. Urban and regional landscape networks stabilise ambient urban temperatures: suburbs filled with native plants and gardens reduce water consumption and heat pockets; building roofs and walls covered with vegetation transform the performance of buildings and surroundings alike; office atrias filled with native land- and water-scapes contribute to the energy performance of the building; urban agriculture and natural surface water management can improve household water, food supply and biodiversity. These wonderful efficiency and sustainability measures are an excellent platform on which to build the Renewable City. All contribute to reducing urban energy input requirements, for heating, cooling, water management, food production and transport. On the urban engineering front, ground, air and water heat pumping, aquatic energy exchange systems, waste heat extraction and landfill gas harvesting are efficiency measures, too. Gradually, they take hold in building practice and policy, from Berlin to Beijing.

Efficiency is essential while the inclusion of measures to conserve energy is basic to good urban design, planning and development practice. It is central for all cities on a path to a more sustainable practice. This guide refers to several best practice templates containing such efficiency and energy conservation measure that may be readily adapted and adopted. But the rising consumption of fossil fuels and uranium cannot be overcome voluntarily in this way, only somewhat slowed in its growth rate. The challenge lies not only in embracing efficiency and conservation measures but also in embarking boldly on paths to achieving community- and city-wide renewable energy autonomy. Cities must move rapidly into defossilisation mode, in addition to any efficiency efforts that can be mounted. While this section touches on several key urban efficiency measures (see especially Section 4.2 below), its primary emphasis is on urban renewable-power generation techniques.

## 3.3 RENEWABLE CITY FORM AND FORMATION

Renewable energy technologies are exceptionally diverse in every sense – in scale, mode and application. Their complexity is both their strength and their weakness: the conventional supply systems that gave rise to cities and their shape and culture during the 20th century have also spawned extraordinary illusions of a simple, anonymous, invisible, silent, steady source. The reality outside the urban cocoon is different: fossil and nuclear sources are highly complex and elaborate systems, staggeringly prominent in power plants and transmission wires and masts; massively visible in their pollution impacts, mining and generator accidents; and potentially always at risk of minor outages and catastrophic failure. But cities in industrialised countries have managed to stay largely disconnected from this reality.

For a very long time the word *energy* did not even enter the urban planning vocabulary. Since the 1970s this has changed, but only slowly and with a primary focus on 'saving energy' – the increase of fossil fuel use efficiency, often while ignoring new supply sources. Now the concept of energy has emerged as the central policy focus it should always have been. Peak Oil is with us now, Peak Uranium follows closely behind – especially with accelerated use, and a virtual Coal Peak is precipitated by a mounting emissions reduction mandate. The false promise of an infinitely growing and quietly humming fossil or nuclear power supply is giving way to an embarrassed admission of a global naïveté, while the perceptions of reliability and safety in supply take on a more realistic shape. They will have to be pursued through a primary resource and power productivity gain by means of efficiency, reuse and reinvention, and through the ubiquitous and intelligent deployment of an ultimately virtually limitless renewable energy resource stream. This means a decided move away from the singular vision of a perfect, global electric grid, towards a much more diverse energy-scape.

Individual buildings, facility groups, streets, neighbourhoods and cities can become 'energy islands': autonomously supported urban domains, entirely or partially detached from the wider grid, except for emergency back-up purposes. The capability of autonomous operation and even net energy surplus generation is built into the very nature of urban renewable energy technologies. Several different technologies can be deployed in arrays and networked in wider web formations. Different systems have different geographic characteristics, engendering different forms, modes and styles of deployment. For example: rooftop solar water heaters and some other simple energy capturing methods do not easily produce electricity; these are intrinsically isolated, *insular* renewable-energy collecting appliances. And solar-thermal power plants and wind-energy generators produce electric current indirectly, while photovoltaic arrays do so directly. All three can be used in insular or grid-connected mode. These and other forms of renewable power such as biofuels can also be translated into electricity and as such fed into public grids: long established as central feature and end-user supply backbone of the fossil fuel regime. In principle, electricity-generating renewable systems are especially flexible in their applications. They are not only available in numerous energy media, levels of sophistication and scales of output, but can also be used either as stand-alone devices or networked into local area networks or public grids.

Numerous small towns are already becoming renewable energy self-sufficient, such as Germany's bio-mass powered village of Jühnde, population 1,080 in 2005; and southeast Colorado's rural, wind-power rich city of Lamar, population under 10,000, a net exporter of wind electricity. It is the seat of Prowers County, proud site of a major AC/DC current switching station, and expecting soon to host the northern hemisphere observatory for high-energy cosmic rays which, it is hoped, will be a renewable energy source of the future, within the theoretical realms of *new energy* (Eurosolar 2005; ProColorado 2006).

## From plain old grid to intelligent energy web

The following paragraphs offer a prediction. In the near future, power grids or networks – termed here the emerging *energy web*, or *e-web* – will be fed by an increasingly diverse combination of conventional electricity sources, to be phased out or converted over time, and a growing array of decentralised, individual generators, stabilised by large-scale, multi-media, or hybrid renewable plants. Such larger suppliers include hydropower, solar or wind parks, and biomass based or hydrogen cogenerators, all of which will supply both heat and power. The input from ubiquitous *e-web nodes and servers* will be two-fold. One source will be supply-side based and consist of dedicated renewable energy plans and farms harvesting bio-fuel, wind, photovoltaic and solar-thermal power on intra- or peri-urban fields, or those positioned in distant locations, in North-African deserts, for example, supplying southern European cities (see also Section 3.4, 'Space, time and energy').

The other source will stem from demand-side located energy machinery, networked and automatically configured to sell surplus energy produced by individual generators into the web. This can range from single, small rooftop wind generator to PV-clad office buildings, and large bio-fuel or solar-thermal powered cogeneration plants for schools, factories, business parks or hospitals. This source does not have to be limited to large new projects or city expansion areas; the upgrading of existing cities can commence today, by ensuring that every building upgrade or infrastructure replacement effort embeds renewable power sources, while ensuring good, efficient building design. It takes limited time to refurbish and even rebuild an entire city, without added effort: a changed policy environment suffices entirely. Given annual building and infrastructure turnover rates of between only 1 to 5 per cent, cities are completely transformed every 20 to 100 years.

## Renewable urbanism

The prevailing central-power supply regime freezes a region or city's infrastructure architecture into a specific regime of immutable conditions. This forms a straitjacket for the supplied communities who now are at the whim of systems vagaries in price, service quality and power source. Even energy efficiency programmes or the supply of *green power* – portions of electricity provided through renewable and so-called alternative sources such as municipal waste combustion – are provided without much choice, largely at the utility's discretion and only after the exertion of enormous consumer and political pressure. In contrast, the attributes of the Renewable City's energy infrastructure – diversity and responsiveness to local conditions – open up extraordinary opportunities for more flexibility and innovation in urban management and virtual city form. The geography of the Renewable City is fluid, networked to allow for supply redundancy, ubiquitously supplied and consumer controlled. At the individual level, its future infrastructure may soon manifest itself in isolated, stand-alone, even mobile elements that are small enough to perform as intelligent *energy jewellery*, *energetic apparel* or *energy couture*, powering personal information exchange or processing devices. Basic public systems such as solar powered streetlights, phone booths and parking metres have long been in use and give rise to *converged civic armature*. While independently powered wireless communication nodes may take the familiar form of plain old curb-side metres but is likely soon to evolve into interactive attendants: a hybrid civic appliance combining a parking meter, local area and traffic information tool, personal communication console and an energy-supply station for electric vehicles.

Renewable urbanism begins to manifest itself also in small power networks, operated independently from the main grid: renewable-energy power connected settlements, houses, dwelling groups, industrial estates and institutional complexes. Distributed power may be supplied by any or a combination of the primary sources in the renewable world: sun, water, wind or biomass based and is often also provided through cogeneration. During and following the Californian power crisis precipitated by Enron's machinations, some Silicon Valley server farms and plant compounds were kept off the main grid for energy security reasons, operating primarily on generators and cogeneration systems originally conceived as stand-by support. These can well be powered by renewable energy systems: biomass based, solar-thermal steam supported or driven by renewably fed hydrogen fuel cells. The German parliament – the refurbished Reichstag building – operates in this fashion, relying on the public grid only for backup. Another good example of an urban renewable energy island is Los Angeles's new Audubon Center, supplied independently of the grid by storage-supported solar energy technology for cooling, heating and power (Perlman 2005). And buildings as renewable energy islands can also serve as urban net surplus producers, moving from the zero-emissions (ZET) to the net-energy export tower category (NET). Skidmore, Owings & Merrill (SOM) hope to convert their March 2006-announced competition-win, the Guangzhou-based Pearl River Tower into a 2006–09 implementation schedule. The 69-storey tower is proposed as a highly efficient construct, and designed to generate surplus energy by deploying building-integrated wind turbines and various solar energy devices (Meyer 2006). Given the vagaries of such competitions, it remains to be seen what actually will be constructed but the commitment by one of the world's great commercial firms augurs well for the proposal's implementation.

Micro- or mini-grids are sub-grids independent of main power network and they can be referred to as *energy local area networks* (E-LAN). Besides urban institutions or business parks, these also supply remote villages, settlements or facilities. Several million Europeans live without electricity, in isolated hamlets and villages throughout mountainous regions, on islands or other remote spots. Applying insular power, this splendid isolation will in future be determined by life-style choice, not technological necessity: the Greek island of Kythnos, for example, is now supplied by a stand-alone renewable energy system, independently of the national grid (Dürrschmidt et al 2004, p 85).

## Islands of autonomy

Close to half the world's population exists not only disconnected from the largely urban power grids, but entirely without electricity. Given this stark energy iniquity, and contrasting the genesis and historical logic of fossil-energy enabled electric grids with the diverse technological and cultural characteristics of renewable energy systems, it is not easy to argue that large, connected electric grids have a plausible future in the evolution of human settlement infrastructure or, given emerging technological scenarios, even that they offer a desirable vision. Conventional power grids tend not to extend to rural and other remote communities or to favour programmes designed to support the poor. The Global Village Energy Partnership (GVEP 2005) and, even more significantly, the enormously successful poverty alleviating micro-lending programme aimed at enabling autonomous solar electrification programmes in rural and other areas and among poorer populations (Grameen Bank's Grameen Shakti division which combines micro-credit with Renewable Energy Service Company (RESCO) functions (Wimmer and Barua 2004, 2005)), usefully divert policy focus from expensive, conventional power grids to locally empowering renewable systems. In doing so, they squarely confront the dilemma inherent in earlier, conventional electrification schemes which generally favour urban or less disadvantaged populations even when projecting into rural areas, while perpetuating the massive risks and costs of fossil and nuclear power schemes. In Europe, the United States and other so-called advanced and urbanised countries electric grids constitute a massive, central-supply geared public infrastructure investment. The embryonic renewable energy revolution focuses on them both as an urban reality and a development opportunity. But for future, emerging communities that are not yet saddled with this historical peculiarity, they may one day seem like strange cobwebs of the past.

## 3.4 SPACE, TIME AND ENERGY: STORING AND DISPATCHING RENEWABLE POWER

Modern cities have evolved with and along electric grids: as ominously humming high-tension, overland conduits strung between giant masts, wildly criss-crossing the urbanising countryside, raising hairs and fears for those dwelling under or near them. Within cities and towns, as the old urban power pole networks, they are strung above ground like laundry lines, or dropped in street-side conduits. They were a great icon of progress since the dawn of the 20th century, but had raised anxieties about carcinogenic radiation, urban despoliation and landscape destruction by the time its dusk had fallen. Urban electric power is associated with the most glorious visions of urban hope yet also the darkest moments of collective existential anxiety: from Berlin's pioneering rail electrification in the 1920s, to the great blackouts of the US Northeast on 9 November 1965 and 14 August 2003. As discussed above, the plain old grid, or POG, of the 20th century is likely to give way to its post-fossil incarnation as an intelligent energy web, hosting a vast community of renewable energy producers and consumers – the rising class of the *prosumer*.

### Internal and external supply

In power grids characterised by renewable energy sources, two basic methods of generation prevail. There are widely dispersed, *end-user based* systems: domestic photovoltaic installations fall into this category. And there are concentrated, *supply-side* installations such as large hydropower facilities, large wind farms or solar-thermal and photovoltaic field arrays. The larger systems become the more they emulate, or even go beyond, the traditional centralised power structures of the fossil and nuclear power empire. The plans for large-scale concentrated solar power electricity production in developing countries, Morocco or Algeria in northern Africa for example, are designed to help supply southern Europe as are other Projects of Pan-European Interests funded under the umbrella of the European Community (Arlinghoff et al c 2004; Morse 2004).

But there are limits to this analogy to POG power: fundamentally different principles are involved. Distributed end-use systems can be organised in ways that create virtual arrays across an entire city, region or nation. In this manner they could collectively perform as virtual power plants, quasi-centralised systems by virtue of controlling protocols. But in order for this radical energy regime to spring to life, new regulatory, market and technical management institutions must be put in place, along with national or international incentives and pricing regimes designed to support both distributed and centralised renewable power, essential to help sustain and grow healthy energy markets.

Many renewable systems are not constantly active; they operate in a stochastic or less-than completely predictable fashion. New storage systems and dispatch protocols are needed to allow both dispersed and centrally produced power to be supplied on demand, emulating the familiar, theoretically better, regularity of conventional supplies at times of plentiful coal, oil, nuclear or hydropower, feeding a docile population of families and industries, resting and busying themselves at regular, daily and weekly cycles of intensity. Unlike well-fed and carefully backed-up atomic plants, constantly active solar, wind and some other renewable power systems capture and convert energy intermittently or at various levels of intensity: as the sun shines or the wind blows. And others, like the early coal industry, are geographically bound: wind farms, for example, or hydropower. But neither of these physical constraints creates fundamental difficulties for a reliable and abundant urban renewable-energy supply. Innovative thinking, persistence and appropriate technical, finance and planning protocols are the only new ingredients required for success.

An important aspect emerges in this new thinking, organised around locally captured power. Locally generated renewable energy from sun and wind sources is most efficiently consumed locally, and ideally as soon as it is provided. If intermittently produced renewable energy cannot be applied immediately it is lost unless it can be stored or converted into more transportable forms of energy. In other words, it needs to be transformed so it can be dispatched for use on demand. The key to successfully combining centralised with dispersed energy sources in a single, reliably managed web lies in the distributed embedding of large and small-scale, ubiquitous storage systems. The total storage capacity inherent in a mature, fully functioning renewable city system is provided in a redundant and distributed manner, capable of buffering and balancing all highs and lows that make up urban energy demand and supply cycles. Energy storage is hence not only useful in making decentralised energy management systems (DEMS) effective, but also in achieving urban power balance: high levels of reliability in grid-connected, renewable-power based, *uninterrupted power supply* – also known as UPS in the electricity storage jargon. For a city or community aspiring to be renewable-power based, the physical needs of distributed storage can be addressed in a build-as-you-go manner within new and refurbished buildings and facilities. In accommodating any larger-scale storage apparatus deemed necessary to guarantee the bliss of UPS, however, some land acquisition, service commissioning and urban design challenges may surface.

## Balance and storage

How does urban power balancing through storage work? Its oldest and best-established example is water storage. Pumped hydropower is the trump card in the finely tuned, highly reliable energy balancing system managed by the Tokyo Electric Power Company (TEPCO), keeping metropolitan Tokyo the unnervingly well synchronised and, arguably, best-serviced metropolitan infrastructure system in the world, particularly given its size and density. Accepted outage tolerances lie within a few minutes per annum. Unused nuclear and fossil energy lifts river and lake water, filling mountaintop reservoirs at night and during other off-peak times. During the day, the stored water is released down mountainside drop channels into generators, to help meet daily peak demand levels. This system, long in use also in Alpine Germany and other mountainous regions of the world, is capable of near-instant response in compensating for sudden outages caused by other sources in the grid. In the event of failure of a nuclear power plant, a sudden lull in a wind-generator studded region, or another unexpected power shortfall, additional electricity can be mobilised within two to three minutes'. Also, water power, solar or wind energy and other forms of renewable power can be used as sole supply of pumped-hydro storage, helping reduce the overall carbon emissions of a city significantly. While the approach is ideal for balancing large wind power inputs, for example, its application is geographically limited – not many cities are endowed with nearby mountains capable of accommodating artificial water storage and associated generation structures.

Fortunately, there is a wide array of other methods and technologies available to help buffer or compensate for power shortfalls, surges and irregularities in grids. Traditionally, network redundancy has been applied, affording the ability to draw from a large number of different power generation sources, typically conventional power plants. The technical response needed to integrate large-scale intermittent energy flows into a traditional electric grid can be substantial. Germany, for example, has set a target of a 20 per cent renewable energy share between 2015 and 2020, much of it from large new off- and onshore wind farms. A recent German Energy Agency (dena) study projected a cost of nearly € 2 billion in grid upgrade and extension works required by the year 2015 in order to be able to balance the introduction of the 37,000 megawatt in new offshore wind power capacity that are expected by that year alone. Some 1,250 kilometres of the highly urbanised country's 380 kilo-volt grid are either to be upgraded or newly constructed (dena 2005). This dramatic initial response measure is likely to prove characteristic of the early stages of significant energy transformations. It is highly significant and instructive, given the country's status as the world's largest national wind energy power today. Integrated, ubiquitous storage protocols have not yet been considered in German infrastructure upgrading plans. But grid integrated and distributed large-scale storage, along with protocols for ubiquitous mini- and micro-storage systems will prove essential in establishing and maintaining a well-balanced and secure overall service level. In principle, what are termed *ubiquitous distributed energy storage* (UDES) systems will allow substantial reductions in new grid capacity construction for developed nations, and cost minimisation in new power infrastructure of developing countries, by helping integrate renewable power generation within cities and human settlements, and allowing necessary new grids to be designed for average, rather than peak use.

For individual renewable energy users and generators such as households or individual small companies, the ideals of UPS – uninterrupted power supply – mean enhancing demand-side energy management systems with small storage devices of below 10-kilowatt capacity, typically standard solar system batteries (Jacques 2005). Larger end-use storage systems are available for urban neighbourhood, village and small town, or even settlement-scale applications, as well as for larger facilities and institutions such as schools, universities, defence installations or hospitals. Such higher-capacity systems include: (a) *mechanical storage*, consisting of pumped-hydro power, the long-established, reliable method with an excellent 75 per cent efficiency record; compressed air energy storage (CAES; for a good example of which see Crotogino et al 2001); ultra-low friction flywheels for short-term energy release or absorption;

(b) both conventional and advanced *chemical storage*, consisting of biomass, methane reforming or hydrogen based, for example; and (c) *electrochemical storage*, which consists of aqueous, flow, organic and high-temperature forms of batteries. There are also (d) *electrical storage* systems, such as super-capacitors and super-conductive magnetic energy storage (SMES); as well as (e) *thermal storage* systems for latent-heat and sensitive storage; below-ground water or brine systems, or deep and contained aquifers (Dürrschmidt et al 2004, p 89; Fischedick and Nitsch 2004; Jacques 2005).

## Hydrogen city?

Several countries, some cities and a number of innovators and investors in non-fossil, non-nuclear options have begun to bank on the fact that hydrogen can be manufactured from a range of renewable sources, from bio-fuel to wind and solar power and not only from natural gas, coal, oil or nuclear power. Used in this way, it promises to become a superior storage medium, revolutionising the manner in which renewable power can supply cities for both transport and stationary energy. As one example of a legion of current innovations, the Canadian Solar Hydrogen Energy Corporation (SHEC) works to produce hydrogen via solar-thermally generated steam, at temperatures capable of splitting water, in its solar catalytic hydrogen generator (Sklar 2005). These and other approaches promise to combat the threat of nuclear and fossil-fuel based hydrogen stigmatising this embryonic industry.

Hydrogen as urban energy carrier is highly promising in the mid- to long-term; its widespread and economic use as renewable energy medium is not, however, expected until the 2030s to 2050s (Fischedick and Nitsch 2004, p 5). Meanwhile, cities will do well to explore future urban infrastructure requirements for accommodating both hydrogen-combustion and fuel-cell based power conversion, for stand-alone and back-up purposes, transport and combined heat-power generation. Hydrogen is widely seen as relatively unproblematic to generate, store and distribute, but for technical and economic reasons still remains remote from becoming a reality as soon as sometimes promised. It is not a renewable energy resource: produced electrolytically with significant energy input, hydrogen is a *form of energy*, a power carrier like electricity, not a source. As such, it is increasingly touted in 'hydrogen economy' promotions, but also groomed into a Trojan Horse, concealing the re-entry of coal and nuclear power in a seemingly clean guise. One major international advocate for a hydrogen future is veteran efficiency guru Amory Lovins, founder and director of the venerable Rocky Mountain Institute. He spells out the potential advantages of the technology most persuasively. These include an established fuel infrastructure that is partially suitable to conversion and use for hydrogen generation and distribution, its relative safety, efficiency and flexibility of use (Lovins 2003).

For urban applications, hydrogen promises to offer a critical breakthrough as energy carrier and storage medium, provided the following, promised technical virtues are translated into a widely and purposefully applied fossil-free and non-nuclear urban reality. First among hydrogen's extraordinary characteristics is its capacity to act as an efficient recipient of renewable energy in almost all forms (see also Section 4.3 for the most commonly used urban renewable power systems). It can be readily generated from electricity, and lends itself to concentrating and intensifying the energy generated from a range of both continuous and intermittent renewable sources such as biomass, solar and wind. Second, excess, or temporarily unused, renewable energy can be stored in both decentralised and centralised ways, and assist in managing load differentials in the electric power grid. Third, hydrogen can be deployed as fuel in a range of other applications: in transport; for cooling and heating; cogeneration, or combined heat and power production; and as peak load compensation medium in conventional power plants. Fourth, it can be treated as a commodity, and stored, transferred and traded across seasons and markets. And finally, it can, indeed, be distributed via established infrastructures (Fischedick and Nitsch 2004, pp 4 and 5).


## 3.5 RENEWABLE CITIZENSHIP: SUPPORT COMMUNITIES AND PROGRAMMES

### Networks and support programmes

A search for greater intelligence and even only common sense in city planning and design has long been a feature of city development and management practice around the world, amid mounting calls for environmentally sustainable urban development. In its pursuit, associations and alliances, the internet, conferencing and other means of networking are increasingly pursued. Early and fragile signals of a post-fossil, nuclear-free urban era can be detected among these loosely structured, shifting communities of cities and towns. These multiply and ephemerally networked 'sustainability communities' are a lively feature of the wider phenomenon of networking among cities. City networks as ancient dimensions of urban development and competitiveness were greatly advanced in the information-technology augmented contemporary era of globalisation (Friedmann 2001; Sassen 2002), intensifying meaningful exchanges, other growing more superficial, elusive and ephemeral. Renewable energy and efficiency questions make up perhaps the most vital theme within the some 50 mostly only recently proliferating *sustainability-oriented city networks* carefully documented at the Eidgenössische Techniche Hochschule (ETH) in Zürich, Switzerland in 2006. The study traces the beginnings of this phenomenon to the years 1913/14 when the International Union of Local Authorities (IULA) and the International City/County Management Association (ICMA) were formed (Keiner and Kim 2006). Renewable city issues feature within this network genre, but increasingly also among other thematic clusters and network galaxies; notably those of renewable energy and efficiency science, engineering and industry on the one hand, and those focused on urban planning, development and design on the other. There is considerable confusion about the priority to be assigned to various discussion topics in both sustainability and planning networks. Most featured are tighter land use and transport integration, greater reliance on public transport, car sharing, urban design and management initiatives to promote bicycling and walking – the energy predicament has only very recently returned to centre stage but still not fully gained the pre-eminent position it deserves. Here stricter building controls, construction standards, rating tools and performance measures are popular means in attempts at overcoming darker legacies of the 20th century, by lowering fossil energy consumption – and, hence, securing more time for the necessary freeing of cities from their dependence on fossil, nuclear and other environmentally deleterious, centralised power systems. Renewable energy as an only recently emerging, active component of generation is as yet not well linked to the older efficiency networks.

Indeed, within the network communities and related web-based services, demand side management, conservation and efficiency are most frequently seen and promoted as the foundation of a healthy urban energy practice, and rightfully so since they form the working basis for a rational introduction of renewable energy in cities and settlements. Several initiatives with a primary focus on urban energy efficiency have surfaced during the 1990s, paralleling the rise of the worldwide web as well as the emergence of new public initiatives, particularly across the European Union and the United States. These are listed among the web references of this guide. Several of these stand out as being particularly well established: the transport-efficiency geared, petroleum-reducing Clean Cities efforts by the United States government, pursued in partnership with states and cities (DoE 2006b); Energy Cities (E-C Energie-Cités 2005) in Europe; a number of energy-minded Green Cities programmes; and the worldwide Cities for Climate Protection (CCP) campaign of the International Council for Local Environmental Initiatives (ICLEI), founded on Local Agenda 21 (CCP 2005). It is important to note that although many programmes are country- and region specific, such as the United States and European based initiatives, as web based platforms all can offer valuable insights and resources to interested cities anywhere in the world. Some are run by government agencies, renewable energy industry and non-profit and non-government organisations as a public or promotional service; others as membership organisations for intelligence sharing; and a third category involves governmental or regional, inter-city arrangements aimed at information exchange.

**Clean Cities** has offered a web-based resource, partnership arrangements and funding for a number of years in the area of private transport fuel use reduction. Its stated mission is 'to advance the nation's economic, environmental, and energy security by supporting local decisions to adopt practices that contribute to the reduction of petroleum consumption' (DoE 2006b). The Clean Cities Programme comprises a network of over 80 voluntary coalitions focused on urban transport goods, services and administration. It promotes alternative fuels and vehicles, fuel blends, fuel economy, hybrid vehicles and engine idle time reduction, working through public–private partnership agreements.

**Green Cities** – this label connotes aspirations, visions and political platforms. It describes no single programme in pursuit of well-rounded urban design and management. Numerous Green Cities efforts aim at making urban development more benign by attempting to limit the damage the process wreaks on natural, pastoral and cultural environments, human health and natural resources. Increasingly, however, these efforts support or reward renewable energy commitments. The United Nations World Environment Day in 2005 promoted the theme of Green Cities with 'urban power' recognised as a major issue in many, if not most, of the locally organised events. This was a breakthrough given that the global and massive human-habitat geared *Agenda 21* conferencing process, commencing with the Earth Summit in Rio de Janeiro in 1992 and its *Rio Declaration on Environment and Development*, has been agonisingly reluctant to acknowledge renewable energy as a major, if not *the* major issue in sustainable development. While it did not figure at all in the programme of the first United Nations Conference on Environment and Development (UNCED) in 1992, it was raised in the most recent of these mega-events, the 2002 World Summit on Sustainable Development (WSSD) in Johannesburg, albeit sometimes still drowned in fossil-friendly protests. The seemingly innocuous cause of renewable power was opposed by a group of petroleum exporting countries and others committed to the fossil fuel and nuclear power industry and its concomitant, conventional promises of yesterday's progress.

**The European Green Cities Network**, with EU support, has attracted some 50 cities, agencies and private companies to focus on innovative urban housing, promoting and publicising best practice projects, and inspiring designers, investors, builders and government officials. It is built around the experience of 11 such projects carried out in 9 European countries, all concluded in 2000. Its main activities today are conferences, technical training and information dissemination (EGCN 2005).

'Greening', a popular term especially common in the United States, has emerged as a form of mainstream city promotion. Many organisations, including the daily press, attempt to evaluate and rank cities in a popular sense, also on the energy performance within broader 'sustainability' or 'liveability' frames. A United States consumer information magazine, the *US Green Guide* runs a Top Ten Green Cities list, with one of the leading 2005 winners – Austin, Texas – described as qualifying due to its being 'clean and affordable' and having 15 per cent of its urban area assigned to parklands and an exceptional array of outdoor facilities. This city of 650,000 is home to the largest concentration of solar industries in the US and has set itself one of the most ambitious targets of its kind in the nation, at 20 per cent of its internal, primary energy use in electricity scheduled to be covered by efficiency gains and renewable power by the year 2020. Another source of local green pride is a portfolio of nearly 20 buildings and projects registered under the rating and certification criteria of the Green Building Council's 'Leadership in Energy and Efficiency Design' (LEED; see Chapter 5; Green Guide 2005).

**Energie-Cités**' membership has increased steadily since the association was established in 1990. The association now has some 125 individual subscribers, mostly towns and cities, but also, additionally, regional and inter-city organisations, local energy agencies, municipal corporations and clusters of communities. The Energie-Cités network extends over 21 European countries, representing 475 European cities, institutions and other groups. Energie-Cités provides information to the public as well as guidance on energy efficiency practice, renewable energy and mobility; and serves as a partnership action platform and lobbying organ with European government (E-C/Energie-Cités 2005). The programme is distinct from the Swiss **Energiestadt** – energy city – proprietary labelling programme, which comprises some 150 cities, towns and villages competing for advanced status and recognition in a point and seniority system of performance (Energiestadt 2005).

The International Council for Local Environmental Initiative's (ICLEI) Cities for Climate Protection™ (CCP) campaign was launched in 1993, since when its membership has grown considerably. Actively participating cities adopt energy change policies and implement ways of quantifying community greenhouse gas (GHG) emissions. A proprietary subscriber-based programme sets five milestones aimed at supporting participant communities in producing targeted GHG reductions, overall air quality improvements and a general boost in urban quality and sustainable conditions. Over 650 local governments participated as of 2005, pledging to build climate change mitigation into their planning. In 2005 ICLEI operated the programme in Australia, Canada, Europe, Japan, Latin America, Mexico, New Zealand, South Africa, South Asia, Southeast Asia and the United States.

CCP's action framework – a system structured around five milestones – aims at: (a) creating an emissions inventory and forecast model; (b) setting basic reduction targets; (c) developing an action plan; (d) policy implementation; and (e) monitoring and verification. Local governments are assisted in understanding how planning choices impact on the use of energy. CCP represents the most widely applied method of accounting for, and ultimately reducing GHG emissions at local government level today.

Participating communities are promised (a) lower utility and fuel costs to local government, households and businesses; (b) improved levels of local air quality and community health; and (c) economic development and employment growth since investment in local energy products and services is hoped to retain more local assets in local circulation (ICLEI 2005a). Emission savings are allocated in economic or urban sectors rather than measured as end-user, ie individual-consumption based. These can range from municipal attention to energy standards in street lighting, municipal fleet use, to building efficiency controls; to initiatives for reduced fossil-energy embodied in materials in construction and services; to energy consumed at a domestic household level. ICLEI provides regionally specific tools and technical assistance to help city governments control local greenhouse gas emissions. (See also the paragraphs on local greenhouse gas accounting methods below, under, 'Climate stabilisation and city programmes'.)

**European and International Solar Cities Initiatives** Two other recent international networking efforts are outgrowths and apply ideas advanced as part of the Solar City® effort, which was commenced under the umbrella of the International Energy Agency from 1999 until 2003 (see below, Chapter 6, and

Droege 1999a). They are managed through the offices of the International Solar Energy Society (ISES). When the European Solar Cities Initiative (ESCI) was founded in 2003 it was a call for membership to a wide range of European players interested in and focused on municipal greenhouse gas emissions reductions, many of the participants had been nurtured in the earlier Solar City® process (ESCI 2005). The International Solar Cities Initiative (ISCI) was launched in South Korea in 2004 and began to point even more strongly to technology solutions. Indeed, ISES's efforts are aimed somewhat more narrowly and directly than ICLEI's in its CCP campaign, favouring sun-energy generation solutions – notably, solar-thermal and photovoltaic systems – with the intention of addressing community-wide emissions targets and wider urban challenges, or other energy-sensitive planning needs of cities. The conferencing programme continued in 2006 in Oxford, and Adelaide in 2008 (ISES 2005a). Although as somewhat more industry-focused, supply-side oriented efforts they appear to challenge ICLEI's more demand-side focused CCP programmes, there is potential for mutual compatibility, particularly since the ISES initiatives have not yet evolved into fully fledged action programmes, but rather are, successful settings for concept comparisons and conferences, as programmed in the original Solar City® effort.

**Brundtland Cities and RESETnet**. Brundtland Cities Energy Network (BCEN) is a closely related network of smaller European cities and has its roots in the 1990s. It is contributed to by ISES and established its own formal, somewhat similar five-year programme in 2003, aiming at a reduction of up to 30 per cent in (fossil) energy consumption within five years of being 'appointed'.

**Renewable Energy Strategies for European Towns** (RESETnet) is a well-established, action-oriented support network focused on a number of renewable energy and efficiency-geared pilot projects throughout Europe and has been active since 1994 (ISES 2005b).

## Long-range needs and short-term horizons

Every community is confronted by a great challenge in terms of change. This is inherent in the dichotomy posed by two great urban change dicta: '*look before you leap*' and '*he who hesitates is lost*'. The urge to phase in renewable energy technology as quickly as possible must be tempered by the need to carefully evaluate and select the best long-term, energy-sensitive emissions reduction strategies, including efficiency and conservation programmes. To understand the entire energy matrix of a city, as well as the emissions behaviour of its community, is an essential foundation for the intelligent deployment of all urban infrastructure, not only of renewable energy systems. Indeed, in an ideal world all municipal planning would be rational, well tempered and strategically geared towards targeted and measured reductions. And this agenda would best be sustained over a significant period: the five decades that are required substantially to transform a city's building stock and energy base, while reducing overall greenhouse gas emissions by the amount necessary to achieve some 3 to 4 tons per person per year, or a global reduction of 60 per cent over 1990 figures (Byrne et al 1998).

Yet, in reality no city could submit itself to such exemplary control, discipline and perseverance. When it comes to decision-making, modern cities follow the laws of chaos rather than cool rationality, even – and, it seems, especially – where they maintain rolling five-year plans. Cities' planning apparatus is subject to great changes in direction, and virtually non-existent when it comes to not only weighing and making long-range choices, but also implementing these. A difficulty arises from the fact that shrinking staff turnover cycles do not allow institutional memory to survive for more than a few years, and even significant policies are seldom sustained for longer than an election period, unless these are enshrined in more durable legislative or administrative frameworks. Yet the resolve to persist is steeled, and ultimate success quite attainable, when a sense of urgency arises, single-purpose causes and projects are commenced, or levelheaded and charismatic leadership gains support. As an example, the 'municipalisation' of Sacramento's power supply – the conversion of private utility supply into city-controlled assets – took eight years to accomplish, and continues to have enormous impact. A tangible, focused goal helped drive motivations. The Sacramento Municipal Utilities District (SMUD) successfully moved to increase the renewable energy share of that city more assuredly and accountably than any distant, privatised supplier ever could.

The key to success is to disaggregate long-term aims into operational, tangible goals, while reforming municipal organisational structures with a sense of purpose: to introduce important legislative and institutional changes at several levels of government at the same time. The result may include reformed local government structures; municipal utilities such as SMUD or Silicon Valley Power (SVP) and its Santa Clara Green Power renewable energy programme; urban charities such as London's Sustainable Energy Action/Renewable Energy in the Urban Environment (SEA/RENUE 2006); public–private partnerships – or a combination of all. This promises to anchor and embed decisions in the local institutional framework as well as the collective memory – two necessary success factors in purposeful and effective long-term decision-making. The Solar City® programme recommended in Section 6.1 aims to assist in that.

## Climate stabilisation and city programmes: local efforts

New urban renewable energy applications proliferate with great speed. Many are described in this guidebook (see Chapter 4). Examples include both centralised and dispersed photovoltaic installations; large solar thermal plants; building-integrated wind power; bio-fuelled cogeneration plants combining heat and power production; or ground-heat pumping. Tangible and substantially pursued commitments to planned urban energy practice, however, are still rare, and they spread more slowly – but interest mounts steadily nonetheless. As individual nations and regional emissions markets such as the European Union refine and clarify their greenhouse, energy and environmental accounting frameworks, the prospects for tighter urban emissions and energy practice are likely to strengthen, and with these the incentives to foster new local institutional arrangements.

Transportation, land use, built form and the fossil fuel content of urban goods and services – all aspects of local energy use – are about to come under public scrutiny, revealing a long-concealed yet fundamental dimension of modern urbanism. All aspects of a city can be understood in energy consumption terms – buildings, services, food, mobility, and so on – and translated into fossil fuel content. Hence, it should be possibly to guide cities, towns and other settled communities in a steady quest towards sustainability through targeted and monitored carbon emission reductions. City leaders and communities could adopt overall, long-term targets towards total energy autonomy and steep $CO_2$ reductions, guiding urban behaviour through pricing, regulations and other inducements – in theory. In practice, this concept faces certain difficulties. Cities and human settlements are imperfect, even chaotic systems and lack the control levers to influence human behaviour beyond short-term timeframes, and outside existing institutional structures. It is therefore important to focus on fundamental performance measures and institutional accountability structures first, to re-engineer administrative and organisational software in ways that make the phasing out of fossil and nuclear power use an inexorable reality. This guide contains several action templates that are suitable to attain this goal, but to apply these requires an awareness of the historical determination of urban political and administrative cultures, and the logic of the fossil fuel city's rise and fall.

Given intelligent national and international frameworks, cities, communities and urban regions may well emerge as distributed energy managers and even carbon credit and debit trading entities, especially as interest in greater local autonomy grows at the same time. While not yet researched or modelled well, it is fairly easy to grasp cities and city regions as power systems, settings of energy and resource flow; and to see the modern city as a great nidus of fossil fuel use, and hence a of consumption-triggered emissions. As a result, there is a strong argument for augmenting urban planning processes with community-planning models referenced to measured baselines, monitored improvement targets and replicable, ideally easily understood means of accounting for greenhouse gas emissions. This idea was advanced early in the 1990s by Cities for Climate Protection™ emissions accounting innovator and software developer, Canada's Ralph Torrie and his peers (Kates et al 1998). It helped inspire others, including solar-thermal physicist and entrepreneur David Mills and his colleagues at the University of Sydney, into promoting equity-based per-capita emissions accounting concepts (Lenzen 1997) not unlike the simplified popular emissions calculators that have been distributed by a number of international government agencies for some years now (EPA 2006b; EPA VIC 2005; GC 2005). Instead of approximating local emissions based on sectoral performance, Mills and others advocated creating total, goods- and services-consumption based greenhouse gas (GHG) accounts per capita, and then specifying long-term local planning targets aimed at notional, absolute per-capita emissions credits of 3.3 tons per annum to be reached by 2050. In contrast, Australia and the United States approach 30 tons per annum per person; most developing countries, including India, still lie well below this level, but are trying to reach it as fast as they can. This thinking, concerned with advocating fair development and emissions equity among nations and people, had been informed conceptually by policy research developed by John Byrne and his Centre for Energy and Environmental Policy (CEEP) at the University of Delaware, based on earlier scientific findings by the United Framework Convention on Climate Change (UNFCC) on the GHG absorption capacity of terrestrial systems such as oceans and forests (Byrne 1998). While compelling in its conceptual commitment equity, in practice this method has not yet found its way onto mainstream local agendas, but in principle the prospects are good. There is great sympathy with the notion of population based emissions equity, especially among local leaders and communities.

Several other local or place-based emissions accounting tools have existed and been applied since the early 1990s. The United States Environmental Protection Agency has long provided support to states in compiling greenhouse gas inventories, usually sector-based, producing action plans and staging demonstration projects. The emissions approximation approach developed for the Cities for Climate Protection™ programme operated by the International Council for Local Environmental Initiatives has already been described above. Another, NASA-funded accounting approach tracks the behaviour of large geographical units – 1 degree of longitude by 1 degree of latitude – developed by the American Geographers, Research Association in its Global Change and Local Places initiative (AAG 2003). There is also the potential to apply modified aspects of the Advanced Local Energy Planning (ALEP) approach developed under the International Energy Agency's (IEA) Building and Community Systems programme (Jank 2000), or basing tools on the physical model of the economy developed by the Australian Commonwealth Science, Industry and Research Organization, CSIRO (Cocks et al 2000; Foran et al 1998, 2005 ).

Despite the obvious difficulties in defining a city as a closed system in carbon accounting terms – or, perhaps better, because of it – the Swiss alpine ski resort city of Davos, site of the World Economic Forum (WEF 2005), is heralded as the world's first city to develop its own carbon accounting method, termed by its protagonists 'complete' in proud hyperbole. Encouraged by the success of its WEF-sponsored Climate Alliance (DCA 2005) in helping to offset the enormous carbon footprint created by the international airline traffic of passengers bound for this popular destination, it engaged in a new set of partnerships to study the overall greenhouse gas emissions profile of the community and its visitors. Davos is one of roughly 150 Swiss *energy cities* committed to reducing fossil fuel consumption, receiving labelled status points, on the road to Switzerland's reaching its Kyoto goal of an 8 per cent greenhouse-gas emissions reduction over 1990 figures by 2010 (Energiestadt 2005). The project examines the total emissions load from a wide range of data sets, including waste figures, resource flows, energy data, demographics and soils profiles and compares these with municipal and sub-regional emission sinks, or carbon binding or sequestration opportunities – local forests areas, mostly. The community of Davos has set itself a fossil-fuel consumption reduction target of 15 per cent by the year 2014, and may some day aspire to become locally carbon-neutral: its inhabitants, industries, services, visitors and other constituents netting zero greenhouse-gas emissions. This study will provide the essential baseline profile for moving to this goal in a planned fashion, perhaps a world first in this comprehensive way (Alt 2005e).

The notion of a total-flow carbon accounting model to be introduced to cities and towns fell on fertile ground particularly among scientists, engineers and some planners: why should a city not accept responsibility for the environmental damage created by its economic gains and prosperity, fundamentally linked to the global economy and its basis on discounting external costs, especially those created in a fossil world (McEvoy et al 1998; Roaf and Gupta 2006)? Yet while it is tempting to anthropomorphise the culpability and behaviour of cities acting as collective persons, or communities speaking in unison, it is important to remember that most cities are rather loose agglomerations of groups, financial flows and cultural signals – and only weakly defined as entities, anchored in what is recorded about their history, in frameworks of government and civic institutions. Their floating populations at times can exceed the numbers of their resident denizens: their products roam globally. Precise carbon tracking systems and attempts at apportioning exact accountability at a local level belong to the realm of closed-system experiments in physics, not to urban communities. Cities don't *do* – people, organisations and near-chaotic interactions between them, following the rules under which they operate, result in an evolutionary track. Fossil globalisation has served to weaken further an understanding of what a city is – perhaps renewable post globalisation will reaffirm it, be it as a result of community unity or government enforcement. Indeed, all individuals have carbon accounts and leave carbon trails and hence, their casual or formal assembly in cities constitutes the carbon world of a city, capable of being tracked by governments bent on Orwellian 'Big Brother' tactics. But such carbon tracking and profiling, if it is ever implemented, may not be able to adhere strictly to an urban enforcement perimeter: in some countries, carbon cantons or communities may turn out to be target units of counting and enforcement in other contexts, national or even geo-regional realms. Meanwhile, in the world of the built environment, the buildings, infrastructure, production facilities and transport settings are specific nodes and networks of carbon emission: these can be mapped and registered in geographic information systems, and spatially as well as economically assigned – and a number of such initiatives are in place, as inaugurated in the United Kingdom (Droege 1997).

Given the nature of cities as politically ephemeral entities, compelling arguments, such as those that led to the commitments by the Swiss energy cities, do not suffice always and everywhere to bring about lasting local change. The psychological dimension and ephemeral nature of any community action needs to be understood, if one seeks to link emissions reductions to local development opportunities, climate change risk management expenditures and concrete rewards. Also, while most greenhouse gas emission sources and practical mitigation efforts are inherently local, their effects range from the global to the regional. Hence, while local action is critical, the identification of globally diffused emission levels carries little practical, local, socially experienced meaning, unless it is made tangible in personalised carbon credit and debit systems. This paradox presents both technical and psychological challenges. The carbon counter's dreams of a perfect, universal and locally meaningful accounting system may never be realised in most communities, but the search for these and local efforts to contribute to the accounting debate will be useful in stimulating more informed local action – in different guises. The fixation on carbon instead of on technology transformation and source substitutions can deflect action. It also ignores the majority of the world's population: a great gulf exists between rich and poor cities in their relative capacity to carry out emissions inventories, and particularly in the need to do so: populations in poorer cities do not generally have a greenhouse gas debt, and a carbon credit flow is a very distant dream indeed, even if it did promise an overall reduction in emissions. Underdevelopment is still defined as a relative absence of fossil-fuel driven forms of industrialisation; the status of Developing Countries in the United Nations Framework Convention on Climate Change (UNFCC) parlance confirms this. Their urban emissions problems are related to immediate health and local air pollution, but, as yet, not to significant greenhouse gas emissions release.

In sum, an unwavering focus on renewable energy systems introduction and the phasing out of fossil-fuel and nuclear technology can be achieved in many ways, and carbon counting certainly is an important tool for measuring conditions and progress. But the adoption of renewable and efficient infrastructure, and not the counting of emissions, is the end of Renewable City planning, and hence must remain the paramount focus of any urban energy transformation effort.

### Solar edifice

France once was a pioneer in renewable power technology: the solar furnace in Odeillo was constructed in 1969. The structure supports a large parabolic mirror, sunbeam target area and control tower. It vaguely resembles contemporary deconstructivist and other postmodern forms, those expressive flowers of high fossilism in architecture. Yet it boldly anticipates the emergence of a new and renewable language, following the logic of the sun, not a desire to revel in petroleum powered abstractions.

# CHAPTER 4

# Building the Renewable City: tools, trades, technology

## 4.1 FORM FOLLOWS FUEL

Cities are energy. Virtually everything about them is determined by its flow and controlled by the kind of resources available, the manner in which these are supplied and used, and the culture they help engender. Up until the dawn of the coal and oil age, the form and function of cities resulted from the raw human, animal, water and biological energy applied in transport, construction and warfare. The felling and burning of trees was a major factor in this urban energy history. It threatened widespread deforestation in the Europe of the 17th and 18th centuries, until the rise of coal made it practical to listen to calls for sustainable forestry, such as that by Saxony court official Hans Carl von Carlowitz (1645–1714) in his *Sylvicultura oeconomica* (Carlowitz [1713]2000). This 1713 programme built on Jean-Baptiste Colbert's (1619–83) pioneering *Grande réformation de forets*, the 1669 *Grande ordonnance* promulgated to safeguard forestry reserves and advanced by the powerful French *contrôleur général* (finance minister) to ensure that a sufficient stream of timber was maintained for Louis XIV's massive ship building efforts.

Coal-fired cities began to expand initially in Europe, especially within reach of local coal sources; the rising steam engine channelled their growth along rail corridors. Electricity lit up Berlin, termed by Peter Hall the 'first Silicon Valley,' and endowed with the electric streetcar, in the wake of Siemens', AEG's and other founding factories in the great electrical and communications complex of the 19th century (Hall 1998, pp 377–90). Other cities quickly followed, transformed into magic citadels of bright lights and motorised motion. The far more mobile oil products and natural gas arrived in the first half of the 20th century, and to a lesser extent, nuclear power in the second. These put an end to the previous energy constraints that were placed on both the growth of populations and the cities that attracted and sheltered them so resulting in today's vertically sprouting central cities and horizontally oozing suburbs. The spectre of a threatened oil supply and global ecocide gave rise to the calls for urban efficiency that commenced in the 1970s, and the urban consolidation, compact-city, smart-growth and transit-oriented development efforts that are a hallmark of contemporary urban planning discourse.

## Evolution of efficiency

Urban resource efficiency is no new concept. Many historical urban design innovations resulted from successfully overcoming urban efficiency challenges. Examples are the ancient water management schemes of Egypt or Mesopotamia; early Chinese settlement history from the evolution of imperial city form to the loess-sculpted settlements in Hunan Province; or the classical urban innovations of Europe: the Greek *polis* of the Bronze Age as an efficient city ideal, the amphitheatre, port structures of Asia Minor, or the Roman military encampment. The pursuit of efficiency lies at the very core of urban evolution. When engaged with imagination and determination it translates into purposeful innovation of form and infrastructure, but also into market strength and economic success. Efficiency measures secured greater urban defensibility, climatic fit, smooth circulation and numerous advantages drawn from local geological and other resource conditions. Urban social control has long been achieved through efficient means of spatial configuration, including the instilling, fine-tuning and efficient reinforcement of fear and awe via urban iconography, both political and religious: temples, cathedrals, palaces, prisons and courts.

The postmodern challenge of urban efficiency is of a different ilk. The overriding mandate in urban development today is not the development of efficient solutions to new and pressing city building needs. Rather, it is the colossal task of undoing the negative effects of almost three generations of planning priorities bred in an era that was gripped by great collective delusions about limitless growth. The new efficiency paradigm is aimed at curbing urban sprawl, oil gluttony and material waste, in a drive to offset the sheer momentum of a century of fossil affluence as burning, all-encompassing aspiration. The new efficiency paradigm is pitched against the blindness of conventional, environmental-cost externalising development economics. In contrast, the new urban efficiency thinking is focused on finding ways of reducing the bloated development footprint – the real size of cities. Herein lies an important performance measure for fossil energy efficiency and conservation drives.

This guidebook touches on three major urban efficiency issues: (a) reforming wasteful forms of mobility and transport; (b) reducing stationary energy consumption: and (c) achieving urban thermal improvements by design. It is important to be mindful of the context of this quest. Much of national and global consumption of resources, products and services across all economic sectors is linked to activities in urban areas, and especially so in highly urbanised societies, such as Japan, the United States, central regions of Europe and, increasingly, China. The achievement of substantially improved systems efficiency through resource cycling and the determined defossilisation of all economic sectors – agriculture, food production, mining and metals, manufacturing and services (Foran et al 2005) – will have a deep influence on how cities are ultimately assembled, managed, used and developed.

## Fossil mobility and the urban energy crisis

Virtually all motorised transport movements are fossil powered. Local and worldwide engine-augmented personal, industrial and freight movements depend almost entirely on petroleum at 95 per cent, with some 5 per cent being propelled by natural gas. Transport accounts for 22 per cent of total fuel-combustion derived carbon dioxide equivalent emissions and for 12 per cent of all anthropogenic greenhouse gas emissions. Of transport emissions, road movements account for 74 per cent of the total share; air traffic for 12 per cent; shipping for 10 per cent and rail for 4 per cent (Lenzen et al 2003, p 52). Of all lead emissions, 90 per cent are transport generated (Hensher 2003, p 3).

The individual, motorised mobility explosion is the most pervasive urban feature of the *Abundant City*, powered by petroleum machines. While many less privileged communities and users depend on motor vehicles for their livelihood and income due to poor public transport options, overwhelmingly, cultural critics such as German philosopher Peter Sloterdijk see the private motorcar as the ultimate form of individuated mass consumption (Sloterdijk 2005). To them, it exemplifies the narcissistic escapism of Modernity. In its mature form it propels consumer culture to extreme heights: the insistence on enormous personal outlays in acquiring and maintaining the machines needed to cover astronomical distances in the expanding metropolitan galaxies of the urban universe – and to assert secure personal and corporate status in the capitals of conspicuous consumption. From the European cradle of auto-mobility that is car-crazed Germany, to the ultimate car emporium of the United States, to congestion-throttled metropolitan Southeast Asia and China's post-Mao motor mania, cities are struggling with the tragicomedy of unfettered growth played out as an existential conundrum of epic proportions. In China today, the very symbols of personal affluence, the ultimate rewards of switching to a 'market' economy, entail seeing its very fruits denied as urban traffic grinds to a frozen, choked halt in a caricature of progress in bloating cities from Beijing to Chongqing.

Barely a generation after the brave new world of mobility machines had been anticipated as radical urban reality in General Motors' *Futurama* pavilion at the 1933 'Century of Progress' World Exposition in Chicago, it began to be fought with great zeal. In the late 1960s, a team of planners preparing the Bavarian capital of Munich for the 1972 Olympic Games visited the United States for inspiration, and returned sobered and subdued. Back at home they worked to avoid the mayhem the motorcar had brought to North-American cities. Almost half a century ago, the city, home of the Bavarian Motor Works (BMW), advanced the very tools proposed by leading transport planners today. It built an extensive subway and regional public transport network, focusing stations on key urban nodes and introducing Europe's most extensive pedestrianised zone into the very heart of the old city centre as a means of reinforcing non-motorised traffic. This served to resuscitate the dying idea of public space, albeit in the commercialised form of an outdoor shopping mall. Still committed to innovation and purposeful planning, Munich is one of the world leaders in urban energy innovation today.

Since then, and particularly spurred by the first great Oil Crisis that immediately followed the Munich Olympics, communities in cities and towns around the world began to pursue large-scale fuel efficiency and energy conservation programmes. Many began to pursue the introduction of renewable energy generation technologies as practical paths to both energy security and economic development through industrial renewal. And leaders in cities such as Adelaide, Barcelona, Chicago, Curitiba, Freiburg, London and Munich understand that the transformation of transport power sources and systems, urban form, human settlement patterns and land management practices presents a critical if frequently ignored dimension of the renewable city building challenge. Stationary renewable power systems, typically photovoltaic panels, are easily and visibly embraced, but form only a part of the array of solutions. The search for a new conceptual and practice framework spans all aspects of the urban energy revolution: from land use to transport to efficiency, financial, regulatory, demand management and distributed renewable energy generation technology. This hunt is about to be whipped into a frenzied search for survivable paths by the three urban change forces of petroleum peaking, climate change mitigation and runaway environmental cost imposed by the fossil fuel economy.

Two Davids taking on a Goliath, veteran urban transport energy researchers and urban sustainability leaders Peter Newman and Jeffrey Kenworthy have in their research and advisory writings since the 1980s reflected a wider, visceral if ultimately somewhat helpless resistance to the privatisation of urban space, as epitomised by the motor vehicle avalanche (Newman and Kenworthy 1987). Their work paralleled that of Peter Calthorpe in the world of planning and his quest for transit oriented development as a foil for reinventing a civic *aesthetic of place* in support of neighbourhood reconstruction (Calthorpe 1993), and Richard Sennett's more fundamental treatise on the shifting balance between public and private life (Sennett 1992). These ideas resonated well with a wider criticism of the amazing shrinkage and evaporation of public space under the onslaught of a gasoline-fuelled cultural shift long in the making: mass privatisation through automobiles, the vexing phenomenon of collective individualisation reinforced by mail order and mall retail and, ultimately, epitomised in the profound impact of new information technology and tele-communication on perceptions and use of space (Droege 1997).

Newman and Kenworthy's simple graph correlating high-density cities with lower levels of per-capita gasoline consumption was perhaps the most pivotal and influential diagram used in urban planning of the 1980s (Newman and Kenworthy 1987, 1992). The simply curved graph became a rallying slide in countless city planning presentations around the world, all calling for 'political will' in 'achieving urban consolidation' and upholding the ideal of the compact city – a battle largely lost in the world's expanding petroleum suburbs of today. Their work culminated in a major manifesto on car dependence and urban sustainability (Newman and Kenworthy 1999). A major Renewable City challenge lies in reconciling the conflicts inherent in a narrowly transport-focused set of policy ideals and the sheer momentum of suburbanisation, driven in part by a lack of choice, and in part by powerful consumer cravings for conformist self-expression, stimulated by excessively low transport fuel prices as well as generally subsidised stationary energy supplies for low-density urban development.

The wider policy environment is already framed with even institutional fossil-fuel protagonists such as the International Energy Agency (IEA) arguing that a large-scale policy push is needed to reduce transport fossil-fuel dependency. A 2004 working paper issued by the agency's Office for Energy Efficiency, Technology and R&D (EET), almost tantamount to an acknowledgement of a problem, argued that 'vigorous action' in improving fuel economy, greater use of bio-fuel for all road transport, and the transition to hydrogen fuel-cell vehicles could reduce greenhouse gas emissions in the transport sector by 30 per cent by the year 2030 (Fulton 2004, p 22). Given the *petrolophile* charter of the organisation, this target can safely be seen as a very minimum, and indeed a highly conservative goal. But the paper fundamentally lacks credibility since it happily projects a US$ 30 ceiling for oil prices even as the oil peak forces the world to rely on mining Canadian tar sands. It also argues mysteriously that 'oil's share of transport fuel use is unlikely to fall very much – remaining around 97–99% in most countries through 2030' (Fulton 2004, p 4) – a stunning feat of projection, given the broad consensus on global oil supply peaking soon, possibly as early as 2010. Since 2004 the IEA has modified its views somewhat: it began to drop between-the-lines acknowledgements that a global rise in oil supplies through 2030 is in fact a more than far-fetched scenario born of wishful thinking rather than an outcome founded on any physical fact (Aleklett 2004; IEA 2005).

The effectiveness of policies relies on their compatibility with cities' institutional, behavioural and cultural environments. In the process of generating intelligent, purposeful and community relevant programmes of change, cities can benefit from decision support tools and alternative scenario models that are relevant in at least the following five ways. They should be meaningful in terms of (a) *policy implementation*: capable of being enacted; (b) *behavioural response*: capable of triggering social and cultural change; (c) *spatial resolution and detail*: capable of being mapped; (d) *decision-making*: helping inform choice; and (e) *outcome*, being meaningful to stakeholders, users and citizens (after Hensher 2003, p 789). Two relevance-responsive, greenhouse-specific urban micro-simulation models stand out internationally: the Australian Transport and Environment Strategy Impact Simulator (TRESIS) and the German IRPUD or Mobility Decision Model (Hensher 2003, pp 793–803).

## Motors, movement and renewable fuels

The raising of fossil fuel costs and the introduction of carbon charges alone may not have a significant impact. Only a small fraction of greenhouse gas emissions – in the low single digits – is policy-sensitive: carbon taxation and its influence on travel behaviour and modal choice appears not to be very effective in reducing overall emissions. One such model, TRESIS, showed that for Sydney's metropolitan region a tax of 20 cents per kilogram of emitted greenhouse gas would reduce annual vehicle kilometres by only 2.3 per cent (Hensher 2003, p 798). Greater change in emissions and fossil-fuel dependency requires efforts that go beyond fiscal market instruments, and pursue policies and programmes that result in: (a) deep changes in urban form and land use integration coupled with wider demand management and public transport reform programmes; (b) fundamental vehicle efficiency efforts in engine operations, hybrid systems and overall weight and behaviour of vehicles; and, most significantly, (c) systematic fuel substitution efforts.

Four cities help to illustrate typical innovations in the next section of this chapter, 'Transport planning and policy imperatives', reported from developing countries at varying level of industrialisation. Attempts at vehicle efficiency are limited to the heroic efforts of isolated think tanks such as the Rocky Mountain Institute, or lonely concept car teams at some mass-market brands, salaried for public relations purposes. Wider change is still thwarted by the present proliferation of tank-like heavier automobiles such as sports utility and heavily horse-powered family 4 × 4, as if these were capable of maintaining fossil rule through the brute force of their countless valves. A growing number of countries is engaged in fuel substitution efforts, either pushed in government programmes, or pulled by regulation-based incentives reform. These range from Sweden, Italy and Germany with their very significant, well-established and growing biofuel production levels in Europe – in early 2006 Sweden announced that the country aims to be petroleum-independent by 2015 – to the Americas: especially Brazil, inexpensive sugar-cane derived ethanol has long ascended to being the most promising motor fuel component. Several states across the US are engaged in fossil fuel substitution efforts, with California in the lead. A growing choice of applications is available in the low-carbon fuels sector, from various combinations of new fuel and vehicle options for greenhouse-neutral forms of personal transport. Three alternative vehicle technologies are maturing and promise soon to join the conventional internal combustion engine vehicle, lovingly referred to as ICEV: hybrid electric (HEV), fuel cell electric (FCEV) and battery-powered electric vehicles (BPEV).

And, pushing to replace gasoline or petroleum diesel, as many as half a dozen renewable energy sources and carriers are emerging, supplying these new forms of propulsion in various combinations, in both liquid and gaseous form. *Methane gas* is increasingly used in buses, taxis and private cars. It is applied either as the evaporating *natural gas* currently euphemistically promoted as a 'clean fuel', ie as an interim, lower-emission alternative to petrol; or, better, in its renewable form: as *biogas* produced through organic decomposition. *Liquid fuels* include *bio-diesel*, plant-based *ethanol*, *dimethyl ether* (DME) and *methanol*. The latter is today still almost entirely applied in its *natural-gas* based form, but it can also be derived from *biomass* in such commonly used forms as sugar cane, maize, rapeseed or wheat (after Johansson 2003). Many of these liquid fuels can pose serious energy efficiency, water use, environmental degradation and pollution challenges in their production. And in terms of energy efficiency, they do not yet promise totally to replace fossil inputs in transport fuels (Pimentel et al 1994).

Corn-based ethanol is heavily fossil-fuel dependent in its production. However, low-cost cellulose conversion techniques may soon permit much higher fossil-fuel independence. Such *cellulosic* methods denote the use of bacteria to convert cellulose and lignin – the hard, fibrous content of plants – into starch. This is then fermented by other micro-organisms into ethanol. Two good candidates in the United States are considered to be switchgrass or tall panic grass (*Panicum virgatum*) and willow (*salix*), but a wide range of plant material can be used, including farm waste. Approximately one billion tons of unused waste is said to be available for ethanol production annually in the United States alone. But even in the current, transitional environment where a significant amount of fossil fuel is used to produce ethanol, the bio-fuel is preferable over petroleum: it offers a 10 to 15 per cent improved greenhouse gas performance over gasoline (Farrell et al 2006).

Bio-energy based renewable transport fuels can fundamentally change the fossil-fuel content of urban life. If their production can be environmentally managed they promise to lower the inherent and inherited toxicity of the fossil fuel city, its massive soil, air and water pollution levels, the incidence of respiratory diseases and, most of all, greenhouse gas burdens. This in itself makes the bio-fuel revolution an existential necessity. It is long overdue if only from a public health perspective; and would doubtless have been in train were it not for the cynical financial accounting approaches to optimising public policy that commonly weigh narrow, industry-internal economic costs of improved vehicle emissions performance and car efficiency against the external burden carried by society and countless individual victims.

But without shifts towards public transit systems and reinforced traditional city forms, fuel substitution and vehicle efficiency will do little to help heal the widespread erosion of urbanity and public space, but instead give further impetus to peri-urban sprawl, traffic congestion and the rising automobile dependency that is so characteristic of the fossil-fuelled mass consumer society.

Without other planning and policy measures, bio-fuelled traffic jams may be as plausible a prospect as solar-boosted suburban sprawl, by softening current development constraints imposed by pollution costs and grid-dependency. If deployed merely to substitute for conventional fossil and nuclear sources, neither transport nor stationary energy technology revolution promises to deal with the structural, physical urban development issues of the 20th and early 21st centuries. Wider, innovative urban planning policy and practice will retain acute prominence and importance in these areas.

## Transport planning and policy imperatives

Transport-energy reduction advocate Jeff Kenworthy reinforces three axioms, tried and tested as effective antidotes to what is termed here the *post-urban syndrome*: a legacy of urban energy ailments that express themselves in peri-urban sprawl, chaotic central cityscapes, and congestion. These axiomatic imperatives are: (a) a paramount insistence on prioritising public transport in all urban development choices; (b) an abiding commitment to a pedestrian and bicycle culture; and (c) the single-minded enforcement of compact, mixed-use, integrated and connected forms of urbanity, anchored in rich public transit networks (Kenworthy 2001). These three canons of postmodern urban planning policy are also among the paramount principles guiding the cities of Singapore, Quito, Bogotá and Curitiba, all widely recognised and praised for their leadership in urban transport policy and programmes. Their success highlights the technological, institutional, policy and planning breakthroughs that can be achieved when pursuing exceptional performance in transport-based energy innovation.

### City leaders in reducing fossil energy use in transport

(after Karekezi et al 2003)

Singapore: integrating planning and pricing
**Planning**. Like Munich, Singapore began to integrate land use and transport-ation planning early on, even before the OPEC-triggered so-called oil shock of 1973. Here the issue was tackled as a matter of national pride after independence was achieved in 1965. In 1967 a State and City Planning Project was initiated with United Nations Development Programme (UNDP) funding that set a 25-year time horizon for implementation. Singapore adhered to its plan with

trademark assiduity, mobilising its housing and settlement policy to ensure its success. Its social housing programme commenced in the early 1970s, delivering affordable high-rise flats in designated areas, clustered around mixed-use centres, and funded through its well-known enforced wage-tied savings programme. Most of Singapore's residents – close to 90 per cent – live in high-rise residential edifices administered by the powerful Housing Development Board. Later looked upon as a rather monotonous and place-less approach to social betterment, this elementary approach to land use patterning has nevertheless engendered a textbook case of efficient and effective transportation. Today, high-rise, high-density residential neighbourhoods, industrial estates and urban sub-centres ring the central business district, all accessible by the Mass Rapid Transit network and ubiquitously networked, micro-demand responsive bus, van and taxi systems.

**Pricing** In the decades since 1972 Singapore has introduced numerous means of restricting both the ownership and use of private cars as one method of boosting public transport use. An *area licensing scheme* (ALS) was devised to impose levies for accessing the city's central activity district during peak hours. This halved total motorised traffic in the target area and reduced its private vehicle movements by 75 per cent. The ALS has since been augmented with electronic tagging: the drive-by delivery of road pricing and congestion charges. This brought overall and private motor-traffic reductions by a further quarter and one fifth, respectively. Average vehicle speeds have risen by as much as one-third, a measure of traffic efficiency. And as a further restriction, vehicle ownership and registration fees have been applied, rising from 10 per cent of an automobile's price in 1972 to 175 per cent in 1983 (Karekezi et al 2003, citing Fwa 2002; World Bank 2002)

### Quito, Ecuador: unifying public transport systems

A round dozen of agencies ruled over Ecuador's urban transport world until 1995. Supreme among these was the Consejo Nacional de Tránsito, which represented the central government, automotive unions, the police and armed forces. National decisions, in as far as these were ever reached, resulted from deals made between these often rivalling factions. In the capital city of Quito, 90 per cent of the public-transport fleet consisted of vehicles run by licensed associations, the city government, and wildcat operators. Owners leased their buses on a short-term basis to individual drivers for a share of the fares. This arrangement created a fatal incentive for loading up these lumbering people lorries with as many passengers as could possibly be squeezed in, and to man vehicles virtually around the clock, far beyond acceptable levels of driver fatigue.

Finally, National Congress stepped in to abolish this dangerous system and at the same time boost public transport passenger numbers. It endowed the capital city government with the authority for 'the planning, regulation and coordination of all matters related to public and private transport'. Through a dedicated technical unit, the city began to monitor and manage Quito's transport infrastructure. An integrated public transport system resulted, featuring a central, exclusive, articulated trolley-bus corridor; dual interchange points linking this line to a network of regular feeder buses; and more than three dozen trolley-bus stops that operate on an advance-purchase based fare system. A new, large public transport fleet featured feeder buses with a capacity of 80 passengers each for the urban periphery, and trolley buses accommodating 180 passengers each serving central Quito.

These measures have halved public transport travel time and saved some 18,000 person-hours a day previously lost waiting for and in buses. An important reduction in air pollution levels has also been achieved along these central trolley-bus lanes by replacing rusting people-haulers and their sputtering engines and by reducing bus idling time by coordinating traffic signals (Karekezi et al 2003, citing Arias 2002).

### Bogotá: banking on buses

Bogotá, Colombia, ranks high on the list as one of the world's most densely populated cities. Its municipality has developed TransMilenio, an advanced *bus rapid transit* system as a way of overcoming a class divide in transport. The city's key arteries become heavily congested, constricting traffic flow in the morning and late afternoon, with rush-hour speeds averaging a mere 10 kilometres per hour. The jams are caused almost exclusively by the minority of Bogotans wealthy enough to afford personal cars. While some 70 per cent of all motorised journeys take place on buses, 95 per cent of all road space is taken up by personal automobiles moving less than 20 per cent of travellers.

TransMilenio is a central tool in Bogotá's strategy for managing the use of private vehicles. Other efforts focus on the design of designated bus lanes; new stations positioned every half-kilometre; inter-modal terminals; and new bus depots and maintenance shops. Rigorous efficiency drives in the private bus operating system have focused on assisting operator companies, and on fleet management measures based on geo-positioning systems. Employee relations were improved. And a more transparent fare collection system was implemented: it features a single-fare, single-card-based access mode, collection-equipment upgrades and enhanced financial management. Key to success was the establishment of a dedicated public organisation charged with overall planning, operation and control.

In addition to these exclusive bus ways, the City of Bogotá constructed 230 a kilometres network of bicycle lanes, to be expanded to 350 kilometres; widened sidewalks; constructed more than one thousand new parks; and a 17-kilometre long pedestrian zone. Among the demand management measures instituted were the banning of private cars in central Bogotá during morning and evening rush hours. Parking fees were doubled, and the gasoline taxes boosted by a fifth. A battery of bollards prevent wanton sidewalk parking. To garner popular support, a festive car-free day is held annually on a weekday, and car-free Sundays are celebrated on certain streets (Ardila and Menckhoff 2002; GEF Arias 2002; Hook and Wright 2002; Karekezi et al 2003, citing World Bank 2002).

## Curitiba, Brazil: mass transit pioneer

Curitiba is the Camelot of sustainable transport and planning policies – her programmes are still the stuff of legends at policy roundtables South and North The city's famed fusion of intelligence and action keeps transport fuel consumption one-quarter below that of other, comparable cities in Brazil: of all journeys, 70 per cent are made by public transport. The city's innovations have informed and inspired many others, including Quito and Bogotá. Its mass transit innovations were, however, not driven by a desire to conserve energy, but introduced to protect and revitalise the city centre, to keep it from being drowned in the waves and eddies of cars washing through it with the daily regularity of a lunar tide. Bold measures were taken, and a lower-speed traffic ring around the city was combined with a network of fast roads linking key metropolitan centres. It allowed the central business district to remain dedicated to pedestrians and local traffic only.

The first dedicated bus way opened in the mid-1970s. It stretched for 20 kilometres between the city's north and south, and their respective bus hubs. Over the next five years several new transport terminals were constructed, and an east–west bus link established. In 1980, a single fare system was introduced: short journeys subsidised long ones, proving a boon for residents in the outlying lower-income areas. Four ring lines were added to the local and regional branches, now connecting the entire city in a fast and efficient network. The vivid memory of the 1973 fuel crisis helped boost the system's popularity. As early as 1981 high-capacity buses for 150 passengers commenced service,

assembled in a local Volvo plant. Bus rides were roundly cheered, comparably cheap at 10 per cent the cost of tram fares, and 1 per cent of subway
tickets. By 1990, the system increased bus capacity to 170 passengers, boosting
the hourly passenger stream per lane to 14,000. In 1991 express services were
added (Karekezi et al 2003, citing Lerner 2000; Menckhoff 1999)

The rest is history. Bus sizes and frequencies have been steadily rising ever
since, and the city found pleasure in embracing a sense of civility, relegating
cars to dirt tracks, while celebrating the pedestrian with massive linear parks,
sidewalks and public space networks, anticipating future urban development
and favouring the needy.


## 4.2 CITYWIDE EFFICIENCY

### The end of the techno-fix

Fossil City air is thick and hot. Fossil-fired electricity production and transport
systems pump noxious gases and particulates into the lungs of urban dwellers,
and in advanced industrial countries ensure that a rich cocktail of greenhouse
gas is being expelled as well, and in copious amounts. Many conventional
technologies are offered to solve the problem, but in leading to a continued
reliance on fossil power only serve to worsen the situation. Such local bandaids
to cover up a tumour include industrial carbon sequestration in the form of
simply pumping emissions into the ground. This is currently studied at a global
scale by the coal industry and is supporters; it is a technology of only limited
use and best applied at or near the point of fuel extraction. Nuclear reactors,
too, are proposed as a seductive techno-fix, but their power offers no real
relief from carbon emissions, while carrying frightening public health, waste
storage and weapons proliferation implications. Significant greenhouse emissions result from the deployment of nuclear power, in the energy embodied in
the mining, processing, distribution, storage and disposal of the fuel; and in its
plant, associated hardware, maintenance and upkeep.

In many cities of hot summer climates abundant fossil power production
feeds an often subsidised, globally swelling army of air-conditioners, straining
to battle broadly rising temperatures. Deployed in excess, air conditioning –
even solar-powered systems – is to ambient air what urban desalination is to
fresh water: one is used to compensate for a city's stock of badly designed
buildings, and the other to augment antiquated and wasteful drinking water
supply and sewage systems. Both are superficial technical fixes cementing fossil

dependency and contributing to climate change or perpetuating its causes. They exacerbate the very conditions that have led to their need: warmer tempera tures and declining fresh water resources. Many conventional power plants – oil, coal, nuclear – have enormous fresh water use rates, for cooling and fuel processing, yet water is increasingly a scarce commodity in many urban and peri-urban settled, pastoral and native areas alike, and frequently in areas tradi- tionally well-served by precipitation. Coal-fired generation is infamous for its airborne pollution, reducing local and regional precipitation (Gleick 1994). And finally, electricity generation and transmission systems become less efficient with higher temperatures for all forms of power production.

There are conventional technologies available purporting to solve all of these problems, but since they derive from the very same conditions that led to the present difficulties, are unable to combat them successfully. In contrast, all Renewable City design approaches genuinely and permanently fight such fossil afflictions helping to leave behind the era of the false technology fix.

## Heat island relief: the ancient wisdom of renewable city design

Atmospheric and climatic conditions may seem to operate above the scale of cities, but this is a misconception. The manufacture of agricultural, industrial and, increasingly, urbanised landscapes fundamentally transforms the dynamics of energy flows across water and land, and through the cycles of the atmosphere. Local settings influence flows, temperature, humidity and chemical composition of the lowest air stratum, the thin atmospheric boundary layer in which human life is staged. As humans change natural settings by expanding cities and other cultural land uses, the local energy exchanges that take place within the boundary layer are affected. Landscape changes hence impact the local, regional and global climate (Arnold 2005).

Cities and their suburban and rural surroundings engender greatly varying climatic conditions. The hinterland is generally cooler than the central city: the latter can build up considerable heat under the sun. In traditional cities, particularly those in hot, arid regions, ambient climatic design has tempered urban climates – through the construction of white surfaces, narrow passages, shady gardens, elegant water courts and the organisation of streets to facilitate the flow of cooler, fresher air.

The southern European, North African and middle-eastern city cores of Grenada, Marrakesh, or Sana'a are famous examples of such thermally driven urban design. Cold-climate cities are traditionally designed to attract and retain warmth through the darker colours of their roofs and walls, and the geometry of their buildings and open spaces. These climatic distinctions and character-istics have all but disappeared in modern, petroleum-powered communities. In modern suburbs surrounding old city cores, or in the relatively recent fossil creations of Houston, Sydney or Dubai, air-conditioned boxes float on a cruel sea of piping hot pavement. These cities and their suburbs encrust bulldozer-stripped deserts, forests or farmlands and have been devised in abandonment of all inherited renewable urban design intelligence. Asphalt city roads and roofs turn sunshine into blistering heat, causing their surface temperatures to soar to up to 100 degrees Celsius above the surrounding air temperatures. This has the effect of further heating already sweltering city air, through convection and radiation.

This 'summer in the city' effect is part of mid-20th century fossil-city folklore and reality. Excessive heat accumulates within and above modern urban cores. Disappearing vegetation and shade; dark, expansive, dry and hard surfaces; blocked breezes; and an absolute reliance on air conditioning are characteristic elements of historic fossil towns. Fossil cities are nurtured on the relatively cheap and easy – and in design intelligence terms stupefying – supply of coal and oil. They exist in artificially conditioned spheres. Their denizens, grown unaware, could not care less about outside temperatures or local climate. In the past, this has limited the need for thermal design creativity and imagination. By contrast, Renewable City design not only applies time-honoured funda-mentals of good city planning but also challenges ideas in new infrastructure planning, technological innovation and building design alike. Post-fossil, or renewable citizens, are keenly attuned to local thermal conditions and the global climate, and demand greater intelligent city design. At a minimum, this entails adherence to basic conventions: designing cities for climatic benefits, and deploying such simple-minded techniques as designing streets and open spaces to create cleansing airflows to relieve summer heat, or to remove winter air pollution.

In existing cities, opportunities for creating new airflow channels may be rare but a city's prevailing surface characteristics can be altered methodically and over time. Various surfaces have different *albedo* values by virtue of their specific grain, texture and colours. Albedo denotes the degree to which solar radiation is reflected by a surface, particularly at the short-wave end of its spectrum. Surfaces with lower albedo values generate higher temperatures as larger amounts of energy are absorbed. Albedo is described on a scale of 0 to 1; a value of 0.0 suggests that a surface absorbs all solar radiation, and 1.0 indicates total reflectivity. In analogy to this scale, albedo is sometimes also expressed as a percentage between 0 and 100 per cent. As surfaces in a low-albedo town heat up, ambient air temperatures rise. This common feature of fossil or blissfully uninformed urban design has been grandly called the *urban heat island effect*. It can increase urban air temperatures by 10 degrees Celsius or more over peri-urban areas. Once this happens, the vicious cycle of the fossil city is set in motion, stoking a veritable urban inferno. Rising temperatures lift artificial cooling efforts to greater heights, expelling more and more hot air into the environment. Electricity costs soar. Increased electricity generation by coal or oil fired power plants boosts emissions of sulphur dioxide, carbon monoxide, nitrous oxide and airborne particulates. During summer, heat islands can add fatal smog to urban health risks such as excessive heat: nitrous oxide and volatile organic compounds react photo-chemically, producing ground ozone (EPA 2006a).

**Cool roofs** are one of the many efficiency response mechanisms available to cities, building owners and architects to improve both the urban microclimate and the energy performance of buildings. Most building roofs in the United States, for example, are dark. This created needless insulation requirements, uncomfortable interiors, inflated cooling loads and electricity bills for individual owners and tenants. Excessive peak power demands, generation costs and stressed grids are the urban flow-on consequence. Overheating roofs age prematurely by going through extreme cycles of contraction and expansion, and sheer material fatigue. This boosts both repair bills and landfill burdens incurred by roofing waste. By contrast, roof surfaces designed to be light-reflective and heat emitting can stay up to 40 degrees Celsius cooler, with many other benefits experienced throughout the urban system.

Much can be done to transform hot building tops into 'cool roofs', rejecting and reflecting radiant energy and hence heat gain across the full bandwidth of sunlight. The coolest materials also very effectively expel already absorbed heat gain. Two core features, thermal emittance and solar reflectivity, combine to lower internal and external temperatures. This is of critical benefit in climates where summertime cooling – electric air conditioning – loads are a greater challenge than heating in winter. Cool roofs have specially devised smooth surfaces that display both properties – the Energy Star's Roof Product Program specifies the performance of flat and sloped roofs to have albedo values of at least 0.65 and 0.25, respectively. A survey of 10 converted buildings in Florida and California demonstrated energy reductions of between 20 and 70 per cent, yielding higher savings where cool roofs were installed over buildings with low insulation provisions. Flat or low-slow cool roofs, made of white thermoplastic-coated metal or other suitable material, require annual cleaning or replacement once a decade to maintain peak performance. Sloped roofs are less susceptible to heat-absorbing dust accumulation: their surfaces are more readily cleared by rain, wind and gravity.

Several United States cities and states have introduced cool roof requirements and incentive programmes. California's Cool Savings Program is administered by the state's Energy Commission and offers rebates to owners for roofs of high reflectivity and heat emittance. The City of Chicago fights its heat island conditions in its energy regulations where it by stipulates that most low-sloped roofs over air-conditioned commercial buildings have an initial albedo value of at least 0.25. And the state of Georgia has instituted a White Roof Amendment, demanding that additional insulation be installed if roof surfaces test below 0.75 for solar reflectivity and emittance and thus exceed a 1994 congressional provision (EPA 2006a).

## Trees, parks, urban wilds and agriculture

Rich and diverse webs of wildareas, parks and gardens naturally supported by locally sustained water regimes are among the simplest and yet most powerful ways of making an overheating city more tolerable. Belittlingly referred to as urban greenery, these networks are more than attractive backdrops to urban real estate, recreational facilities or solemn settings exuding civic aspirations. Throughout the history of urban evolution city parks and gardens have been cherished as climate modifiers, vegetable and grazing fields, or stage sets for political expression. They have long been under pressure from built development, but their multiple purposes and strategic uses have never led to their complete demise. And the more benefits they bring, the easier it is to justify budgets for them. To this end, external economic and social values are assessed, quantified and budgeted for by city or state governments or groups of developers and property owners, raising funds from private beneficiaries or the citizenry as a whole, not infrequently also to protect or boost local property values by enhancing status and views. They are vital assets when accounting for the wealth of services they provide: ambient temperature regulation, shade, pollution control, water purification, flood and erosion control, pollination, bio-diversity and habitat support, food production, carbon dioxide absorption, moisture conditioning, shade provision, tourism and cultural values, reduction in human health costs.

There are countless tangible and intangible benefits to be derived from creating urban public open spaces to lift civic spirits and property values. In Tang Dynasty China, the south-eastern city of Ningbo's Moon Lake park was built as a water conservancy in the 7th century, but quickly emerged as an important gathering and living area for wealthy academics and important poets. Civic initiatives to build *English gardens* mushroomed in the 19th century, with Amsterdam's Vondelpark one of the most explicitly calculated ventures, banking on the benefits it would bring to stately houses and civic institutions adjoining and surrounding it. And 19th century Boston saw the construction of the 'Emerald Necklace', a string of civic spaces, public parks and reservoirs ringing the inner city, providing water and wetland management functions, clean and cool air, and visual delight. They also served the cherished civic purposes that were pursued in the works of architects Andrew Jackson Downing (1815–52), proponent of New York's Central Park, and its final designers, Frederick Law Olmsted (1822–1903) and office partner Calvert Vaux (1824–92). Olmsted developed Boston's Emerald Necklace idea, and rallied support for it. What commenced as an exercise in civic empowerment is today admired for its memorable city design and identity building genius, real estate value creation – and, increasingly, for its securing of urban thermal comfort.

Recent bold public domain building efforts in Bogotá and Curitiba are of this very tradition and current plans for Kuala Lumpur and Singapore, too, are direct conceptual descendants of the great civic park tradition that preceded the democratic innovations of the 19th century. Singapore's island-wide green systems agenda of 2004 is a particularly good example of a systematic, metropolitan-wide open space plan, in part founded on an ambition to achieve ambient state-wide cooling, to make urban outdoor life more naturally pleasant and to deflect focus on to the humble air conditioning system, not information technology, as the first facilitator of Singapore's commercial prowess. The plan was founded on the country's early 1990s' trademark 'Tropical City of Excellence' campaign, a hybrid planning and promotional programme connoting the soothing moisture and breezy coolness of a verdant isle-in-the-shade.

Increasingly, cities throughout the developing and developed world search for ways of protecting or nurturing authentic forms of urban agriculture: putting open spaces to additional productive use. Urban agriculture should be an essential planning priority of all Renewable City programmes. It has traditionally been nurtured for cultural or institutional reasons, as in Japan's diehard tiny remnant rice plots peppering bustling inner city neighbourhoods; in the

US Victory garden during the Second World War, or the Germany *Schreber-garten* immediately after that war, and with its roots in the cities of the First World War. These and similar traditions elsewhere serve as prematurely fading icons of urban subsistence and survival, and are sporadically still present in every small and large city of the industrialised world: in unused plots, tiny backyards and on roofs, terraces and balconies. Urban agriculture will continue to be essential for income generation and subsistence food production throughout eastern and southern Europe, Asia, Africa and South America. It is an essential element, part of essential and hybrid infrastructure of urban energy autonomy – and open to massive implementation through simple legislative measures.

Indeed, significant benefits in urban climate and image do not always require a major and expensive planning effort or dramatic shifts in land use. Simple, dense rows of street trees alone provide important psychological, cooling and aesthetic benefits. This should be part of a basic local regulatory tool kit: at the very least, streets should always be heavily lined by trees; and tree and green space preservation, regeneration and compensation require-ments are absolutely basic for all development sites, as implemented even in Japan's national and Tokyo's local regulations, such as the 1999 national Low-interest Financing Programme, aimed at roof greening; the 2001 Property Tax Cut Programme on Greening Facilities or Tokyo Metropolitan Govern-ment's Mandatory Greening Standard of the same vintage (Akagawa 2003). However exceptionally or rudimentarily, leaders, planners and communities seek to invert the logic governing urban-area development and metropolitan-wide strategies from those traditionally based on built development to a firm focus on nurturing open green and water environments. This approach seeks to provide wild and biologically productive open spaces first, at the periphery and throughout the urban setting – before allocating new land for urban expansion or infill. Such often humble and traditional, yet utterly visionary beginnings are about to be elevated to priority status in mainstream planning research and practice.

## Planted walls and roofs

From Tokyo's towers to Chicago's big box retail outlets and the new Dutch bedroom suburbs city governments increasingly promote, encourage or require *roof greening* efforts to increase internal energy efficiency and fight the heat island effect outside. Singapore has carried its park promotion efforts onto office building skin, promoting facades of chlorophyll. Japanese designers have created plant-coated buildings since the 1990s, providing urban-temperature attenuation with aesthetic appeal. Kathryn Findlay and Eisaku Ushida's 1994 *Soft and Hairy House* in Tsukuba City near Tokyo is still a major milestone in surreal rationality, a quiet monument to the dwelling as organic organism. Commercial and residential structures are being literally greened, and inhabited by various species: including grasses, ground cover, even a range of common garden vegetables and herbs. On Japan's new commercial rooftops the preference is for hardy plants with minimal watering requirements such as sedum. This genus of low-growing flowering rock plant sporting fleshy leaves is typically installed over thin soil layers and waterproof membranes. To promote the programme, national and local government regulations and incentives have been put in place. In 1999 a low-interest finance programme commenced at national level, lending up to 40 per cent of the total building construction cost if more than half of the roof area is being greened. The national government also introduced a five-year property tax cut programme for buildings located in designated 'intensive greening zones' that achieve more than 20 per cent of the site area in roof, wall and ground greening. And in Tokyo, the heat island capital of the world in terms of research and empirical evidence, in 2001 the metropolitan government began to require that one-fifth of rooftop areas be greened, in addition to the 20 per cent of ground area already required to be plant-covered. A development bonus is now granted if at least 30 per cent of a rooftop is covered by grass, sedum, trees or other plants – except for moss (Akagawa 2003).

Across the United States and Europe, too, rooftop gardeners apply a wide range of plant material on lofty growing media. Planted roofs are broadly differentiated into *intensive* green roofs for public access, with greater soil depths, larger plant species and greater load bearing requirements, and so-called *extensive* green roofs. The latter are usually not accessible to the public, feature thinner soil and plant layers, require less maintenance and simpler irrigation and drainage and are less costly to construct. Besides heat island reduction through shading and *evapotranspiration* – the release of water into the atmosphere by plants – green roofs reduce rainwater runoff, remove air pollutants, protect roof material and buffer noise transfer to the building interior. They also help insulate buildings against heat and cold infiltration or loss, improve the cityscape as observed from surrounding higher buildings and assist in safeguarding biodiversity by creating an urban habitat for birds and other city-dwelling animals (EPA 2006a).

## Water in the renewable city

Ponds, lakes, creeks and rivers are the most powerful heat island fighters, capable of lowering local ambient summer temperatures by up to 10 degrees Celsius, particularly when convection is aided by breezes. Their numbers can be readily increased in expanding cities and redeveloping urban areas, and should be planned for while anticipating urban fringe growth. And increasingly, opportunities are found around the world to restore inner-city creeks. The most recent example is Seoul's metropolitan government plans to remove a series of highway sections, some elevated, covering the Cheong-Gye stream in the city's Dongdaemun area, and to replace them with a linear park bordering the restored river channel. While the measure was not primarily motivated by urban climate concerns but to eliminate a source of great blight, noise and pollution, it will have an extraordinarily beneficial effect here as well (Ichinose 2005; Ichinose and Bai 2005). The power of blue and green parks is well demonstrated by some of the United States' finest 19th-century urban innovations. Boston's Emerald Necklace is, too, a fine if scientifically understudied example of contemporary, multifunctional thermal design, here combined with advanced principles of water management in what, in part, is today called *water-sensitive urban design*.

Water-sensitive urban design aims to manage the total water flow of a city or urban water cycle in three ways: through stormwater management, wastewater minimisation and water conservation. The tools to achieve these principles include the reuse of both grey and black water – lightly polluted household water and sewage – and rain or storm water; storage and retrieval of captured and filtered water in aquifers; and overall demand management. Water sensitive urban design relies on the integration of water and urban systems at all levels – regionally, in built environments and institutionally (Wong 2005). In achieving substantial flow reductions of up to 80 per cent or more when applied to standard low-efficiency areas, it makes a massive contribution to reducing water supply and sewage pumping energy requirements – in conventional cities to a large extent provided by fossil or nuclear power. It is difficult to overstate the significance of these water-based efficiency gains: in worst-case environments such as large US conurbations, up to half of a city's electricity consumption is accounted for by the pumping and processing of municipal water supply and sewage flows. At the same time, approximately half of the United States freshwater uptake has traditionally been wasted on the cooling of oil, coal or nuclear-powered electric power plants (Gleick 1994).

The capturing and channelling of rain water as well as grey and black water flows (ie, household waste water) allows them to be processed through surface or subsurface wetlands, or in miniature sewage treatment plants that can be installed in buildings and neighbourhoods. Examples of such mini-plants are *sequence batch reactors* or *rotating biological contactors* which are currently in use throughout Europe, with an installed area requirement of only 0.1 square metre per 500 users. Subsurface or partially exposed wetlands require much more surface space – 1 square metre per user – but can be distributed very effectively in small courtyards, parks, median strips, sidewalk planters and even individual tree containers, while their design and engineering are already well developed, tested and implemented (Wong 2002). If deployed methodically and ubiquitously their combined ambient cooling effects through evaporation can be very significant. Linked micro-wetlands are hence a core element of Renewable City planning.

Hard pavement, too, can serve as urban summer heat cooler, when they are water permeable. Permeable and evaporative pavement systems allow moisture to seep directly into the ground, or draw up humidity, which aids cooling. Unfortunately, much urban pavement is constructed above structures such as underground garages, subways or service tunnels where natural absorption and evaporation of moisture would not occur even with permeable surface materials. To overcome this problem the Japanese construction giant Obayashi has developed a self-contained 'watered paver' system in its Saitama-based Technical Research Institute (TRI), which also houses one of the world's oldest continuously monitored solar buildings. The pavement system emulates the effect of water areas on hard surfaces – sidewalks, parking lots and even tennis courts can become summer cooling machines. In their dry state hard systems have the advantage of functioning as heat collectors in winter (Obayashi 2005, pp 8 and 11).


## Designing buildings with daylight in mind

While shielding cities from unwanted solar radiation, it is still crucial to ensure that their buildings are richly and intelligently suffused with natural light. Herein lies no contradiction; the paradox lies in the very logic of fossil fuel driven design and construction. Modern urban edifices are profuse transformers of energy, extremely effective in attracting heat through their minimal roofs and glass-thin walls, but also in throwing large amounts of unwanted glare and radiant heat onto their neighbours. But when it comes to absorbing useful daylight, most modern office structures are virtually impenetrable to natural light in their centres: their enormous floor plates mandate artificial lighting – and more air conditioning – to make their unventilated, dark and cavernous innards useable.

Renewable City legislation would demand – as basic performance requirement – that every office worker has access to adequate levels of direct daylight at her or his workspace, through windows that can also be opened to enable natural ventilation. Daylight-conscious design is as much an informed art as a science. When handled well, it boosts the thermal comfort, psychological health and visual delight of workplaces. Its principles apply to residential buildings and, in different ways, to industrial work environments as well. While most local planning regulations specify sunlight exposure to residential spaces, specific daylight quality criteria and quantified natural light levels are less frequently called for, and as key performance dimension largely ignored, in the commercial building sector. Siting, obstructions, fenestration and both external and internal spatial relations are critical factors to consider. Daylight, thoughtfully and creatively filtered and guided, has a profound effect on the thermal comfort as well as energy performance of a building, either through its absence, excessive presence or, indeed, optimal levels. Light shelves, atria, screens and skylights are among the basic spatial devices employed together with the more complex light-guiding glass, ceilings, conduits and other devices, while solar blinds and other shading systems rank among the more advanced (Ruck et al 2000). However, most are ignored in the speculative office buildings that populate the central business districts of many cities. Renewable City planning frameworks seek to incorporate such elements through industry guidance, regulations, performance measures and rating tools.

## Urban heat pumps: city power from the ground, water and air

Ambient city heat can be an enormous, untapped resource. As an analogy to the desire to suffuse buildings with natural light, there is a corollary benefit and opportunity to be gained from the fact that soil, air and water absorb heat from sunshine and surrounding temperatures. Heat pumps generally are semi-renewable, ie hybrid systems, mobilising limited quantities of conventional power to derive – or 'pump' – renewable energy sources in the form of solar energy manifest in ambient heat, stored in the ground, in rivers, lakes, groundwater and in the air. Heat pumps are productive: they produce three to four times the energy in heat as is used to drive a particular system (GSHP 2005).

There are two types: *compression heat pumps* work like refrigerators in reverse, with mechanical compressors powered by electricity, natural gas or bio-fuel, condensing heat derived from ambient sources. And *absorption heat pumps* use low-maintenance thermal compressors powered by heating oil, natural gas or bio-fuel, and are typically applied in industrial waste-heat recovery processes. Domestic- and urban-scaled models are on the market as well. Air heat extraction is most commonly applied, but not very efficient. Most effective are heat pumps using brine-filled pipes placed in the ground horizontally at a depth of up to 2 metres, or vertically, at up to 150 metres depth, configured to harvest and concentrate the differential heat. The vertical arrangement is more space efficient but also more costly, and may also require ground water rights permits (Dürrschmidt et al 2004, pp 74–8). Heat pumps also sometimes tap into the heat differences in surrounding water bodies, where, increasingly, hollow coils are also laid to help cool nearby buildings. However, artificial cooling or warming of river and lake water cannot be seen as envir-onmentally sustainable unless to correct an industrially disturbed condition in a controlled manner or, more rarely, where it is determined as having an ecologically negligible effect.

As potentially emerging infrastructure, citywide heat pumps can be deployed on a large scale. Industrial strength power converters can be embedded ubiquit-ously: Installed in sidewalks, streets and roads, under parking lots, in office facades and roof structures, pumping at the hot heart of the heat island city, cooling it and, in its fevering arteries, by generating power. Embedded, some-what non-renewably, in urban waste discharge streams, heat pumps are effective in deriving energy from the elevated temperature levels in sewage, waste and cooling water flows, and the myriad of urban vents and exhaust systems that expel industrial gases, steam or coolant air. In residential neighbourhood and home applications heat pumps work best when integrated into walls and floors. Generally, it is not cost-effective to retrofit structures for heat pumping. Rather it is best if this system forms an integral part of the life-cycle budget of a building or complex at the design and construction stages. Until now, oper-ating energy has been largely fossil-fuel or conventional grid power derived, but in the coming renewable-energy economy solar, wind, water or bio-fuel energy will drive these quiet and efficient energy concentrators, operating ubiquitously as standard features of all buildings and urban infrastructure works.

## Renewable rights and development control

Significant inner-city buildings often undergo wind tunnel and other environmental performance tests. While plans for new urban areas and cities should be subjected to the same rigorous analysis, that is only rarely the case. Prevailing winds can not only be taken into account in a general design sense and as environmental fact, but also be carefully channelled, and finely tuned in their flows. Unwanted exposure can be blocked by taking intelligent and informed urban design measures. Energy gains through building-integrated power wind devices can be maximised in this way. The optimisation of wind power flow gains – and the mutual interaction between buildings to assure equitable access to gains – is about to become a subdiscipline of urban renewable energy design and engineering, in itself an embryonic professional and creative activity with an enormous future.

Through the careful determination of solar access rights, shade can be created and glare across buildings reduced, while adequate sun exposure of photovoltaic facades and solar-thermal roofs can be ensured. The assessment of solar power generation potential represents a growing and hybrid field of urban design: the application of urban configurational efficiency principles in support of active power generation systems. Where there is a desire or incentive to install photovoltaic or solar-thermal devices, maximisation of solar exposure turns from an urban amenity question to a financial issue. *Solar generation equity* emerges as contentious issue as soon as the electricity productivity of buildings and sites is factored into the urban development equation. To be able to gauge the total, theoretical or technical solar electricity generation potential of a city allows important planning considerations to be made, and requires powerful tools. Key variables involved are: level of exposure or available irradiation; collector system efficiency; and the potential building area that can be covered by such sun radiation converting devices (Cerda 2001, p 23; see also below, the subsection on photovoltaics).

A number of local governments have begun to specify planning restrictions seeking to limit the obstruction of solar generation potential by new or future building activity on adjacent lot, but the experience is episodic at best. Common sense needs to prevail, and much of any solar access legislation to be introduced would be trivial. There is a direct analogy to existing legislation in many communities, ensuring sunshine access to land and structures, for traditional amenity and public health aims. And to state the obvious in terms of built form: solar access equity is easiest realised in urban areas of common building heights.

Despite United States resistance at the federal level, and relatively undeveloped local regulatory support, in various states and government agencies involved in land development and administration there is a long and continuing tradition of securing solar rights as a fundamental civic entitlement. Some of it is little more than legislative lip service, but much of it also establishes an important foundation for broader regulatory initiatives and provisions. The Californian Solar Rights Act of 1978 has been formulated to prevent local governments from restricting solar energy use (CERES 2006). And the State of New Mexico's Solar Rights Act of the same year, post-OPEC Oil Shock, recognises the economic benefit of solar energy to its citizens and identifies the use of sun energy as a commercial activity. It asserts that 'the right to use the natural resource of solar energy is a property right, the exercise of which is to be encouraged and regulated by the laws of this state. Such property right shall be known as a solar right' (SC 2006). And the US Bureau of Lands Management (BLM) and agency of the US Department of the Interior, administering 1 million square kilometres of public lands across some 12 western states, has sent out encouraging signals in support of renewable energy development in a memorandum setting policy for the 'processing of right-of-way applications for solar energy development projects on public lands and evaluating the feasibility of installing solar energy systems on BLM administrative facilities and projects' (BLM 2004).

The development of urban renewable energy rights is about to explode. Local governments are advised to embed sensible new legislation within their existing regulatory framework, whether encouraging development or safeguarding sun rights. Analogous to the situation in respect of solar rights as propounded in the 1970s, in principle similar rights exist for the harvesting of urban wind power, the operation of external heat pumps, the efficient performance of buildings in optimising daylight access and passive solar gain, but also rights to harvest and use rainwater, the latter also fundamentally an energy issue.


## 4.3 THE RENEWABLE CITY TOOLBOX

This section focuses on the urban potential of renewable energy. It is by no means intended as a technical exposition of the systems involved. Other books are recommended for a both wider and deeper understanding of renewable energy, notably Godfrey Boyle' *Renewable Energy* (2004).

# Overview of tools

| Source | System | Sub-system | Example applications |
|---|---|---|---|
| **Solar** | **Photovoltaics (PV)** | **PV panel** | Buildings, infrastructure |
| | | **Thin film** | Building integration (BIPV) |
| | | **Arrays** | Buildings, energy farms |
| | | **PV concentrator** | Buildings, infrastructure |
| | **Solar-thermal** | **Parabolic trough concentrator** | Industrial/commercial/ plants Infrastructure/ energy farms/grid supply |
| | | **Compact linear Fresnel reflector (CLFR)** | Buildings, energy farms |
| | | **Parabolic dish/Sterling concentrator** | Buildings, energy farms |
| | | **Multi-tower solar array (MTSA)** | Energy farms |
| | | **Solar chimney/solar tower** | Major buildings, urban supply |
| | | **Solar water heater** | Buildings |
| | | **Solar pond** | Regional and remote locations |
| **Wind** | **Turbines** | **Large turbine** | Grid power |
| | | **Offshore wind farm** | Grid power |
| | | **Small turbines** | Buildings, remote stand-alone |
| | | **Vertical axis turbines** | Buildings |
| **Bioenergy** | Biofuels/wood | Black liquor | Power stations: grid |
| | | Forestry crops | Power stations: grid |
| | | Forestry residues | Power stations: grid |
| | | Timber/paper industrial wastes | Power stations: grid |
| | **Biofuel/agro fuel** | **Dedicated agricultural crops** | Transport, grid power and cogeneration |
| | | Agricultural residues | Transport, grid power and cogeneration |

| | | | |
|---|---|---|---|
| | | Bagasse | Transport, grid power and cogeneration |
| | | Animal waste | Transport, grid power and cogeneration |
| | | Food industrial waste | Transport, grid power and cogeneration |
| | Biofuel/municipal | Municipal solid waste incineration | Grid power |
| | | Sewage | Heat mining, transport, cogeneration |
| | | Landfill gas | Transport, grid power and cogeneration |
| Hydropower | Hydro-electricity | Conventional hydropower | Grid power |
| | | Mini and micro hydropower | Small grid, stand-alone generation |
| Geothermal | | Geothermal | Grid power |
| Ground heat | | Heat pump | Distributed applications |
| Aquatic heat | | Heat pump | Distributed applications |
| Air heat | | Heat pump | Distributed applications |
| **Ocean** | | **Ocean thermal** | Grid and stand-alone |
| | | **Tidal power** | Grid and stand-alone |
| | | **Wave energy** | Grid and stand-alone |
| Hydrogen (energy carrier, not source, | Combustion | | Transport, cogeneration |
| For heat/power, transport, storage) | Fuel cell | | Transport, cogeneration |

Technologies printed in **bold** are fully renewable. Many energy sources labelled 'sustainable,' 'alternative', 'new' or even 'green' in urban or national energy statistics are not strictly renewable or even environmentally sustainable in their use, such as those relying on domestic waste incineration. Some of these are nevertheless referred to here, largely because many cities, countries and development agencies account for them in their 'renewable' or 'sustainable' energy statistics – as does the International Energy Agency (IEA 2002). Misleadingly, these non-renewable, waste encouraging and net-carbon emitting sources can represent a very large share of some statistically declared 'sustainable' energy components. In this spirit, less damaging and more efficient fossil-fuel systems such as 'advanced' coal and natural gas applications are excluded here altogether. They are clearly neither renewable nor sustainable (matrix adapted from Droege 2004, p 307).

# Citywide renewable energy mapping (C-REM)

Numerous sources are available to the motivated urban renewable energy resource cartographer. The United States' National Air and Space Administration (NASA) has developed global datasets to calculate the ideal angle for photovoltaic positioning and other design considerations. These are available over the Internet, such as a 1984–92 satellite solar radiation dataset translated into a software application, *SolarSizer* (Solar Online 2006). NASA has adapted to the reality of a rising renewable industry and assembled a global partnership promoting solar prospecting services based on satellite data, *Environmental Information Services for Solar Energy Industries* (NASA 2005). By contrast, and measuring from ground stations, affiliated to the World Meteorological Organisation (WMO) is the World Radiation Data Centre which offers on-line global sunshine data (WRDC 2005). For the United States only, renewable energy resource maps as well as a wide spectrum of solar radiation and other renewable resource data are provided by the United States National Renewable Energy Laboratory's Renewable Resource Data Center (NREL 2005a,b).

An urban equivalent of a general mapping project should produce an assessment of the overall urban generation and efficiency potential. It will be useful in forming a basis for any citywide renewable energy strategy plan. This can be done in layers of different technologies, and queried individually by energy resource; it is best assembled on a geographic information system (GIS) platform. An approach to solar mapping aimed at optimising the application of photovoltaic systems has been developed in Europe as a basis for developing a local renewable strategic plan. It is described below pp 159–162, examining how to determine the sheer physical potential of a city. Similar maps can be generated for effective solar-thermal locations; for urban wind potentials; air, ground and water-based heat pumping; and for regional bio-fuel, solar and wind resources. And the absence of solar incidence is mappable, too: San Francisco aims at becoming the United States' largest municipal renewable energy generator, and its distributed, rooftop radiation monitoring Solar Energy Monitoring Network has helped produce fog maps for a number of years (Murphy 2002).

The heat island behaviour of a city may form an important base layer for such maps, for heat pumping and ambient cooling efforts as well as other important micro-climatic dimensions, such as humidity, precipitation and wind direction patterns. A building-by-building analysis across the residential, commercial and industrial sectors will produce other important layers, and complete the picture by mapping both greenhouse gas emission and fossil fuel consumption centres as well as urban efficiency improvement potentials. This can help pinpoint and guide building upgrade, refurbishment and renewal programmes.

## City-integrated photovoltaics (CIPV)

The ability directly to convert solar radiation into electricity via simple, surface-mounted or integral, highly durable panels means that every sun-exposed element of a city – stationary or moving – can generate power. To the CIPV-minded observer cities are vast oceans of sun-drenched roofs and enormous batteries of sun-exposed vertical surfaces, inhabited by moving objects that are capable of carrying individual collectors. Once clad in photo-voltaic material, they become a massive electric power plant. Mono-crystalline or the lower-quality polycrystalline cells convert sunlight in semi-conducting, mostly silicon-based elements, whereby negative and positive charges are stimulated by photons – the photovoltaic (PV) principle. Thin-film technology using amorphous cells is often referred to as the second generation of PV, ultimately promising lower cost. And, more recently, screen-printed dye solar cells have emerged as the so-called third generation of PV, manifest in translucent, nano-crystalline structures emulating plant photosynthesis. These are being rivalled in promise by organic solar cells, capable of emitting as well as receiving light. All hope to get ready for a booming market, but the original and durable mono- and polycrystalline cell panel continues its progress as the major work horse in buildings and other urban applications.

While the trusty roof-mounted panel makes significant inroads in the domestic PV markets of Japan, Europe and the United States, building integrated elements in the form of traditional PV, thin film applications and the third-generation photovoltaic systems are still found only in comparatively few settings. It is perfectly possible and indeed sensible today to prepare for powering an entire city from within via the electricity that can be generated on its rooftops using existing technology – yet deep urban integration seems as far from realisation and wide application as the ubiquitous use of microcomputers was in the 1960s. Manufacturing costs and prices are declining while sales rise, yet general and strong systems, market and political bias in favour of fossil fuels, both overt and covert, make this still a significant challenge to confront. This clarifies the very nature of the struggle. Cities acting as concentrating, integrating PV and other renewable energy markets can contribute greatly to accelerating wider breakthroughs.

## Mapping the urban PV potential

The Spanish publication *Solar City Guide – New Solutions in Energy Supply* was completed in 2001, the result of a programme supported by the European Commission to motivate scientists and engineers, policy-makers and market leaders to embrace economically viable, cleaner and more efficient solutions that also help strengthen European competitive advantage in new energy technologies. It aims at promoting urban photovoltaic applications. The document persuasively identified three key variables as important in considering the photovoltaic or primary solar electricity generation potential of a city. These are (1) the amount of sunshine reaching building surfaces, or *level of irradiation*; (2) the degree of photovoltaic system efficiency; and (3) the area that is potentially available for installation. The document suggests a simple formula to estimate the potential for roof-integrated photovoltaic systems in European cities:

> Annual production of solar electricity (kWh) = population size x maximum solar irradiation (kWh/sqm per year) x module efficiency x net area per capita (sqm/capita) x (global system and area factor = Population x maximum solar irradiation (kwh/sqm/annum) x 0.1 x Net area/capita x 0.4) (Cerda 2001, pp 23–4)

## Space requirement

As with most other urban or embedded renewable energy systems, electrical power generation capacity requires no additional or specially dedicated land or building area: the PV elements are installed on existing structures and replace conventional building elements in new construction. The realisation of its potential depends on urban form and the degree to which PV is acceptable in particular settings. The level of public or institutional acceptance is usually determined by non-technical variables: (a) aesthetic, planning and construction traditions for existing and new buildings; (b) historical and cultural values; (c) local design capacity and talent for integrating PV successfully; and (d) general levels of planning regulatory inertia (Cerda 2001, pp 31–2). Urban form variables include a number of key urban design dimensions, outlined below.

- **Irradiation** The level of radiation received is a function of the orientation and degree of incline of potential carrier surfaces. At the risk of stating the obvious, the highest yield of a stationary surface is achieved when it is optimally tilted towards the sun. Less optimal surface orientations receive less radiation but can still be useful for the generation of electricity. For example, a strategic urban plan for solar electricity production will place priority on areas of highest solar yield – but building areas with less than ideal solar yield should still be considered where ownership restrictions, visual impact, building design and seasonal or daily supply and demand issues are important considerations (Cerda 2001, pp 23 and 24).

- **Urban form** Compact development with even roof heights – the traditional city – is ideal for roof-mounted PV. An open built form with a range of heights – the modern city – has good potential for building-integrated photovoltaic (BIPV) facade systems. A key characteristic mapped for this purpose is the *relative building height variability*, colourfully termed *urban roughness*. Many other aspects can be usefully identified, too, such as the *sky view factor*, the extent to which surfaces are exposed to the sun.
- **Orientation** Streets with west- and east-facing facades provide the lowest potential for solar access, while a street pattern that is diagonal to the cardinal directions gives better overall solar access than a street with south- and north-facing facades. But the precise orientation is not critical: there is flexibility in planning for PV (Cerda 2001 p 28).
- **Shade** In areas with highly glazed buildings opaque PV elements can be incorporated to provide shade or as tiled or translucent thin-film applications incorporated into glazing systems. Where small window openings prevail PV can be deployed as cladding. In both cases, photovoltaic elements are most effective when placed high on facades where obstructions to sunlight are less likely.
- **Higher surface to volume ratios** These indicate a higher proportion of facade area available for facade integrated PV, but this also implies a higher risk of vertical obstruction by adjacent buildings. Lower ratios indicate larger uninterrupted roof areas for solar panels (Cerda 2001, p 29).
- **Vertical obstruction** Planning legislation should ensure that building heights regimes help maximise overall urban solar electricity productivity.
- **Reflectivity** Higher levels of surface reflectivity mean that there is more diffuse light available for facade mounted PV: orientation optimisation becomes less important in such environments. The corollary is that the lower ambient reflectivity, the more PV systems need to be configured for direct solar orientation. *Irradiation maps* allow an accurate representation of the total annual solar energy received by all surfaces within an area. They can be used to pinpoint areas of high irradiation and to quantify the effects of shading of planned new construction (Cerda 2001, p 31).

The massive introduction of *building-integrated photovoltaics* (BIPV), too, is part of a successful citywide renewable energy strategy. Photovoltaic elements come in all sizes and a range of applications, making this technology currently the most versatile of urban renewable energy systems. It has the potential to replace roof elements, facades and windows. Greater efficiency in construction can be achieved through modular PV integration systems that permit the ready replacement of elements. A comprehensive municipal strategy should incorporate a building-integrated PV framework consisting of technical guidance, design standards and industry incentives. It begins with applying its principles to city-owned structures – but does not end here, as in so many symbolic efforts involving PV, popular but wrongly perceived to be expensive. Solar access and building rights need to be safeguarded, as was anticipated in the early US solar rights legislation enacted in the 1970s and 1980s (Luce 2006, p 1). CIPV makes particularly good sense in large, sprawling metropolitan regions: in low-density cities, suburbs and other urban regions in the sunnier regions of the world the use of as little as one third of the total roof areas can suffice to generate all domestic electricity requirements through PV (Akagawa 2002).

- **Outlook** Photovoltaic urbanism is beginning to make some inroads, whether integrated elegantly in advanced glazing and exuberant wall elements or fitted clumsily in awkward panels. There are many coordinated efforts to promote it within and in addition to the programmes referenced in this book. While the fundamental principles are basic, residential and commercial applications emerge in a very wide range: a growing number of urban facilities is being augmented, from noise attenuation walls to streetlights and traffic signals; and numerous residential developments throughout the world carry sizeable PV plants on their roofs, from the many demonstration suburbs in Northrhine-Westphalia and various other German states to the 2000 Olympic village in Sydney. The Dutch city of Amersfoort has presented a somewhat self-conscious display in the PV-new town of Nieuwland, in which the elementary elements and management arrangements of the suburban system are expressed, documented and monitored in an instructive, International Energy Agency coordinated effort (IEA PVPS 2003).

But within the conventional world of urban planning, development and management, photovoltaics – like other renewable systems – are generally still introduced only in an isolated and *ad hoc* fashion, advancing haltingly in the hostile conventional energy environment so entangled in fossil and nuclear infrastructures, institutions and market arrangements. Comprehensive change strategies are best commenced by not only mapping the physical urban deployment potential but also through understanding and working with structural challenges, partnership opportunities and market resources (see Chapter 6 for approaches to planned renewable energy transformation). Increasingly efficient and versatile, as basic technology photovoltaics may well emerge as a primary urban-integrated renewable energy system along with biofuel, solar-thermal and both integrated and regional wind generation. Prices shrink while levels of efficiency and technological sophistication increase. Sun-tracking concentrator modules are available as space-saving alternatives to the more rigid panel installations. With a hardware lifetime of 20 years or more, first-generation photovoltaic systems lend themselves to mass production and distribution, the key technology in most solar-roof programmes.

Yet despite enormous opportunities, photovoltaic systems still play only a minor role in most municipal fossil fuel displacement or greenhouse gas emission reduction drives. In the world of urban energy reform they are dwarfed by somewhat simpler yet frequently fundamentally fossil-friendly efforts to cut back on the massive waste in the system or substitute them with other sources euphemistically labelled 'clean': urban efficiency campaigns, public transport improvements, distributed gas-fired power-heat cogeneration schemes or the substitution of coal-fired power plants by natural gas or, worse, nuclear power schemes.

## Solar roof programmes, and other dos and don'ts in national efforts

In several countries urban photovoltaic systems play a significant role at national level. Most *solar roof* programmes and initiatives are photovoltaic-systems based, aiming at the 'shaving' of peak-power demand – or supply supplementation – and the consumer empowering mechanism of fairly compensated grid feeding. The immensely successful 100,000 Solar-Roof programme in Germany has reached its capacity target of 300 installed megawatts of PV well before its target date and had its parallel in the United States Department of Energy's Million Solar Roofs public–private partnership programme (MSR 2006). President Bill Clinton introduced the measure as the *US Million Solar Roofs Initiative* in June 1997. Its declared aims were to help reduce the United States' dependence on fossil fuels and boost commercial solar power use by prompting communities and businesses to invest in rooftop PV, solar water heaters, transpired solar collectors, solar space heating and cooling, and pool heating (DoE 2006a). The programme aimed to have one million solar powered installations in use by 2010 – but the programme was ended five years early. The expectation had been for the creation of 70,000 new jobs, strengthened industry competitiveness and the addition of a new, locally available and hence reliable power source. The US government began to acknowledge the difficulties with this somewhat laborious approach as the concept gave way in 2005/06 to a new initiative, labelled with considerable ambition, Solar Powers America (SPA). It is hoped that in the process the earlier commitments could revive with a more planning and infrastructure-procurement integrated focus on renewable energy.

The old programme did have an impact, but it was limited due to a lack of funding and a narrow hardware focus. Described by some as little more than an elaborate public relations effort, the programme was cheered by others as providing important impulses to state and their local partnership efforts. Indeed, its success was reflected in a number of state-based, homonymous policies and programmes, such as those of North Carolina since 1999, or of California or Oregon. Across the United States, most significant initiatives take place at state level; the Database for State Incentives for Renewable Energy provides a good directory of these (DSIRE 2006). North Carolina has issued a solar resources toolkit for local governments throughout the state which is a good illustration of the kind of structural and well-managed changes that have been pursued (NCSolar 2006). The state-level bipartisan Million Solar Roofs Initiative bill introduced by California Governor Schwarzenegger, rein-troduced in a new incarnation after renewed challenges, and finally approved by the California Public Utilities Commission (CPUC) on 12 January 2006, is billed as the largest solar energy initiative in US history. It supports an 11-year, $3.2 billion incentives programme, promising to contribute 3 gigawatts in solar capacity. This would substitute for 10 coal or 2 nuclear power plants and multiply 30-fold today's solar photovoltaic capacity. Once implemented it would turn California – as an independent state it would rank as the world's sixth largest economy – into the leading PV market, ahead of today's top consumers, Germany and Japan (JSP 2005; Little 2005; SN 2006).

The countries ostensibly most concerned with establishing market mechan-isms for renewable energy introduction have also chosen the most elaborate, indirect and ultimately limited paths towards achieving these. The politic-ally petroleum entangled United States proffered a plethora of small-grants-and-carrots based partnership options, prodding communities and businesses into committing their own funds to raise a million solar roofs. And Australia, hampered in progress by the cursed blessing of abundant coal and uranium resources, gave birth to a complex and slow Solar Cities programme aimed at selected local trials involving competing consortia. Neither of the programmes has been provided with mechanisms that will ensure market performance such as electricity feed-in laws or mandatory renewable energy targets set at usefully high levels. Australia and the United States may have placed the cart before the horse, seeking to battle a difficult market, instead of shaping and then riding it. Yet it is difficult to see how a radical shift can be achieved without a fundamental reform of the energy finance regime.

Japan's major rooftop programmes and projects such as the Ministry of Economy, Trade and Industrys (METI; formerly MITI, the Ministry of International Trade and Industry) New Sunshine (NSS) programme of the early 1990s was an integral part of substantially funded, government-research led photovoltaic and other renewable power efforts. These helped boost substantial innovations such as the late 1990s' solar-house prototypes of prefabrication giant Mizawa Homes, which were developed and marketed in collaboration with the Tokyo Electric Power Company (TEPCO). The Japanese programmes relied on subsidies, tax credits, utility partnerships and practice change, virtually enforced in the construction industry via ministerial fiat. A major outcome of this industrial development programme was the creation of the world's largest and most advanced photovoltaic cell and element production capacity which is today the most significant foreign manufacturing source for Germany's solar installation miracle.

By contrast, the US initiative eschewed national market legislation or bold programmes. It sought to incubate fragile domestic solar plants in the stifling jungle of subsidised fossil and nuclear dominated energy markets. This faint market stimulation attempt was also in part grants-based, supporting start-up ventures to expand the commercial application of solar energy with a US $5 million award programme. Its mission lay in assisting with securing low-cost loans, grants and other financial assistance measures, distantly reinforced by a Department of Energy research division, the National Renewable Energy Laboratory (NREL).

To lower costs by increasing markets, partnerships were encouraged and commitments to help install model photovoltaic elements and systems were sought from communities, businesses, state governments and utilities. In 2002, a tax credit of 15 per cent of the installed cost of a solar generation system was proposed, to further prod homeowners and businesses into adopting the technology, now limited to a 1999–2005 window. But the lack of a significant support budget meant that during the first half of the programme's life progress was less than had been hoped: by the end of 2003 the 89 regional MSRI partnerships reported the implementation of a disappointing 229,000 residential solar roofs. But as soon as support was enhanced, state and local MSRI partnerships grew to 100 by 2005, still aimed at removing market barriers and building demand. New participants have since joined the building industry, other federal agencies, state and local governments, power companies, solar power providers, banks and non-governmental organisations of civil society (NREL 2005c; MSR 2006).

The extraordinary interest, energy and imagination displayed in the United States is not matched by national commitments. Theoretically, by harnessing the former the world's greatest greenhouse gas emitter could be dramatically reformed, by creating the market framework to allow all the nation's cities, towns, homes and businesses to become renewable energy producers. The world's most powerful market driver, and a useful model, is Germany's national legislative framework designed to stimulate the national mushrooming of solar roofs, PV power plants and other means of renewable electricity generation. This is the country's legendary *electricity feed-in law*, setting tariffs for the mandatory purchase of renewable power by conventional utilities (see also *Energieeinspeisegesetz (EEG)* [The German Renewable Energy Sources Act (Act on Granting Priority to Renewable Energy Sources, 1 April 2000)], below). Germany has introduced and quickly implemented its solar roof programme as means of implementing its larger market objectives. In Germany, low-interest loans were combined with other financing measures – not large government subsidies – in a programme that was designed to be 'unbureaucratic', compatible with existing schemes, conducive to nurturing industry competition and independence, as well as flexible and expandable (Scheer nd). By 2005, some 30 countries had either begun to study or implement their own version of the initiative. It has informed the renewable energy legislation of Brazil and China. And in Canada, both the city of Toronto and Prince Edward Island are moving to adopt such feed-in legislation.

Among the range of current renewable energy promotion policies and laws, none is as useful and effective as a national, state or even locally selective feed-in law, ie the requirement that electricity utilities purchase renewable power at set tariffs, thereby creating a market for renewable power that is open to all and free of subsidies. It is especially helpful to local communities in terms of their interest in fostering effective means of ubiquitous, integrated renewable power generation.

These other approaches include renewable energy portfolio standards (RPS), such as those enacted in several states in the United States, or the Mandatory

Renewable Energy Target (MRET) in Australia; or tax or finance incentives; funds, subsidies and grants; public tendering for renewable generation; and drives for various voluntary activities (Wiser et al 2004). The RPS, for example, is useful for pursuing known targets among generators and suppliers, but none of them offer the range of advantages: embedding of renewable energy generation at the point of consumption. MRET is cumbersome, biased towards large and established producers and notoriously aimed too low. The others are either too weak or unfocused as instruments or do not lend themselves to the establishment of viable markets. Feed-in provisions are fair, capable of being set according to various levels, and transparent.

The German Renewable Energy Sources Act sets acquisition pricing policies for power utilities, requiring them to purchase renewable energy produced and fed into the grid by individual generators.

The United Kingdom's £20 million, three-year PV Major Demonstration Programme had set a somewhat modest goal of 3,500 solar roofs to be developed by 2005, only moderately more ambitious than the City of Melbourne's federally funded 100-roof programme, which was designed to help strengthen a fledgling domestic industry with the aid of local utility company, CitiPower (AGO 2003).

And in 2004 Australia announced a AUS$ 75-million (US$ 50 million) Solar Cities Programme designed to be carried out at a measured pace and with a narrow focus, to develop and test local solar-electricity – photovoltaic – supply models in grid-connected urban development sites. Indeed, after a lengthy start-up and orientation period, the effort embarked upon a cautiously administered, staged-bid based procedure focused on giving preferred status to consortia composed of local governments, development industry groups, solar equipment suppliers and power utilities. It was structured to run from 2004 through 2013 to implement such trials. Some industry participants could not resist from ironically commenting that the programme was so structured that it lampooned the coming solar transformation as a complex, overly technical and painfully slow change prospect – serving to reinforce certain popular and industry prejudices against renewable energy, and putting a dampener on broader change in the interim.

Guidelines have been developed to delineate tasks and outline the roles of each consortium participant. Consortia resemble stiffener versions of the US partnering efforts: eligible participants included state agencies, local governments and other organisations with ties to the community or with responsibility for electricity pricing, or regulatory and planning arrangements. Other stakeholders and consortium members are electricity generators, retailers and network service providers aiming to deliver service without consumer cost increases and via demand management techniques – that is, of limiting peak demand by rewarding energy savers. Manufacturers, suppliers and installers of solar generation and efficiency technologies contribute their industry capabilities. Providers help in the adoption of standards, education, accreditation and testing procedures. Further assistance is to be provided to consumers – still defined in the nomenclature as passive participants rather than as microgenerators – in finding and installing the most suitable equipment. Financial institutions are to provide funding packages and help manage initial outlays. Developers and architects are expected to 'raise consumer awareness'. The interests and roles of individual households – seen as the very foundation of the German and US Solar roof programmes – are not represented in the consortia, but the programme has called for a 'consumer engagement strategy' in all Solar Cities consortium proposals, designed to 'include' communities and businesses in some form or other (AGO 2004).

In summary, while the United States, United Kingdom and Australian models have provided solid platforms for individual action, the reliance on phantom markets and individual, carefully selected manufacturers for research, production and dissemination, combined with the non-binding, uncommitted nature of industry guidance have left the wider community of energy stakeholders – potential individual prosumers, investors and planners – understandably unenthusiastic about the idea of introducing PV technology in urban development. Meanwhile, in Germany the market is continuing to expand and mature. The formation of numerous entrepreneurial initiatives such as a 'roof exchange' – a commercial investment platform that matches owners of roof areas with investors and installers of PV, allowing individuals to operate solar power generators on leased and pooled roof space – signals the emergence of a broad and ubiquitous, interactive and information technology driven *energy web*, as described in Chapter 3 (Alpensolar 2006).

## Urban sun collectors: city-integrated solar-thermal technology

Compact-lens Fresnel reflector, parabolic-trough mirror and other solar-thermal power arrays – referred to as concentrating solar power (CSP) in the United States context – are ideal for fitting on any medium- to large-scale urban surface such as atop high-rise buildings, schools, bus terminals, parking lots or office parks. These sophisticated and highly efficient systems rely on direct sun presence and therefore work best in areas of the world with high sun incidence. They generate steam, are capable of driving *Sterling* or *Rankine cycle* engines, powering turbines and generators, and yielding a combination of heat and electricity that can be used also for solar air conditioning and freezing and industrial process pre-heating.

The most commonly used and cost-effective of all urban solar-thermal energy applications is the trusty solar collector, in all its guises, which is used for household, pool and industrial water as well as general heating. The most basic and inefficient system deploys black plastic mat absorbers, while the very common flat plate collector, endearingly awkward in its insulated metal case, is more sophisticated and commonly used, channelling and heating water as energy medium against a sealed black surface. Highest efficiencies are achieved with vacuum tube collectors, where very little heat loss occurs at all. Examples of these systems can be deployed in individual units or linked arrays. They are perched atop houses in all parts of the world, and active even on overcast days. But in their more efficient incarnations, they are also happily integrated in larger building rooftops, in industrial installations and public recreation facilities, including as pools and baths, and heating water and space in residential developments, airports and rehabilitation centres alike.

Small cities make the largest progress in deployment of solar water heaters. The efforts of the quasi-autonomous Austrian solar villages have been legendary for a considerable time; and in 2005 the German city with the largest locally integrated solar-thermal area was Rottenburg am Neckar, a small community of 40,000 with almost 1 square metre of collector area per 10 inhabitants installed in the last four years alone, with its district of Oberndorf sporting 1 square metre for every two inhabitants. The town has become a veritable solar theme park, an open-air display of solar thermal installations (Alt 2005d)

## Urban wind power

Wind generators are among the most traditional, direct and productive forms of converting renewable energy flows into mechanical, today mostly electrical, power. Micro- and mini-wind power applications are powerful additions to the built environment and, deployed *en masse*, can help transform the electricity supply profiles of urban areas and city regions. There has been a traditional bias against wind power in urban areas due to the wind flow disturbances created by built-up areas, but in these city eddies and gusts can constitute a vast and to-date untapped resource. Buildings and other structures such as skyscrapers, bridges, stadia, theme and entertainment parks, shopping centres and telecommunication towers are often tall enough to access air layers with effective wind speeds and that generate sufficient turbulence in ambient wind flows to allow the sustained generation of electricity or can be streamlined and designed to drive building-integrated wind energy collection devices.

Cities should pursue wind power as integral to the energy performance of their buildings and facilities and their overall energy web. Buildings should be crafted to harvest the powerful wind forces that can exist at their tops, the edges of structures and internally. This may involve building-integrated rotor assemblies, vertical axis generators for eaves, edges and corners or using the *thermal stack effect*, which harnesses warm airflows in building cores to drive internal fans and turbines, or as solar-radiation boosted air streams in the external, dual walls of specially configured office towers. To facilitate the deployment of wind power generators throughout the city, the mutual spatial relationship of buildings should be planned and engineered to optimise conditions for good wind power generation. In the renewable portfolio of buildings and urban areas, integrated wind power may only play a secondary role, but because of its iconic role as a highly visible expression of commitment to sustainable development, it is becoming a renewable energy source of choice in corporate and civic design projects.

For the first renewable-energy optimised Wal-Mart store in McKinney, Texas, wind power played an important part. There a low-cost, 50-kilowatt generator is one of two small turbines, part of a broad portfolio that includes PV and biofuel-use for electricity production (Broehl 2005b). It is maintained as a highly visible, tangible expression of the many, largely invisible innovations introduced by Wal-Mart and its designers. In New York, Daniel Liebeskind and Skidmore, Owings & Merrill designed the Freedom Tower to replace the World Trade Center destroyed by the terrorist attacks of 11 September 2001. Originally, wind power was to be integrated in the building shaft – perhaps in a gesture symbolic of the petroleum link to the predominantly Saudi attackers. A later design saw this idea dropped. Instead, some other commitments to environmentally sustainable design were maintained such as energy efficiency, internal daylight use, low-sulpher diesel generators and recycled content in some materials (SOM 2005). The Freedom Tower had evolved into a Fossil Tower, albeit one civilised by improved energy standards and controls.

## Urban waterpower

Waterpower has a wide range of applications in and around cities. Hill- and mountaintop reservoirs provide energy storage and generation capacity. For seaside cities, wave and tidal power, too, can readily be harnessed if marine coastal and ecological conditions permit. While their use may seem limited in the context of specific urban conditions and opportunities, emerging techniques achieve extremely high efficiencies in converting ocean movements into electricity. Sydney civil engineer Tim Finnigan has pioneered the mimicking of shark tail fins, obtaining 1 megawatt of capacity from a 12-metre fin, and of sea plants such as kelp, while minimising maintenance requirements and the impact of seabed anchors (Rossmanith 2006). Streams can serve as riverine, small and micro-generation sources. New and open, short-blade technology has been developed for benign river-flow installations that do not disrupt inland navigation or fauna migration patterns. Waterpower has been used for centuries, generating mechanical energy for pre-industrial streamside mills, for example. Much of this use has since given way to electricity generation.

Inner-city waterpower systems are a small part of a massive, global resource. Worldwide, 17 per cent of electricity is generated by hydropower (Dürrschmidt et al 2004, p 33); water-based power constitutes the vast majority of renewable energy that is deployed, excluding biomass. The link between cities and water energy can be intimate, and not only in mountain villages or historical mill towns, such as English and North American textile centres. The Bavarian state capital of Munich is in the process of installing a new inner-city water power generator in the heart of the city, where the River Isar passes Prater Island (Green City 2005). Small and micro-hydropower systems form an integral, sustainable and powerful component in a myriad of Chinese villages and settlements, in India and throughout the developing world and have given rise to indigenous generator manufacturing businesses active in export.

But the great hydropower schemes of the inter- and postwar era, from the Colorado River's monumental Hoover Dam (1931–6), opening up extensive farmland downstream, to the elaborate 16-dam Snowy Mountain scheme in Australia (1949–74), have seen their best days: they may well be remembered as among the first and last of their kind. While a number of urbanisation or resettlement schemes are associated with contentions and socially and environmentally damaging schemes, including China's controversial Yangtze River Three Gorges Dam, or India's calamitous Narmada River Development Programme, such schemes are not usually part of a sustainable urban renewable-energy portfolio. Here, waterpower has been used inappropriately, as external and internal costs soar, returns diminish and overall costs outstrip benefits. Also, large new hydropower schemes can be substantial emitters of net carbon and other potent greenhouse gases – not only in the fossil energy embodied in their materials and construction. Emissions are triggered also through land clearance and deforestation, or swamped biomass left to rot in the reservoirs, as in Brazil's massive Itaipu Dam (1975–82), at Foz de Iguasu. Rated at 12.6 gigawatt capacity, this was the world's largest hydropower installation until the completion of the Yangtze River scheme.

## Regional renewable power systems (RRPS): from intra- to extra-urban generation

Distributed renewable energy systems may dominate the urban scene of the future but they will be massively supplemented by large-scale regional production systems to make up for the limited pace of inner-urban transformations. The electricity for cities and smaller urban communities is typically supplied from regional power plants – coal, oil, natural gas fired, or nuclear. Solar, wind, hydropower and biofuel are perfect media for overcoming this dangerous dependency and supplementing and gradually replacing conventional systems with regional renewable power generation capacity. A number of communities invest in renewable energy plants in various energy media. In Europe and elsewhere, large-scale solar electricity plants are already on the increase. In 2000 five photovoltaic power plants operated in Germany with more than 1 megawatt of capacity each. Five years later there were 50, in PV systems alone. Just outside of its inner harbour the city of Copenhagen has recently opened its 20-turbine, 40-megawatt cooperative offshore wind power plant, aggressively expanding the Danish capital's reliance in renewable energy. In Denmark 86 per cent of wind power is developed by private investment, largely through citizens' cooperatives (Vikkelsø 2003).

In southern Germany the solar production capacities of the tiny towns of Mühlhausen, Günching and Minihof combine in the 10-megawatt PV Solarpark Bavaria, officially opened on 30 June 2005 it is the largest of its kind in the world, and a 100-megawatt farm is on the drawing board. The output of the Solarpark helped Germany reach 1 gigawatt of renewable power capacity in 2005. These initiatives, like many others of this kind, were boosted by a new supplementary regulation, the *Photovoltaik-Vorschaltgesetz*, to the national renewable energy law (*Energieeinspeisegesetz – EEG*), in force since 1 January 2004 (Solarserver 2005).

Sacramento has relied on PV since 1984 and is the largest municipal PV operator in the United States. And the Sacramento Municipal Utility District (SMUD) famously decommissioned its Rancho Seco nuclear power plant in the late 1990s and aggressively built up its large grid-connected solar-array portfolio instead, with a 10-megawatt capacity across some 900 sites. Sacramento diversifies its renewable portfolio: SMUD also advances a new 85-megawatt wind power installation at Solano (GM 2004).

## Solar thermal plants

Cities in sun-baked locations have greater choice in the wider world of solar technology. Indeed, today's solar-thermal plants are ready to be assembled in large arrays as well, to function as primary electricity sources: supplying electricity running absorption chillers for cooling; driving combined heating and/or power generators; augmenting conventional fossil-power plants, or powering solar desalination machinery. Used in combination, these technologies can reach a high degree of efficiency, converting up to 85 per cent of the absorbed radiation into applied energy (Dürrschmidt et al 2004, p 42). Numerous cost-effective and efficient systems are in use: parabolic-trough mirror banks, compact-lens Fresnel reflector (CLFR) arrays in California, multi-tower solar arrays (MTSA) in Spain, California, Australia and elsewhere. Such systems harvest the power of the sun and convert it via steam or hot air into electricity, using Sterling or Rankine cycle engines, or larger turbines. Unlike PV arrays, solar thermal plants work effectively only under direct sun exposure, and are therefore only tested and operated in various reliably sun-drenched countries.

A number of solar towers are being advanced around the world, most to supply urban grids. Among the more ambitious ranks the massive prototype developed by EnviroMission in New South Wales, Australia, partially financed by international investors including the United States and Chinese sources, and applying technology developed and tested by Germany's Schlaich, Bergermann & Partners. The company had planned to develop five 200-megawatt facilities, each a giant circular greenhouse 6 kilometres in diameter, with 1-kilometre pipes rising from their cores. It heats air, releasing it into the chimney, powering turbines at its base, and promising to generate electricity for a million homes. Recently the prototype has been scaled back to 50-megawatt capacity (Enviro-Mission 2005).

## Municipal wind energy

Wind power alone is fully able to meet world commercial energy needs, and provide more than seven times of its electricity demand (Archer and Jacobson 2005). Greenpeace estimates that 12 per cent of the world's electricity demand can be met by wind power by the year 2020 (Aubrey et al 2005). Like solar thermal systems, wind energy has lost at least one century in terms of technological evolution, given the historical detour into the fossil-fuel cul-de-sac the world has taken in the interim. By the middle of the 19th century some 20,000 windmills were in use in Germany, delivering mechanical energy. These vanished for more a century – only to resurface in that country making it the global leader in wind energy generation.

Depending on regional conditions, municipal wind farms can be powerful assets in a city's regional energy production regime: Melbourne in the late 1990s has been an early investor in regional wind power schemes. Indeed, like Copenhagen, new and proud owner of one of the world's largest offshore wind installations, a growing number of cities around the world manage their own wind generation plant, through their municipal utilities, on contract through third-party suppliers, or through so-called green-gold energy purchases, typically rich in wind-power content. Cities, city alliances and city regions find that they can both invest in and integrate state-owned and commercial wind farms in their wider metropolitan region.

Wind farms are sometimes criticised by environmentalists, criticism that is often amplified in the fossil fuel advocacy press. Stigmatised as unsightly, they are said to spoil valuable landscapes, coastal regions and mountaintops or the otherwise clear view out onto the endless sea. To others, they appear as sleek White Knights helping to slay the fossil dragon. Yet whatever one's sense of aesthetics, windmills are not to be blamed for their prominent role in the post-fossil landscape. Heavy energy demand boosted in a cheap-oil era results in their mushrooming, too, to keep up with bloated and ever-rising energy demands. And, sidestepping the question of whether they would exist in ways approximating their present form had cities been created to run on renewable energy and greater design efficiency instead of depending on the fossil fuel drip, in a perfect world they would have had much of their energy generation systems embedded and integrated, rather than awkwardly applied in retro-fit fashion like so many odd-blue PV panel oceans stressing the eye of the architectural aesthete; or the whirling white wind-turbine forests, with blades lazily spinning in seeming mockery of fossil naturalists. Yet such an outcry betrays an almost hypocritical myopia: few complain about the vast and menacing maze of high-voltage masts and humming power lines strangling the cultural landscapes of advanced industrial and aspiring developing worlds alike.

## Bio-energy farms and forests: biomass, biofuel, biogas

**Biomass** is a rather clumsy term for the oldest combustible renewable energy source used by humans. For eons, wood, plants, sap and other combustible organic materials have been burned to warm and heat, to light, cook and roast, to forge, to cremate as well as to repel wild animals and lay waste to enemies and their settlements. And still today biomass incineration is a major source of energy, much of it touted as inherently carbon-neutral: in so-called closed-loop energy crop farming only carbon that has been stored is released, and promised to be re-sequestered in new organic growth. However, biomass combustion is also a major cause of global deforestation, as millions of energy- and food-starved subsistence farmers, nomads and settlers embark on a daily, arduous wood foraging trek to help feed their families – in a so-called open-loop combustion frenzy. And in the richer world, too, wood chips, old wood, grain, harvest residue and organic waste and leftovers of all kind are either directly burned, or turned into bio-fuel to generate power in advanced generators for remote, cogeneration or grid-supporting power. There is an analogy to domestic waste incineration in the sense of rewarding waste and excess – but much of this is done with great efficiency and care, for example by growing dedicated plants in closed-loop biomass applications. Yet there also lies a danger in this technology, warranting caveats. Unless energy crops are farmed in carbon-neutral and ecologically sustainable ways without harm to the environment and human health, and hence producing a truly renewable energy stream, biomass as energy source, like large hydropower installations, remains very much a double-edge sword. Energy generated from old growth, native forests, for example, is an extremely negative application of biomass technology. Poorly managed, extensive monoculture forests, too, have negative impacts on the environment, outweighing their benefits.

Biomass used for direct burning can be polluting, does not achieve very high energy conversion rates and is extremely space intensive: it competes with nature conservation, food production and urban land uses (Pimentel et al 1994). This technique is hence as limited geographically as coal power was in its early days, and found only in regional enclaves of abundant forest resources. Like many other Scandinavian cities, Sweden's Göteborg relies on wood and paper mill waste, in chipped and pelleted form, as the primary source for its district heating systems (Göteborg, Energie AB 1998). Only part of this, the carbon neutral, ecologically managed, closed-loop component, can be regarded as a reasonably renewable power source.

Meanwhile, the combination of rising fossil energy prices and increased carbon costs makes financially expedient the current structural moves to alternatives, as do tougher environmental regulations; moreover, growing awareness and bold civic action in ecologically driven urban recycling and reuse programmes serve to boost the evolution of sustainable, fully renewable bio-energy systems. Herein lies the major bio-fuel challenge: to engender a fully renewable, biomass-centred energy industry capable of supporting the strategy of an aspiring Renewable City, but an industry that does not rely on the direct combustion of biomass or on energy-intensive fuel production processes that emit toxins and are based on water depleting, fertiliser rich and pesticide laden fuel crops.

Modern cities have evolved into enormous waste machines, transforming biomass along with other resources at a precipitous rate (Lynch 1990). They devour life – biomass – in the form of plants and animals (ie in its *phyto-* and *zooform* incarnation) while sustaining and enriching lives and livelihoods. They inefficiently transform these constant and growing, largely finite or declining resource streams – of materials, water, food and energy – into a mass of sludge, solid waste and air, soil and water pollution. Indeed, while up to 200 square kilometres of marine and agricultural land and forests on average are required to supply 1 square kilometre of a large city at the Baltic Sea (not among the most wasteful of cities), up to 1,000 square kilometres ie five times as much natural lands, waterways and woodlands are used to absorb the waste flow created (Costanza and Folke 1997).

Under continual pressure to increase energy supply to satisfy aspirations of never-ending growth, and already in a manic fossil resource-kindling mood, one may be tempted to simply set light to the solid and dried liquid waste streams, and harness their unused power. Indeed, a growing number of cities do, and many have done so for a long time. Tokyo and Seoul are only two of the more aggressive among a legion of municipal household waste incinerators. Indeed, waste incineration may appear like a brilliantly efficient solution, but unless planned for as a transitional measure only, it can serve to delay the curtailing of excessive consumption, and even encourage it. It distracts from the greater challenge of greater sufficiency in curtailed consumption, and in recycling and reusing instead. Domestic waste incineration is not a source of renewable energy, and cities and their waste streams are no biomass energy farms, not even their landfill sites. Still, harvesting methane and other *landfill gases* is far better than releasing it into the atmosphere – methane is a highly potent greenhouse agent, far more powerful by weight than carbon dioxide. And like sewage mining for fuel, fertiliser and filtered water, the composting and digesting of irreducible organic wastes into biogas and fuel, too, is a valid form of reuse – but, strictly speaking, not a renewable source of energy. In the agricultural domain, each cow alone, its excrement duly collected and transformed into gas, stands armed and ready to contribute 1 cubic metre of gas to the powering of the economy each day – the equivalent of 0.6 litres of petroleum heating oil (Dürrschmidt et al 2004, p 60). When produced and harvested sustainably, biogas and biofuel become significant power sources for the Renewable City.

*The use of plant oil as fuel may be insignificant today. But over time such products can become as important as petroleum and the coal-tar-products of today.* Rudolf Diesel, 1912, in his patent application (Eurosolar 2005). Originally, the diesel engine was developed to run on hempseed oil.

**Biogas and biofuel** offer a faint beacon of hope for the post-fossil fuel world. They have begun to supplement fuels for commercial fleets, mass motorists and municipal, institutional and other cogeneration plants, both urban and remote. The combined generation of electricity and heat is the most efficient and effective way of using biofuel and gas for stationary, ie non-transport uses, followed by single-output steam turbines and Sterling engines. When turned into gas, biofuel also lends itself well to use in gas turbines. In the more distant future, like liquid biofuel, it will be a good source for efficient hydrogen fuel cells. Biofuel and gas are derived in part from agricultural wastes such as rice husks, cane residues or grass, the last demonstrated by the world's first grass power plant in Schaffhausen, Germany (Alt 2005a). For dedicated fuel production, a range of plants including rape, lupin, pea, summer barley and linseed is used, to name but a few. Poplars, willows, bamboo and other trees and grasses can be planted for closed-loop biofuel and gas extraction in short cycles of a few years (Dürrschmidt et al 2004, p 59). And coconuts provide a new source of energy and livelihood for remote island settlements of the South Pacific. Coconut oil is a high-quality biofuel when blended with kerosene and diesel, in addition to its widespread use as healing and cooking oil and soap compound. Its role as a fuel can be traced to the experimentation and improvisation with coconut-based diesel carried out by occupying forces in the Philippines during the Second World War (Etherington 2005).

Generally speaking, wood supplies the most effective *biogenous* fuels while sugar-rich plants such as cane, beet or corn are an efficient source of ethanol. Oil-rich plants – sunflower and other seeds – lend themselves to pressing to release bio-oil. Liquid sewage, food waste and other organic matter can be digested into biogas, either separately or jointly with animal waste, via an anaerobic, methane-bacterial fermentation process that has been well established since 1948, the year Germany's pioneer Odenwald plant commenced operations. But wood, too, is readily turned into bio gas and has been prior to and during the Second World War. Wood gas has powered trucks and other vehicles in Japan, Germany and elsewhere.

Biofuel plants can pose monoculture problems, but no more so than modern industrial agriculture methods dedicated to food and animal feed production. Biogas production places less demand on the purity and nature of the processed plant material than conventional agro-industry, and lends itself to environmentally more benign *polyculture* farming. A number of energy plant varieties can be cultivated and harvested either in rotation or in combination. If carried out under ecologically sustainable land management principles of *permaculture*, this is a positive step towards rejuvenating agriculture, and the regeneration and revalorisation of city – regional economic interactions. Biogas and biofuels such as bio-diesel – *esterised* sunflower seed or other plant oil – are part of a series of useful bio- and biochemical products, including industrial bio-lubricants. Biofuel and biogas burn efficiently, and at a lower waste rate than petroleum products. Plain plant oil, in its *unesterised* form, is an excellent and efficient fuel for locally supplied bulk users: dedicated vehicle fleets, distribution centres and courier or transport companies. It requires basic engine conversions, local plant oil manufacture or milling plant and results in cleaner, cheaper transport power.

The German *Energiewirtschaftsgesetz* – 'energy economy law' – ratified by the German parliament on 16 June 2005, opened the doors to the feeding of biogas into the natural gas network during supply bottlenecks. This represents a great boon to applications in heat-power cogeneration plants supplying district-heated urban areas, hospitals, universities and business parks. In Sweden the world's first biogas powered train was introduced in late June 2005, in a country with a growing number of biogas powered cars and buses: 50 per cent above the European Union's average. Sweden sees biogas as an important component in the race to achieve national energy autonomy: biogas can easily be produced locally, yet forms a major pillar of national industry (Alt 2005b). In early 2006

Sweden announced its aim to become petroleum independent within the next decade. As in Sweden, the German success in promoting biofuel was founded on essential tax exemptions to help nurture the industry as an independent market player. Political attempts by the fossil fuel lobby at removing these exemptions and to require a blending with conventional combustion fuels were by the German parliament in 2006.

## Regional and national roles

Biogas and biomass production lends itself well to peri-urban, regional production aimed at urban markets. The rejuvenation of the agro-forestry industry in Germany has been based in part on transforming traditional farmers into energy producers, both for specific fuel plant harvesting and for the generation of biogas from farm waste. In 2006, Germany operates 1,500 biogas plants; it is estimated that a potential capacity of 200,000 may be in operation nationwide: almost 10 per cent of Germany's primary energy needs could be supplied through biomass alone (Dürrschmidt et al 2004, p 63). As a consequence, energy farms are an essential component of modern regional plans aimed at metropolitan and urban autonomy. Comprehensive energy farm portfolios include wind power and regional, large-scale solar farms and power plants. All of these energy products can be used to generate transport fuel, also in the form of renewable hydrogen.

Biofuel production partnerships and networks work to build a strategic asset in a community's regional strength, deepening and diversifying a city's regional economy and employment base. Until open market conditions favour energy farming, a multitiered approach is most useful in helping nurture an equitable market environment. This requires a state, regional or, better, national and international legal framework, dedicated land use provisions and incentives and, if necessary, regional and municipal finance arrangements.

Ultimately, biogas and other forms of agricultural energy production should be allowed to operate in free market conditions by internalising external petroleum costs, and removing fossil and nuclear fuel supports. International trade arrangements should be structured to help boost biofuel access to both stationary and transport-geared fuel markets.

Biofuel can be produced and deployed in virtually all parts of the world, at all levels of development. It transforms the globalised fuel-distribution regime into local or regional production. Its employment effectiveness is high. By 2010, the European Union's biofuel market alone is projected to reach an annual turnover of between €14 and 21 billion, before duty and tax (Ecofys 2005).

**Munich – biofuel city** In Munich, a civic action group, Green City, has founded a specialised renewable energy company, Green City Energy (GCE), to develop renewable resources for the city, expanding its non-profit renewable energy work with even greater focus. In addition to the urban solar installations previously advanced by Green City, the new company promotes a modest inner-city waterpower installation along the city's green River Isar, biogas production, plant oil generation, solar power and energy contracting services.

GCE formed a partnership with a bio-crop concern, Bioland Markt in December 2005 to provide a massive push to the transition between the fossil fuel and the biofuel age: the Organic Oil Company (OOC). The new venture is financed through a Munich-based share and options float. The aim is to produce 10 million litres of plant oil by 2009 for Munich's municipal market, powering some 10,000 re-engineered diesel vehicles. Commercial users such as freight operators are particularly interested. Another popular use is expected to be Munich's traditional district and urban block-based power plants, generating combined heat and power (adapted from Alt 2005c; Green City 2005).

## 4.4 URBAN RENEWABLE POWER FINANCE

To transform a city's power system requires open energy markets. Without such access renewable power systems will not be allowed to gradually and, ultimately, fully replace fossil and nuclear sources. The conventional energy market is very much closed to all but a few players, providers and power sources. Its opening up will come in stages, initially with financial levers and incentives as essential forms of renewable energy affirmative action to enable the process of market transformation to commence. In the mid 2000s, most markets are massively skewed towards fossil fuels and nuclear power; without the present preferential treatment these sources would be far less affordable. This market imbalance is further exacerbated by political bias responding to the influence wielded by powerful and vested interests. Annual global subsidies lavished on the fossil and nuclear industries amount to hundreds of billions in US dollars, a hundred-fold larger than all support of renewable systems combined. Tax breaks, public underwriting of bankruptcy and insurance costs, research grants and a century of direct development subsidies ensure the continued reign of a fatally flawed energy base – while a chorus of feigned protest rises among conventional power supporters whenever the possibility of support for renewable energy is even mentioned (Scheer 2005, pp 227–30).

Distorting markets even further in favour of the established yet irredeemably antiquated power systems, conventional financial analysis does not account for the dramatic and rising environmental risks and costs of fossil and nuclear power: oil spills and radiation leaks, pollution, cancers and respiratory diseases, global warming, fresh water depletion and so on. Many automobile users are aware that the cost of petroleum transport fuel would more than double if only the most rudimentary of these external costs were to be internalised in the price at the fuel pump (Appenzeller 2004). Yet few have a choice of fuel, or the means of altering the financial reward structure for petrol production. By the same token, the conventional economic model does not account for the corollary environmental benefits of renewable energy. If fossil fuel's external costs are not expressed in its price, the external benefits of renewable energy need to be internalised in the form of subsidies and incentives.

Voters and decision-makers in a significant number of countries concur in principle and policy that it is justified to impose limitations on the support and bias enjoyed by conventional power sources, and at the same time build a solid support base for renewable energy until a healthy, fully priced, self-supporting renewable market can be established. Cities have important roles to play in this transformation, both in the reduction of the costs inherent in conventional systems and in establishing the means by which increased and routine efficiency measures, and the use of sun, wind, biofuel and other renewable sources can begin to take root. To expand the use of one increasingly popular and versatile urban power source alone – photovoltaic systems – a range of tools is available to facilitate investment in its deployment, operation and innovation such as fostering the integration of energy systems and building construction. The European Community (EC) funded 2001 *Solar City Guide* was assembled by Madrid's policy and research organisation Institut Cerda working with a group of a half dozen other organizations and companies. Written to help the broad introduction of photovoltaic systems in European cities, it classifies the most widely applied financial levers into two categories: those supporting the development and production of renewable energy technology; and those stimulating their commercialisation (Cerda 2001, p 40). Other good generic overviews of financial support instruments are contained in the US focused *Database of State Incentives for Renewable Energy* (DSIRE 2006).

## Development and production

The Cerda Institute and its EC-funded partners identified a range of production finance arrangements. These are variations of these, not alternative approaches.

(a) Feed-in tariffs denote legislated requirements for power utilities to compensate renewable energy generators at set acquisition fees, loosely referred to as *buy-back rates* in the United States. Spain's photovoltaic boom was to a large extent triggered by a December 1998 law making it mandatory for privately generated renewable electricity to be purchased at minimum or prime rates. Main aims were the immediate development of local, also urban markets involving largely private customers, as well as the stimulation of renewable markets. The German and Spanish *Renewable Energy Feed-in Tariff* laws – dubbed here REFIT in deference to the standards of EC acronymic poetry – served to accelerate renewable energy generation capacity, and particularly that of wind and photovoltaic power. The time horizon of financial guarantees is as important as the REFIT prices themselves, usually differentiated according to various sources of renewable power to take account of generation costs. While rates are guaranteed for a time period sufficient to secure an acceptable investment return (Cerda 2005, p 42), these are also often scaled to decline and be phased out over time in anticipation of the establishment of a self-supporting market.

The German 100,000 Solar Roof programme was introduced as a REFIT-based implementation mechanism. It was designed to structure and channel investment in a simplified manner, focusing on stimulating the interest of individuals and small- and medium-size companies to invest in grid-connected photovoltaic installations. The country's Renewable Energy Source Act (EEG) originally provided for €0.49 to be paid for each solar kilowatt hour supplied into the grid; it greatly assisted in meeting the solar roof target early. It was so successful that it temporarily exhausted supplies.

A good example of urban production incentives for PV power is offered by Aspen, Colorado. The example shows that even without national and state support, cities can establish their own incentives – but it helps greatly if the electricity utility is owned and operated by local government. Aspen's tradition of solar support goes back to the 1990s: the city pioneered production encouragements for residents, rewarding the installation of photovoltaic systems with up to $3,000 in incentives. The city formed a non-profit organisation, the Community Office for Resource Efficiency (CORE). In running the programme it rewards participant homes or businesses with payments at 3.5 times Colorado's retail electricity price. The programme was started with support from the International Local Environmental Initiative (ICLEI) and Aspen's Municipal Utility, with continuing assistance from Aspen and Pitkin County's Renewable Energy Mitigation Program (REMP). State government also provided credits, helping to lower installation costs by one third. The recovery of investment through actual electricity generation was presented and experienced as a crucial benefit, stimulating demand greatly (ICLEI 2005b).

(b) Renewable bidding processes are used to ensure that the most economic renewable projects are selected for implementation. Cities can contract for a given amount of renewable electricity or biofuel supply on the open market – provided, of course, suppliers can be found.

(c) Green energy pricing is a means of financing renewable energy bidding procedures while allowing energy customers to specify and pay for a given amount of guaranteed and certified renewable power content in their supply. Green energy pricing typically applies to electricity supply.

(d) Solar stock exchanges are forming in a further elaboration of this new reality. Spearheaded by the pioneering Swiss municipal utilities of Birseck and Neuchâtel in the 1990s, and dubbed *solar stock exchange* by the city of Zürich's electric power company, the system operates as solar power purchaser and retailer, acquiring renewable electricity at cost from grid-connected generators and selling it at the same rate to end-users – a pro-active, city-based version of the feed-in law concept (Cerda et al 2001, pp 43 and 44).

**Renewable energy certificate system** (RECS) and **Renewable Portfolio Standards** (RPS)/**Mandatory Renewable Energy Targets** (MRET). Through their utilities, countries, cities and states can issue renewable energy certificates (RECs) that reflect the renewable power produced, such as that generated by home-based or other small solar energy systems. Applied in this way RECs in effect substitute for the net metering of solar electricity and associated feed-in tariffs. New Mexico in its new REC programme values each certificate at one kilowatt-hour, for example. Government authorities typically grant certificates or credits to satisfy their *Renewable Portfolio Standards*, also sometimes known as *Mandatory Renewable Generation Targets* for a state, city region or nation. Certificates, or credits, are issued to reflect these targets, guaranteeing a narrow market for the new generation of renewable power. This approach allows electricity purchasers to acquire a certain amount of renewable power from renewable generators – but it also can penalise them if they fail to do so. In Australia's case one certificate equals one megawatt-hour of renewable energy generated or an equal amount of fossil energy displaced by a solar water heater. The system fails to work properly if the targets are set too low, or an insufficiently long operating time frame is provided to secure market and planning certainty. RECS systems nominally operate in Europe, Australia, the United States and other parts of the world. At the time of writing this book the United States certificates were not tradable in a market sense, but issued and reimbursed by a utility (DSIRE 2006; ORER 2006; PNM 2006; RECS 2006).

**Production partnerships** The Cape Light Compact example. In 1997, 21 towns on Cape Cod, Massachusetts, created the Cape Light Compact (CLS). The aim was to secure lower electricity rates for their citizens and at the same time develop renewable energy, using power contracts in a voluntary arrangement. CLC gives consumers the choice of collectively securing power through local governments, at a financially advantageous rate. By hammering out supply contracts, municipalities can set the proportion of renewable energy provided. Communities can also provide preferential prices and support for disadvantaged citizens (CLC 2005).

## Commercialisation

The Cerda Institute also found a number of commercialisation aid systems, mechanisms applied to reduce the initial capital costs of photovoltaic installations. These were essential to the success of these projects, especially in Japan, world leader in such applications. All countries granting such commercialisation supports recognise their artificial nature but see them as essential as temporary measures.

(a) Grants or subsidies are the most commonly used forms of investment support. Almost every European country has subsidy programmes aimed at compensating for 30 to 50 per cent of the capital expenditures for photovoltaic and sometimes other renewable energy systems.

Japan has recently begun to phase out subsidies, while the market for photovoltaic applications is expected to grow at 20 per cent annually – even without support. Subsidies are sometimes scaled according to particular sources used. As an example, while photovoltaic electricity production costs exceed those of wind generation, the photovoltaic output cost is identical with the final cost to the customer: building-integrated photovoltaic systems do not incur transmission and distribution costs. Hence photovoltaic electricity can compete with lower-cost but remote resources, particularly if subsidies reflect these differentials. Also, subsidies can be fine-tuned to reflect the needs of cities and their citizens. In Japan residential photovoltaic systems make up 85 per cent of the overall PV share: here cities focus their implementation strategies on new urban dwelling construction programmes. It proved to be important that government subsidies were relevant to different types of development in Japan's cities, supporting installations in individual homes, area-wide supply networks for residential developments, or assisting local organisations chartered to introduce residential photovoltaic systems (Tanaka 2004).

(b) Fiscal incentives are both effective and popular in limiting cost. Many countries in Europe provide tax credits towards the cost of photovoltaic systems and other energy sustainability measures, or allow the acceleration of capital depreciation. As an example, the Italian government offers a tax reduction of up to 36 per cent for investments in renewable energy sources, which can be written off in five or ten years. The United States commenced with a limited national solar tax credit scheme in March 2006, adding to its national incentives portfolio also aimed at efficiency (Luce 2006).

(c) Low-interest loans are often granted at below market rates to help lower system cost. Interest rates are often fixed throughout the loan term, usually for between ten and 20 years. Grace periods for loan repayments can be granted as well (Cerda 2001, pp 40–1).

(d) Renewable energy bonds can be issued by cities or states. The best-known example is that of San Francisco where a US$ 100-million solar bond initiative was adopted in 2001, supported by voters to fund efficiency measures, wind turbines and solar panels for municipal structures. The bond was secured from funds that would otherwise have been invested in conventional power, and its expenditure was combined with a financial method of buffering the risk of photovoltaic power by combining solar projects with commercially viable wind power and short-payback efficiency measures (Vote Solar 2006).

(e) Another form of commercialisation support, not of a financial but of a market-creating nature, is the introduction of regulatory requirements. One of the most progressive of these statutory paths to renewability in urban development is Barcelona's *Ordenanza Solar*, inspired by an earlier ordinance drafted in Berlin. Barcelona calculated its solar energy supply potential, and on 1 August 2000 introduced a regulatory system requiring households and industrial users to provide at least 60 per cent of their hot water requirement through solar systems. The scheme is focused, specific and practical. It was also based on intensive community engagement. An early inquiry revealed that 80 per cent of Barcelona's citizens were willing to pay 10 per cent more for renewable than fossil energy – another important factor in initiating the programme. Solar ordinances following Barcelona's example are increasingly in use in other urban communities, such as Mardid, Seville and a host of other Spanish cities and towns, and elsewhere in Europe, such as Vellmar, Germany (Barcelona 2000; Dürrschmidt et al 2004).

### Italy's solar roofs: targeted deployment to boost commercialisation

As an example of a traditional, outright grants programme, the Italian Ministry of Environment commenced its national Photovoltaic Roofs programme in 2001. This entailed the installation of grid-connected plants on buildings, roofs, in facades and other elements of urban infrastructure, modestly sized at capacities of up to 50 kilowatt per installation. The focus was on highly visible features of the civic infrastructure, and the general population; ie on (a) facilities in provincial capitals, municipalities in regional and national parks, provinces, universities and national research institutes; (b) small cities, corporations, households; and (c) buildings of architectural significance. The Environment Ministry grants up to 85 per cent of pre-tax investment cost (Cerda 2005, p 42).

### Urban project finance through partnerships

To advance renewable urban development projects, few support mechanisms are ever used in isolation; combinations of support mechanisms and partnerships are typically employed. As a broadly well-liked example, the so-called zero emissions development in Beddington, BedZed 6, in the United Kingdom was advanced by a consortium of private investors and companies and both government and non-government organisations. Seed capital was provided by BioRegional Development, a charitable agency devoted to commercialising sustainable enterprises, with additional marketing resources granted by the World Wildlife Fund, prior to site selection. Finally, an innovative and well-established social housing association, the Peabody Trust, was introduced as investor and developer (Dunster 2005; Stockholm Partnerships for Sustainable Cities, 2006).

## Financial benefits of distributed energy: direct renewable power and cogeneration

The merits of energy decentralisation have been discussed earlier. This is a good opportunity to reflect briefly on the intrinsic financial advantages of distributed power to urban users – as opposed to grants, incentives and other market correction mechanisms. There are two basic choices: direct renewable power supply such as solar panels or wind turbines, or combined heat and electricity generators – cogeneration – using conventional or renewable fuels, or a combination of these.

## Direct renewable power

When purchased outright, solar cell modules and other direct renewable energy equipment may well seem more costly in the initial years, but this investment does not only achieve good amortisation rates but also translates into lower risks, for both small and large customers. Such renewable energy sources can serve as a financial hedge: once installed, their generation costs remain stable. Indeed, producers of renewable energy other than biomass sources – sun, wind, or water – avoid the cost or price variations that are the bane of fossil and nuclear producers. Renewable energy systems can also be more readily implemented incrementally, sidestepping the risks of large initial outlays in central plants. Individual, institutional and commercial users can install distributed systems without initial systems outlays by contracting specialised providers. These finance, develop and manage plants, and invoice use rates that are generally lower than those of conventional utilities.

Renewable energy generation – and its potential – can also improve property values. The United States *Appraisal Journal* cites some regional evidence that home value appreciated significantly in relation to reductions in annual utility bills. This study related to energy efficiency measures, but it would seem plausible that similar dynamics would apply to distributed generation as well, translating into some relative property value advantages linked to sun exposure, for example (Perlman 2005). Such advantages could translate into higher credit leverage potentials, possibly supporting the commercial financing of renewable energy capture systems.

## Cogeneration

This technology uses a wide spectrum of generators that work with a range of fuels to produce both electric power and heat. Depending on power prices, cogeneration may prove less costly when aiming at producing a significant share of the total power used locally. And cogeneration delivers greater operational reliability, translating into reduced financial risk for companies and institutions. After decades of development in major applications from universities to hospitals, cogeneration is growing in popularity in an increasingly wide range of applications as a stand-alone alternative to unreliable and unsustainable power grids as new biofuel and hydrogen options become available. A generic method of converting a range of fuels into electricity and heat, the technology is emerging as a central player in the evolution of Renewable Cities. Cogeneration is a powerful, reliable, non-intermittent pillar in any distributed power regime – an energy *server* in the evolving e-web. A wide range of robust machinery is readily deployed, capable of handling a range of fuels: it is not only a good conversion medium for biofuel and biogas, but can also be adapted for a range of different sources over time. This mature technology lends itself to several urban applications that are more affordable than utility power, even when considering short payback periods. Owners and operators save or earn the price of power, depending on whether the electricity is consumed locally, sold to a larger power supplier, or directly provided to other users. The power company purchasing surplus cogeneration electricity receives the benefits of a stronger grid under less strain, but it may bear the marginal burden of having to balance irregular power inputs (Perlman 2005).

Cogeneration can take on a wider purpose as core municipal and reliable, primary power source. In Sweden, the City of Gothenburg's utility, Göteborg Energi AB, pursues the strategic expansion of municipal biomass development for municipal electricity, transport fuel production and district heating supplementation. Biomass here becomes a single source with multiple energy stream benefits, adding bio-oil and diesel production opportunities (Göteborg 1998). And the small town of Jühnde in northern Germany demonstrates through its village-wide heat and power generation the practical feasibility of comprehensive, community-wide power supply utilising only renewable energy. The fuel is provided solely through bio-energy sources: the waste from 2,400 pigs and cows is supplemented with plant-based material (Eurosolar 2006).

## 4.5 MUNICIPAL POWER

Worldwide experience teaches two general rules. One holds that wherever reasonable opportunities exist to introduce municipal power companies, this should be done with determination, energy, speed and persistence. And if any move is underfoot to disband an existing local energy utility and replace it with a regional or private supplier with little local accountability, this should be resisted at all cost.

The reason for this advice is simple: in the battle for planned energy transformation, few government agencies have proven to be as useful as have municipal power providers, lovingly referred to as 'munis' in the United States. Such local utilities can manifest themselves as any or all of the following: accountable policy setting agencies with a charter to specify service levels and provisions according to a strategic plan; fully developed and publicly accountable service providers, ie traditional utilities, or dedicated providers of certain types of energy needs or equipment. Local community involvement can also take the form of full or part ownership in regional or local energy generation assets. Deregulated and restructured statewide or national, private, public or quasi-public organisations are typically not accountable to local area or municipal needs. As a general observation these will pursue their agenda according to abstract market principles, and typically only within the infrastructure and policy parameters of fossil and nuclear energy industries. As a rule, they will pursue some efficiency or green power programmes, but these are seldom more than lip service paid to popular concerns and community pressures.

Large regional utilities throughout the world, whether in Western Europe, the United States, East Asia or southern Africa, see their core business as lying in increasing large-scale fossil and nuclear power supply, not general energy and resource management. To them, renewable energy is culturally alien and an inexpedient nuisance. A typical example was the 2002 lobbying by California's three large utilities, Southern California Edison, Pacific Gas & Electric and Sempra Energy Resources, to undo the state's net-metering laws. The group raised spurious arguments of administrative difficulties and excessive costs (Hochschild et al 2002). Neither proved to be correct, but this small episode is a good illustration of the intrinsic difficulties such anonymous entities face in their organisation and charter when they are challenged to evolve institutionally.

By contrast, some of the most extraordinary advances in urban energy practice were made possible by the enlightened management of dedicated, city-owned and operated power supply companies. The cities of Aspen, Barcelona, Los Angeles, Munich, Palermo, Sacramento, Saarbrücken, Silicon Valley and Zürich – among many others referred to in this book – have benefited enormously from the accountability, commitment and resourcefulness of their local power providers or municipal power departments. The key is local ownership and control: whether comprehensive utilities exist or not, in principle all communities can take an active and controlling share in renewable energy production assets, as in Melbourne's inner-city photovoltaic and regional wind investments, or the community ownership experience in Luxembourg's Heinerscheid wind farm, where the local council sold its shares to local citizens; or the successful local ownership model of heat storage facilities in new medium-density suburbs of Hannover, Germany, in the solar district heating precinct of Kronsberg near the city's famed Messe district.

Municipal influence can be exerted through direct ownership control, policy guidance, or both. This makes the very process of transforming local policy and supply dependence into municipal forms of control so attractive: municipalisation. The story of giving birth to SMUD, the Sacramento Municipal Utility District, in a long, eight-year process of taking over California's Pacific Gas and Electric Company has been described in Chapter 3. Such takeover processes can be expensive and difficult, and the SMUD story is an important warning to perhaps reform and make more accountable, but never to give up existing municipal utilities and public energy assets. While large private operators usually heap scorn on attempts at municipalisation as resulting in organisations that are inefficient, ineffective, inexperienced or worse, evidence from North America suggests that the vast majority of public power companies in the United States – serving almost 20 per cent of the population – operate at lower overheads, more responsively and are cheaper: they charge on average only 69 per cent the rate at which private operators bill their customers (Moore and Rosenfield 2001).

There is one possible exception to the two general rules of municipal power. It would apply if national governments were to mandate the transformation of all energy utilities into renewable energy facilitation operations, policy institutes and separate renewable operators. But, unfortunately, this day appears to be some time in the future. Until then, municipal power assets are still the best path to a renewable future, institutionally speaking.

### Rise of the renewable building
Swiss Re Tower by Foster and Partners, also known as the Gherkin Tower (built 2001–2004) is billed as one of the most advanced sustainable office towers in the world. Lloyds Building by Richard Rogers Partnership (1979–1984) in the foreground, is a monument to high-tech symbolism of another era. Both London buildings are home to members of the global insurance industry, long alarmed about the urban impacts of climate change.

# CHAPTER 5

# Renewable City buildings: guidance and learning

Buildings are the basic building blocks of cities and towns – the elementary operational unit of all human settlements, whether they accommodate families, enterprises or livestock; laboratories, airport functions or assembly lines. This chapter first examines basic tools of measuring and guiding the energy performance of buildings. Following an overview of the assessment, rating, design and planning tools, we will examine what can be learned from the world's most advanced building practices. Only a very small fraction of all buildings are designed by architects; nevertheless, their experience does offer some general lessons for their colleagues, their clients and local governments.

## 5.1 RENEWABLE CITY BUILDING TOOLS: RATING PERFORMANCE

Individual buildings account for the lion's share of urban energy consumption, as constructed, managed and operated systems and as settings of social use patterns and cultural conventions. In response, a rich world of commercially available building rating tools and associated services has evolved, ready to gauge and help improve the performance of these basic building blocks of the Renewable City. This world of tools has flourished amid (a) increased competitiveness in real estate performance and quality; (b) a rise in corporate responsibility drives; and (c) broadly toughening public policy instruments, in energy pricing, fiscal and development incentives and performance regulation. It is a scenario that parallels the rating boom in many industrial and material development and production processes: assessing embodied and operating energy performance in the steel industry, in wood processing, or for motor vehicles, household appliances and other consumer products, in their development, manufacture and reuse. The concept of *lifecycle* has also become redefined as a true cycle, not a one-way-street to the scrap heap, but allowing material to move from one life as an appliance, textile product or building to the next – '*cradle to cradle*', as a United States dean of sustainable design, William McDonough, has trademarked the notion into a handsomely profitable service business (McDonough and Braungart 2002).

Acronyms and labels such as BASIX, BREEAM, Energy Star, LCAid, LEED and NABERS denote but a few among many methods designed for market-driven environments with a low level of statutory building performance requirements, or the ideological aversion to government imposed regulatory direction in bulwarks of business *laissez-faire* such as Australia, the United Kingdom or the United States. Here, they are warmly embraced as tools to help inform, guide and reward investors, developers, owners, operators, designers, clients and users – and to stave off government regulation regarded as intrusive and heavy-handed. But they are also increasingly called for by city governments, or deployed as disincentives for failure to attain certain standards: in the selection of tenders in construction and development bids, for example. Rating tools are used in evaluating and characterising new and existing buildings in their energy behaviour, greenhouse gas emissions and wider environmental performance. However, reliable and sophisticated methods of evaluating urban areas are hard to find. These are often specially developed for specific areas, such as the Australian state of Victoria government's *Ecologically Sustainable Development (ESD) Guide* for the Melbourne Docklands (Docklands Authority 2002).

In the absence of adequate regulatory guidance, rating tools increasingly serve as specifications for the Renewable City's architecture. Urban and regional governments, communities and business alliances can adopt a three-tiered approach in their deployment. They can (a) help promote state, national and industry-wide legislation and regulation; (b) set their own specific and overall performance criteria that take into account both public and private assets, and can be readily benchmarked against other cities; and (c) they can require that developers commit to and demonstrate performance within one of the commercial or government-devised rating systems available. And in planning, development and approval applications they are best used in three ways: (a) during concept development, design and feasibility, to test and demonstrate the cost, design, energy and wider sustainability impacts of programme, material and design and engineering choices; (b) in rating final designs for negotiations, commitments and agreements during the bidding and approvals processes; and (c) in monitoring and assessing the building or facility in question: for the verification of compliance with commitments made, and for post-occupancy evaluations of the overall structure as used, managed and experienced. Different tools are applied to different stages: this Renewable City guide highlights a handful of the most promising initiatives found around the world today.

## Breeam

This is the *Environmental Assessment Method* developed, promoted and applied for a over a decade by the Building Research and Consultancy (BRE), the 650-strong British research, testing and advisory service, to gauge the environmental performance of new and existing buildings. A wide range of environmental parameters is covered. Structures are rated in design or their final built form, and the parameters presented in ways that are easily comprehended and applied by building developers and managers. Buildings can be evaluated on eight criteria: (a) *management*: overall policy, site management and procedures; (b) operational *energy use* and greenhouse performance, disregarding embodied energy; (c) *indoor and external dimensions of health and well-being*; (d) *air and water pollution* impacts; (e) *transport*: defined as location-specific, transport-related greenhouse gas emissions; (f) *land use relevance*: a building's location in a greenfields versus, preferably, a brownfields site; (g) *ecological conservation and regeneration* relevance; (h) environmental impacts of *building materials*, including life-cycle considerations; and (i) *water consumption and use efficiency*.

BREEAM is used to assess and rate structures that include offices, homes, industrial developments, retail space and schools. The tool is promoted for marketing as well as design purposes. It suggests that all involved in the development process – owners, developers, agencies, designers, managers and building researchers – apply it to specify the sustainability performance of buildings in a market relevant way. Designers deploy BREEAM to enhance their understanding and ability to create better buildings. Building managers apply it to monitor facility portfolios and devise management, maintenance and adjustment programmes. Real estate sales professionals incorporate BREEAM ratings to brand buildings and developments in their promotional campaigns (BRE 2005).

## Energy Star

This is a United States government-sponsored public interest programme reinforcing good practice by labelling and rewarding high levels of energy efficiency, and the effectiveness of renewable energy installations. It provides a number of useful software tools and other resources on-line and free of charge. It exemplifies how government can advocate limited but important voluntary individual and business commitments: significant where the government's political leadership does little to promote or implement effective and strategic change. This phenomenon of strong and visible public programmes designed to prod consumers and industry in the absence of a tangible national commitment is a feature common to a number of countries reluctant to embrace national emissions control lest these hamper fast-fading concepts of economic prowess, including the United States, Australia, Canada, South Korea and Japan.

The United States Environmental Protection Agency (US EPA), in partnership with the Department of Energy (US DoE), has long rewarded good energy performance across a range of products and services, from refrigerators to buildings. Rudimentary tools like Energy Star and the *national energy performance rating system* that support it should be critically reviewed in their effectiveness, and aggressively expanded, crossing into city- and state-based statutory controls. In the interim they should be promoted strongly by cities and urban communities as a starting point, in partnership with provincial and national agencies, for use by the entire development and asset management industry, building owners, users and designers.

The Energy Star programme features a set of software tools available to owners and operators of a range of building types wishing to monitor and manage the energy performance of their assets. One of these is *Portfolio Manager*, designed for commercial asset managers to boost their energy-sensitive decision-making capability. It rates buildings on a 1–100 scale in relation to a nationwide reference set of comparable buildings, applying US EPA's *national energy performance rating system*. Scores above 75 qualify for the Energy Star label. Annual weather variability, geographic location, facility scale and type from offices to warehouses, as well as a set of operational aspects are considered. Energy consumption, intensity and overall rating can be viewed at the same time; and access to the system can be networked throughout an organisation. Important portfolio and individual asset management decisions can flow from such insight. A sub-tool, *Target Finder*, is also accessible free of charge and usable via the Internet. It assists architects, engineers and other building designers in creating power targets and budgets. Another tool, dubbed *Delta Score Estimator*, helps relate energy savings directly to the energy performance rating system (EPA 2006b).

## LCAid

This is the *Environmental Life Cycle Assessment Design Aid* software package developed by the New South Wales state Department of Public Works and Services in Sydney, Australia. It is an example of a software tool that allows life-cycle assessments during the building design process: evaluations of environmental performance over the life of a building, from construction to demolition, disposal or – preferably – reassembly or reuse. The tool permits the integration of other computer-aided design packages within most environmental design parameters; assists in calculating the thermal-energy performance of a design in its climatic setting; and accounts for the energy embodied in the chosen materials. It projects annual operational energy data, given the design and energy systems choices made. Importantly, it allows the instant comparison of a number of options across a number of environmental parameters, and the projected, future evaluation of buildings throughout their entire lifecycle (DPWS 2006).

The **International Energy Agency's** Committee on Energy Research and Technology (IEA CERT), through its Renewable Energy Working Party, operates a cooperative research program specifically focused on lifecycle analysis tools for buildings (Annex 31, 2006).

## LEED

The **LEED** – Leadership in Energy and Environmental Design – *Green Building Rating System*® is promoted by the United States Green Building Council (GBC 2006). GBC started as a property industry based initiative by S Richard Fedrizzi, David A Gottfried and Michael L Italiano to create a voluntary, consensus-based set of building standards. The ambition driving LEED was to establish a commercially viable, common standard of assessment; to promote integrated building design practice; reward competition for environmental leadership in the building industry; raise public and client awareness of so-called green building benefits; and, ultimately, help transform the buildings construction market. LEED helps establish a comprehensive framework for site planning, water and energy efficiency, renewable energy applications, materials selection and indoor environmental quality. LEED promotes improved building practice through a system of project certification, professional accreditation, training and practical resources. However, as yet this is not a system for rating embodied energy or for verifying compliance with commitments made or standards established.

LEED standards are either already available or under development for (a) new commercial construction and major renovation projects – LEED-NC; (b) existing building operations – LEED-EB; (c) commercial interiors – LEED-CI; (d) core and shell projects – LEED-CS – and (e) individual homes, LEED-H. A tool for rating urban areas, ie *Neighborhood Development* (LEED-ND) has been advanced since 2004 in a joint effort with two United States advocacy organisations, the Congress for a New Urbanism (CNU) and the Natural Resources Defense Council (NRDC).

The Green Building Council is also represented in Canada (cagbc.org) and Australia (gbcaus.org) with the establishment of a World Green Building Council (http://www.worldgbc.org) in train. LEED has been adopted and renamed as the *Green Star* rating tool in Australia and, as such, has been made available worldwide on a one-time, royalty-free, promotional basis (GBC 2006).


## NABERS

The *National Australian Built Environment Rating System* is, in 2006, one of the most comprehensive post-construction rating tools on the market or under development. Designed for assessing existing buildings, not for evaluating designs under development, NABERS has been developed for the rating of residential and commercial office buildings by tracking the impacts they have on the environment, both directly and indirectly. The approach is simple but sophisticated: the tool helps examine buildings in the resource and waste stream they foster or help stem; and the energy they cause to be used, conserved or permit to be generated, to support light, heating, cooling and ventilation. It rates the way in which water is managed and used for washing, drinking and air conditioning and how rain and storm water is handled. Local biodiversity impacts are assessed as well.

The tool is designed to help understand the use patterns of occupants and visitors, and how people are affected by the quality of air and light in the building, or the level of toxicity in the materials used. It takes into account the life and work style buildings encourage or discourage in their users, but also the patterns adopted by the user community, such as commuting modes and behaviour. Above all, NABERS interprets the edifice as a social and cultural construct: as an outcome of decisions made before and during the use of the building by owners, managers or tenants (DEUS 2006).

## BASIX

BASIX is the Building Sustainability Index and is an example of how rating tools should work: not as voluntary industry standards, but as mandatory performance screens that are part of local and state government development and building control procedures. It has been introduced in Australia within the greater Sydney area and across the larger New South Wales state planning system. The web-based BASIX is focused on residential building only at this time. It serves as a design, planning and assessment tool, measuring the potential performance of proposed residential dwellings against energy performance, thermal comfort and water consumption. BASIX helps enforce the state government's policy targets of reduction in greenhouse gas emissions as well as water use, likely to shift over time. For new construction permits emission performance is currently limited to 40 per cent of those of average homes or apartment buildings implemented before the legislation. To be granted development approval, each development application must carry a BASIX certificate. Certificates are issued once a BASIX assessment has been satisfactorily completed on-line, using either the *single dwelling* or *multi-unit tool*. Building applicants – architects, builders, owners, developers – complete the assessment themselves; plug-in software and specialised assessment services can be consulted in the rating process (BASIX 2006).

## Built integration: the emergence of renewable building practice

The most advanced buildings today are configured to live up to many of these challenges and opportunities; these are frequently 'urban landmarks' – taller building in dense urban environments, often endowed with renewable attributes to convey a sense of corporate prestige and pride. The best efforts by leading developers and city governments have assembled a rich portfolio of advanced buildings since the early 1990s. Several major architects have positioned themselves as energy and sustainability pioneers. On the climate-minded design of tall buildings the spirited and meticulous work by Ken Yeang stands out (Yeang 1994, 1996, 1999, 2002, 2004, 2006). Yeang fiercely eschews renewable energy generation in favour of a radical commitment to the efficient bio-climatic design of the building itself. Other designers of global landmarks have been less puritan, integrating so-called low energy design with renewable power. Developer Douglas Durst's breakthrough Condé Nast Building at 4 Times Square in New York, by architects Fox + Fowle, pioneered the integration of urban energy technologies in efficient lighting and window design and by the integration of a photovoltaic curtain wall and natural-gas fed fuel-cell combined heat and power generators (DoE 2001). Recent buildings by Norman Foster, too, provide tangible guidance – notably Foster + Partners' Commerzbank headquarters in Frankfurt (1997), extravagantly billed as the 'world's first ecological tower'; Berlin's Reichstag reconfiguration into the German parliament's new plenary facility (1999) and the iconic "Gherkin", the 2004 Swiss Re headquarters in London (Foster et al 2005). Numerous new renewable landmarks are on the drawingboards of well-established design firms around the world, such as SOM's Pearl River Tower for a Guangzhou client group, promising to generate surplus power (see Section 3.3, 'A renewable urbanism' (Meyer 2006)).

Such are the guiding efforts of the global Renewable City elite, but renewable and bio-climatic design of the urban building manifest itself also as daily practice, implemented locally and perhaps more quietly, but with no less civic pride. An important recent example is Melbourne City Council's new building, imaginatively called Council House 2 (CH2). The 10-storey design has been flattered by an extravagant six-star rating by the development friendly Green Building Council of Australia. The ground-floor retail spaces are cooled under a four-storey evaporative shower tower. Thermal mass is a main feature in temperate Melbourne, in floor plates, ceilings and walls. Materials capable of phase changes are used to store and release energy: an army of 30,000 large steel balls stands by in the basement, submerged in cooling water. They contain inorganic salts, a good heat exchange medium. Sun-tracking louvres deflect unwanted sun light from the interior, and walls of vines adorn the sunny side of the facade. Wind turbines power air heating and cooling, and the city sewer is mined and filtered to yield 100,000 litres of clear water for toilet flushing, irrigation, to run nearby fountains and supply street cleaners. The active energy plant is comprised of photovoltaics, solar water heaters and cogeneration equipment. When compared to the current council home, CH2 reduces gas consumption by 87 per cent; emissions by 87 per cent and mains water use by 72 per cent. Elevated design, construction and maintenance costs will be recovered within a decade through reduced fossil energy use, employee health improvements and enhanced workplace effectiveness (Warren Centre 2006).

Given sufficient, integrated design input, and an adequate budget buildings demonstrating such leadership in terms of energy efficiency are within the reach of most local governments. They are increasingly embraced as a form of model action by government to respond to voter concerns, demonstrate direction and help build skills and markets.

## 5.2 LEARNING FROM RENEWABLE BUILDING PRACTICE

Regulatory and market frameworks lag behind global performance needs and aspirations. The conditions for a broad-based transformation of the building industry in procurement, development, design and construction are slow to become established: it is difficult to get a notoriously conservative industry and its governmental guidance framework to respond to immediate change, let alone longer-term needs. As a consequence, the highest expectations are still placed on individual acts of improved practice, as pathfinders, trailblazers, in the hope that others will follow, a market interest is awakened, or an already existing need met. The global fossil energy crisis has prompted a generation of exceptional building efforts by government agencies, companies and individuals around the world, at all scales and in all building types and use categories. What lessons can determined city officials, architects, builders, developers, owners, users and investors learn from the most successful of attempts to improve the performance of individual buildings, on the road to the Renewable City?

This chapter contains a set of conclusions as messages, drawn from a broad series of individual building profiles. It began with a search for a good sample of individual building evaluations; we found that United States building data pools are the best-documented presently available. And due to a paucity of national government regulation in the US, and a characteristic reliance on voluntary action rather than government or building code requirements, some of these may be useful in many other countries that lack firm government direction in environmental performance. And as in some other countries where stunning national, personal and political riches were founded on the story of coal, oil or uranium exploration, or the fossil-fuel economy more broadly, the United States has had difficulties embracing much-needed moves towards renewable energy autonomy at the national policy level. Yet, on the state, city and community level, in small and large communities across the country, among investors, owners, developers and individual users, the degree of entrepreneurial drive, civic leadership and environmental responsibility and achievement is striking, indeed, inspiring. And because many of these accomplishments were the work of individuals – single corporate or personal champions – the rich portfolio of long-standing and innovative solutions to the challenges posed by the fight against fossil-fuel addiction is extremely well documented. The achievements became a matter of civic pride.

The following general and thematic insights have therefore been drawn from 80 projects across a range of building types, based on United States Department of Energy (US DoE) documentation of individual building efforts. The DoE supports research into the environmental performance of buildings, in terms of energy requirements, materials, land use and other areas. Its *High-performance Buildings Database* is an attempt to help general performance by gathering and disseminating building project data from around the world, from medium-density residential projects to commercial complexes; from private homes and office interiors to universities and entire neighbourhoods. Inclusion in the database does not require a prior building energy or environmental rating status or certification, nor that buildings excel across all their features, but it does subject each entered project profile to rigorous performance screening, based on the material submitted. The information, however, is provided by individual entrants and has not been audited or verified (DoE 2006a).

Besides the designers and their firms, a diverse set of commissioning players championed, initiated or drove the process, ranked here in apparent order of frequency or importance in triggering change – along with their primary actions and motivations. The drivers of change were:

- state agencies with building portfolios in health, education, administration, corrections, transportation – in their building procurement programmes, as chartered or directed by government and in their efforts to show leadership;
- local residential building cooperatives and associations – in their development aims and through their charters to develop solutions that are durable and environmentally sound;
- community or neighbourhood organisations – in lobbying for responsible building practice, or in demanding environmental commitments as part of development approval processes;

- private developers – in the pursuit of corporate excellence or responsibility initiatives as public identity management and product promotions;
- individual clients – following a vision of personal rationalism, an altruistic vision to serve, or a desire to generate long-term savings;
- national government departments or agencies – through their facility development efforts, in a desire to accumulate assets of value, show prudent management, demonstrate leadership or follow government policy; to create employee satisfaction and satisfy productivity interests;
- societies or non-profit organisations – in acting as responsible clients; serving their corporate identity interests; or advancing enduring assets;
- private companies – as part of their corporate missions; identity concerns; employee satisfaction and productivity interests;
- universities and public institutions – to be seen as innovators and as part of their corporate identity; pursue employee satisfaction and productivity interests; and to demonstrate a concern for asset longevity and long-term operating budget savings;
- private donors – in pursuit of their funding priorities; and
- international bodies such as the United Nations – as clients in pursuit of a combination of the motivations detailed above.

### General observations and caveats

There is a number of lessons that can be drawn from the Department of Energy's High-performance Buildings portfolio (DoE 2006a); the following conclusions have been extracted for this guide by comparing the individual experiences made and documented therein. These, in a sense, are all pilot or pioneering examples. A first and fundamental message to local, state and national government flows from this: it important to seek mechanisms that successfully secure a faster and more broadly based transformation of the entire building industry rather than lavish all hope and focus on the exceptional, pilot or model project, which can provide model performance to aspire to and a satisfying success experience but makes little difference to overall, citywide performance. Moreover, there is no evidence that exceptional building leadership in itself leads to wider improvements across the building design, building and management sector. Rather, fundamental changes in renewable energy feed-in provisions, supports and requirements exert the most significant change impulses worldwide, while leadership in individual building performance is largely useful to demonstrate how these wider changes can be intelligently managed at the building level, as a form of product development.

## The state of standards, regulations, and rating systems

The most striking observation to be made is that each fossil-fuel tran-scending, environmentally well-performing project is still very much hand-crafted, resulting from an individual, specially motivated initiative: a one-of-a-kind labour of love – a post-massproduction artefact. And it is still celebrated as such: an exceptional achievement, a cut above the rest. It is difficult to find evidence for the building production system as a whole – the vast majority of which does not involve architects – as showing signs of improving beyond the general efficiency and environmental performance gains made in the wider economy. Voluntary performance and rating standards are still very much in their infancy. Few precedents and performance benchmarks exist to guide the public or private owner, manager or developer as performance champion. In the United States, West and East Coast states have moved to improve their building standards, following certain European and Japanese regulatory changes: but these changes are far from adequate to help transform the new and renewed building stock in a decisive enough manner to make deep cuts in greenhouse-gas emissions and fossil-fuel dependency. But while some of what is celeb-rated as environmental innovation and energy efficiency achievement in one country is regarded as standard practice in another, when it comes to renew-able energy integration, exceptional leadership quickly stands out everywhere. There is very limited technical support and guidance available to those determ-ined to generate and implement better building practice anywhere. Existing building standards and benchmarks are not consistent, and do not cover all building types.

Building rating systems are seen as cumbersome, as requiring too much or too detailed documentation. Because of the time and financial resources required for most rating efforts, such systems are not suitable for gauging small-scale projects. Many rating systems are seen as having been devised to satisfy preconceived notions of what constitutes good practice, and hence can fail to register unique and unprecedented solutions. To supplement current rating systems, developers welcome simpler tools to quantify the tangible reduction in environmental cost that can be attributed to particular sustainable building measures. This would make it easier to gauge more directly the environmental benefit each unit of capital outlay would realise.

Rating systems and standards can also be dangerous, and even undermine design by stifling creativity in the process. Rating tools are there to test and confirm choices, but if they are applied without a clear and leading design framework they can have the effect of causing the design team to merely add scores against checklists, rather than develop the most appropriate actions. To avoid this risk, it is also useful that potentially achievable credit ranges are reviewed at the outset of a design exercise, and familiarity and ease with the certification process acquired.

Developers leading in best practice often complain about an absence of means to identify and compensate for the financial risk that may lie in uncertain or longer-term payback periods that can be the result of investing in research, development, implementation and management of renewable energy and other systems. A massive challenge lies in overcoming a broad reliance on agreeable but intangible 'greenspeak' – subjective values and feeble standards expressed and applied by local government in assessing sustainable design. Vague 'smart growth', 'sustainable development' or 'green design' notions, too, are frequently adopted as 'benchmarks' by developers and local governments officials. Their tangible dimensions can be difficult, even impossible to monitor and assess. Broad quality aims must be translated into hard performance criteria: most fundamental and clearly identifiable among these are reductions in fossil fuel consumption, and the degree of reliance on renewable power.

Finally, standards all too readily become a means to an end, in the diligent hands of local governments and their approval officers, assessors and professional institutes. Administrators can get quickly seduced into scrutinising standard compliance, while losing sight of their very purpose and hoped-for outcomes, and, due to the absolute and rigid nature of many standards, find themselves unable to improvise when better means of reaching outcomes become available.

## The design process

Buildings are often seen as hurried through an increasingly shallow design development process, in response to investor and local government pressures, procedures and capacities to absorb. But the creation of renewable buildings, and those that excel in other ways, requires a significantly higher intensity in the pre-design process. A wider range of expertise is required, implying a larger consultation team, involving energy, sustainability and ratings consultants. Some successful project design teams formed partnerships with research institutions or university departments to test solutions and identify the best design strategy.

Closer coordination between team members, and a more careful scrutiny of design progress and products are required. A typical feature of contemporary building development processes is the separation of design and construction teams. This proves to be particularly unhelpful: teams cannot work independently and hope to deliver well-performing buildings. Similarly, building and zoning departments and other technical constituents should also be included in the process, consistently and from the outset. This highlights the need for a sound framework of peer and team communications, and a focus on clear priorities during the design process. The lack of wider peer review processes in this area makes such team arrangements even more essential.

Increased levels of ongoing research are needed, including more rigorous scientific testing; and computer simulations and energy modelling should be carried out early in the design process. For example, early energy models based on design orientation and massing allow a baseline, minimum-performance, code-complying energy rating that is specific to site and occupancy. These can then be usefully compared to a series of enhanced design options and measures. A strong and unwavering commitment to performance aims and means is essential, from design to construction. Determination sags easily, and early commitments are readily dropped. Success was helped when project leaders made consistent and unambiguous statements about their commitment to designing and building a carbon neutral, solar or other kind of sustainable building.

There is a tendency to complicate solutions, or arrive at idiosyncratic designs, when innovation or pioneering efforts are required. Design teams should focus on the simplest, even most ordinary design and construction details possible. Similarly, design language and technical expressions require simplicity and precision to establish unambiguous communication among team members, city officials and clients.

## Time is energy

At the beginning of a project it is important to clarify schedule implications. It will take more time to design new and sometimes ambitious post-fossil edifices than to dust off, say, off-the-shelf speculative office plans – but they will not necessarily take longer to build. Significant efforts may be required in research, team coordination and component sourcing and testing. Because buildings are first and foremost financial constructs, all major building and urban development projects are under time pressures: to secure sufficient concept development, research and design time will be a critical achievement. These time pressures may prompt some hesitation to commit to renewable design, especially if regulatory or procurement processes do not require this.

Sophisticated investors and users understand that the design process for renewable, energy-efficient buildings may be more time-consuming than for conventional, fossil edifices. But it is a general misconception that energy efficient and renewable-energy suffused buildings always take longer to assemble and construct. Incorporation of sustainable elements and features such as new energy technologies has little or no impact on the construction schedule if they are taken into account from the outset. Yet such misconceptions are so common, to the point where any delay is falsely attributed to unconventional energy features. For example, when a regulatory change requires a design modification, clients are tempted to conclude that the renewable specifications have caused the delay.

On the other hand, renewable construction can sometimes take longer. Renewable equipment testing or experiments may take time. Building inspections may cause delays if inspectors are unfamiliar with integrated wind power or cogeneration systems, or new materials. Also, local building and safety departments may cause delays: time is required to ascertain the safety performance of new systems.

Therefore it is useful to focus on limiting delays. This can be a process management challenge, or one of crafting unique cooperative arrangements. Integrated local building codes can be augmented by software based choice support tools that make explicit the manner in which renewable energy choices may impact construction – this is relevant for product selection. If the cost implications of each choice are understood and considered throughout the design process, developers and clients will be able to select options efficiently, satisfying statutory requirements and building codes while limiting changes and delays. LCAid is one such tool (see above, Section 5.1).

Many projects have multiple user groups and complex constituencies. Important stakeholders want to be centrally involved in programming a facility – and not only for universities, corporate facilities or cooperative housing schemes – and many of these groups are not familiar with renewable energy and wider sustainability choices, adding to the time needed to manage the programming effort. If not factored in from the outset, consultative and participatory design process requirements can compete with the time required for developing renewable energy and building efficiency measures – both sometimes misguidedly considered peripheral to the core task of building design. But when the post-fossil energy objectives are made a central dimension in the building programming process both the users' space planning and design interests and energy and resource performance can easily and productively be reconciled.

Sometimes a project is deemed too far advanced in design or even construction to accommodate important energy measures when they do surface after a project has been launched. But even when the design process is completed and construction in progress, it can still be possible to take certain efficiency steps, or incorporate generation systems, or make other adjustments, provided logistical flexibility provisions have been made. Finally, much team and office time is needed to stay up-to-date. State-of-the-art energy systems and tools are evolving rapidly.

## Construction considerations

It is important to focus on the construction process itself, managing it in as renewable a manner as possible, ultimately working towards the use of materials and construction procedures that are produced and powered in non-fossil ways. Also, when introducing renewable equipment and building infrastructure, local conventions need to be take into account; these contribute to timing, the quality of workmanship and success of the final result. Communications with the construction team need to be exceptionally good, in technical briefings, training and construction and support documentation. This may require the writing of manuals; photos of equipment assembly and construction practices, and an accessible collection of material suppliers' product literature is crucial. Sufficient time should be allotted to explain the overall environmental sustainability and fuel independence goals to the construction team. Because renewable energy and efficiency design strategies are still new to many contractors, sessions to educate both management and workers are important. Broader project goals can be usefully presented as being on an equal footing with conventional construction considerations of safety, quality, budget and schedule.

Close monitoring of the construction phases is crucial in renewable-energy integrated and high-efficiency projects. It is essential for clients, through their management representatives, leading architects and engineers, to stay intimately informed throughout the construction process, monitor compliance with specification, and be consulted in the approval of substitutions. It is also important to keep in mind that renewable-energy technologies and building efficiency methods bring into sharp relief the risks and costs of design-build and other streamlined methods of delivering large complexes. The structuring of development projects into distinct stages proves to be more fruitful generally: it establishes feedback loops, permits change and encourages innovation by creating cycles of reflective experience, inquiry and learning.

Construction trades and skills are positively influenced, too. The new focus on renewable energy and efficiency also highlights the fundamental importance of resuscitating and nurturing time-honoured construction methods. Yet at the same time it also requires an effort to *normalise* new skills by educating and training all relevant trades in new skills, and to avoid the formation of an artificially specialised caste of renewable energy installers. Any use of specialists to install new systems should be seen as an interim measure – if its very newness is the only distinguishing feature of the new technology. For example, all electrical subcontractors and tradespeople should be able to install photovoltaic systems; this will help manage costs and avoid construction delays due to skills shortages.

## Materials matter

Most players in the industry – architects, developers, financiers and builders – are only beginning to understand the extent to which today's building materials consist of embodied fossil energy, can be toxic, or should be reused because of their limited uses after they have outlived their initial cycle. But being renewable in a fossil city is somewhat akin to being vegetarian in a party of carnivores: it can be difficult to procure high-quality materials with little fossil-fuel content embodied in their making or chemistry, and easy to reassemble and reuse. This is a particular challenge for building facades.

Existing standardisation programmes can constitute a barrier to material innovation, too. Design teams working for local government, schools or other institutions can find themselves restricted in their ability to specify low-energy materials, and be confined to using standard materials and elements, some already purchased in bulk, such as paints or pavement systems. While photovoltaic elements and other renewable energy systems are increasingly considered and specified, sometimes to appeal to contracting agencies or meet bidding preferences, there is also a parallel tendency to delete them at the end of the design process, just as readily. This is not surprising, given the general lack of authentic and market-based incentives in the United States: if they are left merely to volunteer action and temporary commitments, the temptation is too strong to delete modular, backup or detachable elements as soon as it is rewarding to do so. By the same token, experience shows that solar systems and other, similarly performing renewable systems can be added later to a building, but only if appropriate planning has taken place beforehand (Hayter et al 2002, p 12, cited in DoE 2006a).

Given the limited scale of most integrated or clip-on renewable installations and the frequent absence of other supporting renewable energy or efficiency measures, most current solar buildings in the United States have difficulty becoming net electricity exporters within their own footprint. Because of the level and nature of their energy consumption, in commercial buildings this can be extremely difficult even when solar applications are maximised and general building energy consumption is curtailed through efficient design. Still, it has been shown that even a partial supply is welcome as useful in maintaining basic operations during grid power failures (Hayter et al 2002, p 12 *et passim*, cited in DoE 2006a).

## Technical, media and general support

While it is useful to focus on available products and technology, new products and systems demand active support in development. Design and building industry support and supply participation are needed to make existing products more responsive than they are now: photovoltaic panel and solar-thermal systems can be highly rigid in their requirements, and stultify inventiveness, even hamper basic functional requirements. Given a paucity of traditional skills in the crafting and assembly of elements among commercial contractors, there is increased reliance on manufacturers and contractors for the provision of higher quality products. At the same time, in-house contractors become an advantage for companies and institutions: within government agencies, this can ensure project success, enabling reduced construction costs and facilitating testing and monitoring of system and component performance. This can also sidestep the challenge of identifying suppliers willing to offer service contracts. Finally, there is a considerable communication challenge: missing or misleading information on renewable energy products and efficient building systems or cost implications can not only make sourcing and procurement difficult but also reduce design team credibility with local building and safety departments. This is not only a challenge of a technical nature: media support measures are key as well as rating incentives, such as LEED, and other local and international assessment and award programmes. Well-reported design and performance competitions, and other forms of media exposure, help greatly.

## Finance aspects

At the outset, building budgets are always too limited and structured around conventional projects and standard design schedules. It will avoid surprises later if a challenging design and development process is conceptualised and budgeted for. Similarly, standard low-cost development formulas need to be challenged from the outset: the aim is to create, build and manage a better, more durable building with lower maintenance, environmental impacts and external energy costs. A central budgeting challenge lies in prudent cost estimation: the increased complexity in building design and construction can result in difficulties in assessing the cost involved not only in the building itself but also in the costs of ensuring regulation compliance.

Tax incentives, utility rebates, loan schemes and outright grant opportunities have to be identified early in the programming and design process, too. Although it is entirely possible to finance renewable buildings conventionally, without incentives, rebates or other methods, external finance sources always assist in the feasibility calculation. Support funding may come from a variety of local, public and private non-profit sources, such as state government or local tax credits, private company programmes, civic programmes, or access to technology support through working as a manufacturer's research partner. Many sources require verification of renewable power and efficiency benefits before granting support. Renewably powered building financing mechanisms include *credit enhancement* through private loan guarantees; *equity support* through renewable building tax credits; *grants* through public agencies or civic trusts; *private or public loans*; and, in a sense, the nature of the *procurement process* itself, through design-build contracts structured to make renewable power and efficiency possible.

Salesmanship is key to raising funds. To be successful in securing resources for renewable and efficiency schemes one must squarely address issues of profitability. This is no different from other innovative schemes: crucial are persuasively framed bank proposals, clear strategies for managing approval stages and for marketing the project effectively, and the demonstration of where, why and when a profit may be expected. The renewable developer needs to be fully conversant with good industry examples to impress – from knowledge of large and profitable examples of the proposed project type, to employee productivity, to public perception and advertising value. The following four arguments are useful to keep in mind. First, renewable investment goals need to be aligned with sound business planning. For businesses that intend to prosper in the long term, such investments can make good economic sense. Second, opportunities should be sought to expedite development and approval processes. This involves finding subsidies for renewable development, tax incentives or density credits for developers, or assistance with interpreting building code requirements for renewable building measures, but also fast-track arrangements in which renewably powered projects receive the benefit of expedited processing. Third, alternative forms of renewable energy finance can come in many guises. As an example, Chicago has made available the proceeds of a lawsuit filed against a local energy company for damages caused by blackouts. Fourth, combined financing can be used: national grants can be used to support renewable infrastructure, while other agencies may be called on to support added design measures in reducing energy consumption.

It is also useful to distinguish short term from lifecycle benefits. Later benefits and longer payback periods are not always easily incorporated into building feasibility calculations. Therefore, to enhance short-term viability it helps to demonstrate short-term benefits, even indirect ones, for example in prestige, value increase and corporate identity. Reputation benefits often result: owners reported a rise in sales even before construction was completed, attributed to the building's innovative design and the public's desire to support such initiatives. Market visibility improved, and even expectations of increased productivity and lower vacancy rates can contribute to making early viability assessments. There are strong psychosocial benefits to users, including a sense of pride in the values conveyed by the building, a more positive overall workplace experience, and a strong connection to the natural environment. Social benefits reported included improved communication, a sense of belonging as well as feelings of being treated in an egalitarian manner.

Renewable and efficient buildings involve more up-front costs, and hence new lifecycle cost models are required, determining costs and gains not only for developers and owners but also for builders, tenants and purchasers. Economic benefits are typically only obtained over time, in different stages of the building's life. Costs and benefits often accrue to different participants in the process: while it is widely agreed that renewably powered buildings are cost-effective, actual energy savings are enjoyed by the final owners and users of the building, not by the builder or developer. Additional costs incurred by developers are not typically passed on to owners. Some portion of the expected, long-term value increase or profit may have to be allocated to the builder or developer to offset initial costs. Unless this takes place, it is difficult to convincingly attract developer and builder interest.

A range of other budget-sensitive benefits can improve feasibility. Energy-efficient design reduces heating and cooling load: less equipment and plant result. This translates into greater space efficiency, and lowered construction and operating costs. Returns can be higher, through higher resale values, or premiums on leases. Tenants' benefits accrue through low utility costs and a healthier living environment. And net-metering agreements, while challenging to introduce in multi-apartment dwellings, are seen as attractive in generating income.

Separate funding sources should be sought for the post-occupancy study of building performance. Since these may require sizeable management systems, an added budget can be helpful especially for residential developments, due to their complexity and typically smaller core budgets for electrical, mechanical and hydraulic systems. Hidden, unregistered, yet overt and substantial social and ecological costs result from choices made at each step of the design and construction process. Though such costs are difficult to quantify, they must be recognised and conveyed at all stages of a building's genesis (see Orr 2002).

## Building awareness

A fundamental challenge is to battle still-prevailing scepticism, a frequent lack of community support; lagging enthusiasm; or limited involvement – combined with a general paucity of awareness of need or solutions. The active constituents of a major renewable and efficient building or development scheme should cooperate to address this wider image problem – foremost among them, city government, local community leaders and civic champions.

The realisation of sustainable, renewable powered development is easier and takes less time if client, public authorities and local residents are already fully aware of needs and advantages. The following eight measures are particularly successful and tested. First, broader *market awareness* can be reinforced effectively via comprehensive marketing campaigns. Second, there is no such thing as media over-exposure of the subject: achieving *ubiquity of coverage and familiarity of issues* are key. A key measure of success for renewable and efficient architecture lies in it becoming so commonplace that the terms 'renewable', 'sustainable' or 'green' are no longer used. Third, community *lobbying* through frequent meetings with stakeholders will bear fruit, and help garner active local support for the renewable development. Fourth, communication media offering public information in local print or other visual productions, and exposure on television are among the most effective. Fifth, *events* help enormously and more interactively, such as public open houses and neighbourhood consultation evenings. Sixth, *mobilisation* of wider civic resources can see the engagement and transformation of public buildings; the organisation of environmental education programmes in schools; or alliances through community partnerships; engaging, for example, conservation agencies, employment and training bodies, museums, even childcare centres. Seventh: personal *motivation* efforts can help transform anonymous employees, tenants or users into renewable energy champions and environmental stewards. And finally, of supreme importance in promoting a climate conducive to, or even outright calling for a renewable energy revolution, is the firm *engagement of sustainability networks*. Awareness of the need for renewable energy in the built environment is rising, and many are keen to manifest an interest in tangibly safeguarding the environment.

Buildings are socially used and culturally experienced: an important aim lies in nurturing a work culture of sustainability. A staff user guide should be based on a psychosocial understanding of use and user patterns. Tenants require guidelines for energy efficiency: a tenant manual should provide resource and supplier information about low-energy and recyclable, non-toxic office equipment, fit-out and building materials. Now job profiles emerge. renewable property managers will be needed to ensure sustainable operations and maintenance; and renewable systems advisors should be made available to all tenants in procuring healthy materials, and to make the best use of the available building features.

## Before and after

What can be learned from guidance efforts, pilots, prototypes and post-occupancy studies? While a few agencies manage research and development, and national governments still largely control direction in research, much of this activity is increasingly also taking place in industry and universities. But while pilot projects are important in setting precedents – and indeed, small, renewably powered buildings can lead the way, and help change minds in the procurement of larger buildings – many test cases, have remained isolated events, especially in the residential building industry: lessons are not often propagated into standard practice. This highlights the limits of individual industry efforts lacking a national, state and local government regulatory and financial support structure, to adapt, adopt and expand practice. In the absence of such support in a majority of countries, the models available to local governments include public–private partnerships; development approval incentives; corporate practice by the city itself; the support and encouragement of competitions; and the promotion of a culture of innovation at all scales.

Post-occupancy, much is to be learned from pilots, prototypes and normal practice. The concept of ongoing learning, and of future accountability and responsibility is, in a sense, built into the very nature of renewable energy installations. For example, the sub-metering of electricity, chilled water and other services to retail and office tenants is as instructive as the recording of income generating renewable electricity being fed back into the grid on a daily basis. And to ensure effective post-occupancy readings, it will be useful to separate monitoring systems from energy management systems. The monitoring of energy performance is not generally a facility management concern.

Post-occupancy studies are essential for updating and fine-tuning a building's systems. They reveal energy management deficiencies, human errors, or hardware and software problems. They help stop the under-utilisation of features: not all integrated elements and features are apparent to users for example space temperature regulation systems may not be switched on. Post-occupancy studies also help cope with the phenomenon of exaggerated initial expectation: sometimes a renewable building's performance is lower than anticipated, or it behaves differently, due to altered use patterns, system overload, shifting use schedules or system adjustment needs. A building is a socially enacted construct; it is nothing without the actions of current and future users, which, while responsive to opportunities in learning and sensitive to incentives, are largely beyond control. The effectiveness of technology should be achieved by adjusting to use patterns, not the other way around.

Post-occupancy performance standards vary greatly and are subject to constant change. These should be codified and firmly embedded in building approvals and contracts. To gain legitimacy, such standards must also be widely understood and agreed upon: all too often this is not the case. Post-occupancy studies are needed to examine and learn from installation, maintenance and operations aspects, and to see whether these continue to comply with existing health and safety standards. This is needed as basis for future certification requirements, and in order to determine whether and when a new standard is required to respond to technological innovation and other forms of change.

*This section has been developed by screening the United States Department of Energy's* High-performance Building Database *for thematic lessons in renewable building practice (DoE 2006a), and integrating it with experience gleaned from other countries and project settings, including personal perceptions.*

**Gauging renewable city performance**
The renewable city requires careful guidance and assessment: anyone can feel and tell the benefits of a more equitable, healthier, more innovative city increasingly liberated from the shackles of the fossil-nuclear power regime, but it does require rigorous and studious planning and assessment efforts to guide and quantify progress over time.

# CHAPTER 6

# Renewable City planning and action: guides for local government

This book is about achieving local energy autonomy and this section is specific-ally aimed at local government politicians and officials who wish to implement change in their organisations. When it comes to change, no department, city official or political leader is an island – urban energy transformations embrace new forms of practice at all levels: public policy, market guidance, regula-tions, public–private partnerships, joint design and management. New local, regional, national and even international policy and practice frameworks are unfolding, too, to support urban transformations in the post-fossil fuel and post-nuclear age. In keeping with these developments, this section has trans-lated best-practice approaches into a comprehensive model for change, subject to adjustment for local conditions. The new approach seeks strategic plan-ning processes, legislative frameworks and ways of guiding local change in development.

Offered in this chapter is Solar City®, one possible do-it-yourself frame-work for highly committed cities or alliances of cities that seek guided change, Solar City® is an exclusive guide to renewable energy development as a central objective of a local government and its communities, businesses, universities, neighbourhoods and other constituents. Here, the term 'solar' is used in the same way that many renewable energy experts denote all major urban renew-able energy sources (bar tidal power): as related to the agency of the sun. But for other cities interested in evaluating their general performance, or for those that would like to conduct an ongoing, broader assessment, this first section is followed by a rating framework for evaluating a city's more general Renewable City status.

These two sections both provide menus or checklists; they are not intended for linear, narrative reading, but for devising step-by-step action frameworks and evaluation systems. *Renewable City* concludes with a brief celebration of one leading Renewable City of great promise: Portland, Oregon.

## 6.1 THE SOLAR CITY® PROGRAMME

Dynamic cities and urban communities constantly search for new planning and management models. They do so as part of genuine reform efforts, in a search for leaner government, or to devise a more competitive business environment. And many go beyond the normal process of reform, seeking greater efficiency and effectiveness in urban administration to achieve both tangible and visionary outcomes. They see a need to restructure outmoded planning and management arrangements to cope with massive environmental change, but also to deal with the enormous security threats that stem from fossil and nuclear dependency. They want to be ready for the coming global struggle for urban survival. This search is far more serious than the battle for global city status of the 1980s and 1990s to project higher levels of competitive advantage in attracting regional corporate headquarters, creative talent or tourist streams. The struggle to find a path to the necessary energy transition will also be very much a battle, but one that must be won in close cooperation among cities – in a search for practical techniques of prospering jointly while seeking greater degrees of autonomy. This new kind of collaborative competition for increasing independence from energy and carbon risks will yield more meaningful results than the conventional striving for political hegemony and economic supremacy.

The new competition for post-fossil urban directions will be marked by a quest for new forms of urban life, markets, management models, energy supply systems and environmental support structures, pursued within an increasingly unstable climatic environment and uncertain local conditions. It will be a focused struggle for urban innovation: to achieve a sharp reduction in greenhouse emissions; shrinking ecological footprints: the protection and regeneration of water and food resources; and the control of exposure and vulnerability to extreme weather events, migrating disease vectors and other features of climate change. It will enforce a more sustainable context for the development and management of buildings, infrastructures and land use arrangements.

Finally, in this emerging era marked by a quest for settlement autonomy in food, water and energy supply, the new urban competitiveness will be founded on new relations between cities and their regions.

In sum, this is a guide to a new strategic planning process. It is designed to help cities become fossil fuel and nuclear power free: communities large and small, in all parts of the world. The period of time needed to effect this transformation is for the city to decide, and for its population and businesses. To pursue it requires a comprehensive and sustained commitment by local municipal administrations, supported by political leadership and civic champions. Given the policy volatility characteristic of local government this can be a challenge, but it is a worthwhile political leadership goal given its local and international rewards. Provincial, state, national and international frameworks in guidance, incentives, programmes and legislation will help enormously in shoring up local resolve. To flourish, programmatic frameworks such as Solar City® require strong alliances with state and national government, local and regional business communities and citizen' groups, ie civil society. While they do not depend on the phasing in of urban-based carbon trading schemes, they would certainly boost their progress. Local incentives to grasp this opportunity lie in the prospect of economic development and environmental enhancement, employment generation and wider community prosperity.

Strong local championship will be useful for implementing the programme, and the programme will strengthen leadership in turn. In embarking on this path it will be helpful to have a history of local civic environmental engagement, of administrative environmental protection and energy efficiency programmes. In promoting this programme it is also helpful to identify and rally the support of the early winners in a shift away from coal, oil, natural gas and nuclear power: the citizenship at large, as well as new industries, services and employment nodes built around energy efficiency improvements and renewable power generation in all its forms. To bring all these forces into alignment will help to establish important political and planning continuity and to construct policy frameworks that can be sustained across election periods and party lines.

To help make the energy transformation attractive as a fresh, bold and practical initiative, this strategic planning template has been designed for a three-year period only. This means that it can be carried out within one typical legislative or election period. It is designed to transform government as a learning organisation and enable leaders, agencies and communities to achieve not only a better understanding and basis for planning but particularly to help drive change itself – institutional, cultural and political.

Many models have been tried on the road of broad-based urban change towards energy autonomy. Some are founded on community action, others are utility focused and some rely on longterm strategic planning against emission or consumption targets and baselines. The approach recommended here provides a generic template for institutional change. It is based on a three-year effort involving a number of experts from many countries, carried out under the umbrella of the International Energy Agency's (IEA) Committee for Energy Research and Technology (CERT) and, specifically, its Solar Heating and Cooling Programme. Its outcome has been updated, refined and advanced for this book (Droege 2001).

The IEA has provided the organisational context for the committee, teams and individuals engaged in advancing the project, but has neither directed nor endorsed its content. The history and evolution of this arm of the Organisation for Economic Cooperation and Development (OECD) are testimony to the contradictions encountered by policy institutions in this age of fundamental change in the energy paradigm. The agency was established in 1974 in response to the first oil crisis in a move credited to Henry Kissinger. While it oversees a sizeable renewable energy research and policy portfolio, growing since the 1970s, it has not been the most forceful advocate of overcoming the fossil fuel age. Rather, chartered in part as steward of global energy security and particularly of an international pool of oil reserves available to OECD countries, it acted as advocate and steward of conventional energy streams. Now, a quarter of a century later, human civilisation faces a terminal energy crisis brought about by a continued, near total reliance on these inevitably expiring resources. In response, the IEA has begun to acknowledge that a radical petroleum saving plan is needed. For example, it has proposed ways in which OECD countries can cut back on more than a third – 36 per cent – of their transport fuel needs (IEA 2005). The proposal falls short of the magnitude of action required, but were it to be taken seriously and translated into national policies it would significantly increase the pressure to develop urban response mechanisms in demand reduction and crisis responsive, globally accelerated demand reduction as well as bio-fuel and renewable hydrogen fuel promotion.

Solar City® first commenced as a market development initiative. Since the early 2000s the International Energy Agency has sought to find ways of either relating markets to the widening array of renewable energy technology and methods developed since the 1970s, or of using a better understanding of markets and market levers to help guide technological development – matching a sense of demand to the supply-side push of technology development. But change may be some time off because the IEA has not been able fully to transcend its charter and take renewable energy as seriously as have some of its own member states. While there are signs that states are beginning to acknowledge that there may possibly be a terminal oil and gas supply problem, as late as March 2006 a draft study proclaimed that such global drivers as 'the liberalisation of energy markets [and] the international greenhouse gas regulation' will change the market framework for the 'development and deployment of renewable energy technologies' – and, by implication, not for a profound market flaw like the impending peaking of the global oil supply stream. The same study asserts that 'the IEA does not expect fuel prices to increase considerably during the coming 25 years...', lulling its main OECD members into continued complacency. Meanwhile, the calls for action grow, to some extent even within, but far more persuasively outside the agency (Kofoed-Wiuff et al 2006, pp 6 and 13).

While the IEA may look to some like an institution of faith rather than fact, it deserves the credit for providing a rich setting for many engaged individuals and national representatives pursuing important technical agendas in renewable systems development. Solar City® was one of these endeavours. And the urban focus was justified: cities and smaller urban communities have long been among those entities calling loudest for change, seeking models of transformation. The template below provides an outline map only. There are numerous resources available to detail, refine and carry out the programme, including internal skills, external consultants, as well as tools and advice available through members of the World Council for Renewable Energy (WCRE), International Solar Energy Society (ISES), the well-established programmes of the International Council on Local Environmental Initiatives (ICLEI) and many other regionally active networks and programmes referenced in this book.

Several cities declared their intention to adopt the Solar City® path (or a derivation of it) for example, the pioneering South Korean city of Daegu (Kim 2005), Oxford in England (Roaf et al 2005b) or Adelaide in South Australia. The more recently declared European and International Solar Cities initiatives, too, have adopted it, and some of its members have informed its early evolution.

## Programme structure

*The following text is a set of step-by-step instructions for action; where it is repetitive it is so rather in the manner of an exercise programme or a dietary regime...*

## 1 Rationale and background

Why should cities, towns or urban communities adopt a Solar City® or other energy transformation programme to embrace efficiency and renewable power? What benefits can be expected from carefully structured efforts to support the introduction of renewable energy technologies in cities, towns and other urban communities? There are many reasons, each overwhelming in importance. The rapid growth of cities throughout the late 19th and the 20th centuries was driven by the expanding fossil fuel economy. Today, the development and operation of urban areas absorb the lion's share of the world's fossil fuel production. This is a staggering amount given that fossil fuels supply the vast majority of total global commercial energy use – and their use is increasing at a rapid rate. Economic regions, nations, cities and smaller communities worldwide are under great pressure to reduce fossil power use, find alternative sources and introduce these decisively and methodically. Besides the introduction of renewable energy technologies cities will have to be re-engineered in terms of their transport and land-use systems and their building and urban design principles.

To combat the fatal triad – carbon-emissions induced climate change, fossil-fuel supply peaking and mounting environmental damage due to excessive use of oil, natural gas and coal – cities must be powered differently both to mitigate further emissions and adapt to now inevitable climate change. The use of urban efficiency mechanisms and renewable, distributed micro-power systems is on the rise, but the current speed of change is much too slow to counter climate shifts and commercial fossil fuel depletion prospects, or to avert serious crises on international and national scales. Cities, towns and other urban communities are increasingly seen as important settings for coordinated policy implementation aimed at introducing renewable technology and carbon emissions reduction. The Solar City® programme prompts the evolutionary rethinking of planning tools, the determinining of sustainable urban emissions targets and ways of gauging progress. An additional aim is to foster new urban business and industry in renewable energy systems and so also direct attention to the need for a new urban employment base. Indeed, the most advanced city governments hope to distinguish themselves nationally and internationally by offering clean and future-oriented investment locations, employment generators and lifestyle choices.

The benefit of a focused local, integrated transformation project is derived from the increasing numbers of shared challenges that cities face in addressing renewable energy needs. There are, for example, challenges of regulatory reform, technology acquisition, organisation, planning and employment generation. And more fundamentally, many cities seek tangible responses to civic calls for greater development sustainability to cope with air pollution, water and soil contamination, traffic congestion, heat island effects, sub-standard food supply, rural decline and much else. Placing cities on a renewable energy footing is central to solving the urban sustainability question. The Solar City® programme is offered to help solve it.

Such a project, once embarked on by a city, will benefit from international collaboration. There are universal opportunities that can be derived from embracing this paradigm shift: understanding cities as massive and influential renewable energy users of the 21st century. Cities are seats of political power and nodes of intense economic activity – and they are the markets for solar and other energy technologies of the future. Solar City® is aimed at the core of a country, state, region or urban community's market development efforts.

In the past, too many renewable energy research programs have focused on the supply-side development of specific techniques, products and systems. Since the last decade of the 20th century, more emphasis has been placed on demand: understanding and building strong markets for renewable energy technology. Responding to the need for a greater emphasis on community applications and their markets, this programme has been conceived to advance the strategies, tools and industry partnerships a city, town, community or urban region must develop in order to introduce renewable energy technologies on a large scale, within the context of land-use, transport and building performance efforts based on energy conservation and efficiency principles.

Cities, towns and regional governments are well equipped to structure programmes in locally meaningful ways and have access to the technical and policy apparatus required for significant planning innovations. Urban communities can provide an effective environment for the pursuit of the ultimate goal underlying all applicable renewable energy programmes: targeted and measurable reduction of greenhouse gas emissions and lowered reliance on fossil fuel.

## 2 Aims and scope

This step-by-step plan helps cities programme the research, development and communication and organisational transformation work that is necessary to introduce urban renewable energy technologies in a systematic, targeted and purposeful manner within a general energy efficient environment. It includes all major aspects of urban management and support needed to confront this apocalyptic challenge – the planning strategies, energy and emissions frameworks and industrial and business development dimensions.

## 3 Objectives

Solar City® has been designed to help introduce renewable energy systems to make urban communities vastly more sustainable environmentally through a steady and determined reduction in their reliance on fossil fuel and nuclear power. Doing this will also make a city or urban community more viable economically due to the powerful impulses provided to innovate urban technology and infrastructure, develop industries and businesses and generate new employment. This effort will result in important roductions in greenhouse gas emissions within a practical timeframe and inside a transparent framework.

To achieve all of this, this programme template is structured to help nurture a fertile institutional context for change – to develop both the planning tools and organisational arrangements needed to transform a community. It will help overcome the main legal, institutional and cultural barriers currently slowing the introduction of renewable energy technology and broad energy efficiency in cities and communities.

These general goals are translated directly into the three programme areas:

A  Renewable energy based city planning
B  Targets, baseline studies and scenarios
C  Urban renewable energy systems, industry and business development

Before detailing these project areas, here are some key aspects important for understanding them, including their principal stages.


## 4 Key aspects

This section discusses several key aspects that are common to the execution of all programme components and useful in understanding the overall framework in which Solar City® will operate best.

**Participants** An important feature is the collaboration among partners within and outside city government. Such partners are needed to contribute staff, finance and other resources in an active engagement in the programme. In choosing one's collaborators, it is important to begin with those who are sympathetic with and even enthusiastic about the idea of a fundamental energy transformation. Once a programme is running, it is then time gradually to bring sceptics into the fold. Partners can be selected from a wide range of groups: state and federal agencies, private companies and top industry groups, civic foundations, universities or research institutions. But participants can also be selected from many other circles with a stake in a livable, enduring and prosperous city: community groups; renewable energy associations and companies; property development organisations; architectural institutes; economic development groups; future-oriented think-tanks; city planning, industry and professional entities; local and regional power utilities; road and traffic bodies and motorists' associations; environmental groups; anti-pollution campaigners; or pedestrian rights and cycle-way activists.

### Community awareness and incentives
Sustained, innovative and engaging branding, public awareness programmes and communication campaigns are key to success. A city suffused with renewable power needs to be understood as desirable and exciting, advanced and wealth creating if it is to come into being. It cannot be enforced by legislative fiat or plain exhortation. Awareness or compelling arguments alone are also insufficient for success. Incentives such as tax advantages, income generation, legal rights, entitlements or development bonuses will help to create an environment conducive to change.

### Funding and finance
Essential elements include secure base funding and the entrepreneurial financial skills required to launch the programme in the city and to maintain its

administrative life for as long as possible, but at least for the initial three-year period for which this programme, is designed.

## Political advocacy and expertise

Programmes are socially constructed and politically assembled. Hence they are subject to constant scrutiny and change. No programme can simply be introduced, approved and left alone if it is to survive and prosper. It requires constant vigilance and imagination to enhance its strength and steer it through the vagaries of a complex and challenging – albeit rewarding – path.

## Partners

The building of coalitions with other public institutions, community groups and private businesses is another essential feature of programmes that are truly successful in producing transformation.

## Stages

The three-year programme is structured into five broad stages, each designed to deliver early successes and tangible outcomes. The role of the initial stage is to finalise and detail all necessary arrangements, and to commence the programme with important fundamental research and development work. The other four stages are devoted to activities of analysis, strategic planning, implementation, feedback gathering and communication.

The stages are:

1 inventory, partnerships and approach advancement (nine months);
2 practice analysis and strategy development (six months);
3 institutional innovation and implementation (nine months);
4 monitoring, evaluation and feedback (six months);
5 refinement and final reporting (six months).

This work program is intended to form the overall map for guiding the collaboration of all countries and cities involved, to provide a sense of the phases, milestones and outcomes expected, to give a general sense of the resources required and, ultimately, to ensure that all participants gain useful results.

**Deliverables** It is important that the intentions, processes and tangible outcomes of each stage are well documented and disseminated. Published reports, workshops, seminars and both national and international conferences can augment this effort (see also the specified outcomes under each annual activity period below). Annual and biannual citywide workshops will help to carry the work agenda forward. An increasing number of international conferences provides added support: the World Council for Renewable Energy (WCRE) holds annual forums that generally contain an important renewable city element; the International Council on Local Environmental Initiatives provides a good, albeit closed-circle environment for communities participating in its Cities for Climate Protection™ (CCP) campaign; the International Solar Cities Initiative (ISCI) sponsored by the International Solar Energy Society (ISES), too, offers biannual opportunities for congress participation and the sharing of experience. And there is a number of other more regional programmes – most of these offer excellent learning and information sharing programmes: examples include Energy Cities, Green Cities and, until recently, the Solar City® based European Solar Cities Initiative (ESCI) managed by ISES.

**Skills** The diversity, suitability and excellence of the core Solar City® team's skills base are of utmost importance. Depending on the precise nature of the chosen path, required skills may include:

1 renewable finance skills;
2 advocacy and communication;
3 urban market development expertise;
4 urban and regional planning and design;
5 programme design, management and administration;
6 baseline $CO_2$-e accounting and plan scenario modelling;
7 applied renewable energy technology, integration and policy;
8 transport systems modelling and policy, including fuel substitution; and
9 geographic information system, urban climatology.

**Best practice benchmarks** The world of urban innovation is full of wonderful initiatives and success stories. It is important to access these continuously. Because of the unprecedented nature of the challenge, it is important that even the most local of programmes seek access to international information, to both offer and apply useful lessons from elsewhere.

A central feature of the programme is thus the process of identifying, documenting, studying, evaluating, describing and communicating current best practice in integrated urban energy planning, management and projects. The activities will include:

1 identification of scope and criteria for evaluation;
2 information gathering and documentation;

3 study and evaluation;

4 analysis and description, or case study development; and

5 communication and dissemination.

The scope will include technologies and management practices as well as strategies. As a point of departure, it is useful that at least three categories of case study are differentiated: (a) cities and community-wide efforts; (b) precincts and projects; and (c) city networks and programmes.

**Learning in action** Successful municipal programmes depend on the recording, monitoring, reflective analysis and constructive feeding back of programme experience. This is critical in developing a shared understanding of the barriers to, impacts and dynamics of large-scale technological, community, institutional and business change, with a view towards the planned and targeted, GHG-sensitive phasing in of renewable energy sources on a city-wide scale. The results of this activity should not only be useful to the city or community carrying out this programme, but structured to be shared with other cities, city networks and programmes similarly and actively engaged.

## 5 Task A: Solar City® strategies: renewable-energy based city planning

Objective

This effort will identify local planning and development approaches that are particularly helpful and important in the introduction of renewable energy technologies, within an energy-centred urban development approach. Especially pertinent here are issues of strategy, city-wide renewable planning tools, building and planning controls to safeguard renewable energy generation rights, organisational arrangements, legislation and standards, incentive structures, public information and exemplary municipal practice.

While this task emphasises the introduction of renewable energy technologies, it is equally important to focus on reformed land use, transport and urban design and planning practice. It is recommended to use Task A to help integrate the outcomes of Tasks B and C (comprising municipal target setting and industry reform promotion) into a coherent, well-structured outcome without interfering with their own integrity. It is to manifest itself in the generation of a community-wide Solar City® plan.

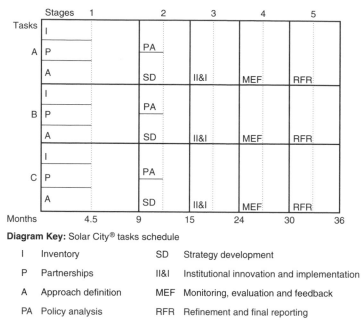

**Diagram Key:** Solar City® tasks schedule

| | | | |
|---|---|---|---|
| I | Inventory | SD | Strategy development |
| P | Partnerships | II&I | Institutional innovation and implementation |
| A | Approach definition | MEF | Monitoring, evaluation and feedback |
| PA | Policy analysis | RFR | Refinement and final reporting |

## A.1 Activity period 1: inventory, partnerships and approach definition

### A.1.1 Inventory

In this period of related activities we will methodically record what measures of renewable energy technology and general energy-conscious planning approaches are already taken throughout the community. This may include the adoption of renewable building, infrastructure and urban design and planning approaches. There is a range of ways in which this can be supported including:

1 direct legislation and standards;
2 the provision of incentives and disincentives;
3 corporate asset management, power purchasing and pricing;
4 institutional reform and improved strategic and general planning practices;
5 community action development, industry alliances, information and education.

Planning tools such as regional and city-internal energy resource mapping of sun radiation, wind power and bio-fuel farming opportunities will be helpful additions to this arsenal, using geographic information systems as database frameworks.

This activity is to investigate each of these in detail and develop means of generating improved urban practice approaches in partnership with the participating cities. An important component is the documentation of the practices already promoted in the city or its state, regional or national context, in other cities as well as relevant international programmes, including those of Cities for Climate Protection™, Clean Cities, Green Cities, Energy Cities.

## A.1.2 Partnerships
In this stage we will also complete the selection of suitable partnership communities and their government, civic and industry representatives. If it has not yet occurred, this may be the right time to enter into agreements with related city programmes or networks.

## A.1.3 Approach advancement
In this activity period we will review, test and advance the overall spectrum of approaches chosen, and frame the work agenda for the following years in coordination with all participants and city partners.

## A.1.4 Reporting
The remainder of this first activity period is dedicated to the assembly of the individual national report components, the first Task A report (*Solar City Strategies)* and the overall Volume 1 of the *Solar City Guide*. Volume 1 might be entitled 'Solar City: Current Practice'. It is the responsibility of the Task A leader to assist in compiling Volume 1 – digesting the results of all three tasks into a single document, drawings conclusions as well as developing instructions for further work.

*Duration of activity*
Up to nine months. The initial three activities are expected to take six months, with another three months dedicated to final approach testing, reporting and publication.

*Estimated time resource requirements*
Task leadership: 4.5 person-months
Activity overall: 9 person-months

*Deliverables*
Task A report for Activity Period 1: *Solar City Strategies*
Volume 1 of the *Solar City Guide*: 'Solar City – Current Practice'

## A.2 Activity period 2: practice analysis and strategy development

### A.2.1 Practice analysis

The important task here is to evaluate the manner in which the city approaches renewable energy technologies in their institutional arrangements, regulatory frameworks and the other dimensions of local government practice outlined in A.1.1. In particular, the analysis is to explore the strengths and weaknesses of the current and/or emerging arrangements, evaluate the opportunities that exist and the threats that may militate against seizing such opportunities. This process is to be conducted after a careful evaluation of the work and in consultation with local government staff, political leaders, community representatives as well as industry and business leaders.

### A.2.2 Strategy development

The development of a clear and shared vision on the expected outcomes is a central step in the detailing of a strategy, based on the analysis carried out in step A.2.1. The careful development of a strategy, or the refinement of existing approaches and methods – such as the Cities for Climate Protection™ five-step approach, Energy-Cities method, possibly emerging future International Solar Cities Initiative (ISCI) processes, or any other suitable approaches including self-defined efforts – will take up the remainder of this stage. A complete strategy will include tangible targets for the urban transformation process.

### A.2.3 Reporting

A careful analysis and strategy report is to be issued in a form that is relevant to the wider community, as well as to other interested cities. This report might be entitled 'Solar City Planning Practice and Strategic Options'. In addition, Volume 2 of the overall Task report, entitled 'Solar City: Understanding Practice – Developing Strategies'. This compilation will cover the work of Tasks B and C.

*Duration*
Approximately six months. The main two activities of this stage are expected to take three months, with another three months dedicated to reporting and publication.

*Minimum time resource requirements*
Task leadership: 3 person-months
Task activity per country: 6 person-months

*Deliverables*
Task A report for Activity period 2: 'Solar City Planning Practice and Strategic Options'.
Volume 2 of the Solar City Guide: Solar City – understanding practice – developing strategies'.

## A.3 Activity period 3: institutional innovation and implementation

### A.3.1 Activity description

This activity focuses on the organisational, skills and tools requirements necessary to transform urban development, strategic planning and design provisions, procedures and processes to maximise opportunities for introducing renewable energy technologies and wider post-fossil energy practices on a city-wide scale, taking into account the work and findings developed in Tasks B and C.

Most cities will have no difficulty in developing effective ways of accommodating this objective institutionally, such as through selective policy change and some regulatory reform. However, few if any are yet fully embarked on a path that aims to place the entire urban community on a renewable energy footing. This programme, this particular task and especially this activity are designed to identify, develop and design but also help implement such paths. The local innovation and implementation programme is best designed as an outcome of Activity Period 2.

### A.3.2 Reporting

A careful institutional innovation and implementation report is to be issued in a form that is not only relevant to local constituents but also other cities. It may be entitled 'How to Build the Solar City – Handbook for Local Government'.

*Duration*
Up to nine months. The activities of this stage are expected to take four months, with another two months dedicated to reporting and publication.

*Minimum time resource requirements*
Task leadership: 4.5 person-months
Task activity overall: 9 person-months

*Deliverables*
Task A report for Activity Period 3: 'How to Build the Solar City – Handbook for Local Government.'

Volume 3 of the *Solar City Guide*, entitled 'Solar City – Implementing Institutional Innovations'.

### A.4 Activity period 4: monitoring, evaluation and feedback

A.4.1 Activity description
By the fourth work period a thorough monitoring programme should be introduced, while the main programme continues. Monitoring should be ongoing and carefully documented. A well-structured evaluation method should be applied that is useful in local, national and international contexts. This is also the key year for providing feedback and reflection in the institutions involved, to enable broad learning from own, other national as well as international failures and successes.

A.4.2 Reporting/task outcome
A careful institutional evaluation and learning report is to be issued for each country in a form that is both relevant to the entire urban system – ie other cities – as well as useful to the cities involved. This fourth Task A report might be appropriately entitled 'Learning from Solar City Planning'. A synopsis of this report, designed for wider consumption, might be called 'Learning from Solar City'.

*Duration*
Up to six months. The main activities of this stage are expected to take four months, with another two months dedicated to reporting and publication.

*Minimum time resource requirements*
Task leadership: 3 person-months
Activity per country: 6 person-months

*Deliverables*
Task A report for Activity Period 4: 'Learning from Solar City Planning'.
Volume 4 of the *Solar City Guide*: 'Learning from Solar City'.

### A.5 Activity period 5: refinement and final reporting

A.5.1 Activity description
In the fifth stage we will refine the overall findings, the operation of local programmes while their implementation and the process of long-term institutional change continue.

## A.5.2 Final reporting

A final report is to be issued, with lessons for the community, as well as other national and international cities. This report might be entitled 'Solar City Strategies: Summary'.

A synopsis of these and the overall programme experience and results will best be digested as a summary of main findings, new knowledge areas, policy recommendations and instructions, and to be entitled 'Solar City Guide'.

*Duration*

Up to six months. The substantive refinement activities of this stage are expected to take three months, with the entire six months dedicated to final task reporting and publication.

*Minimum time resource requirements*

Task leadership: 3 person-months

Task activity per country: 6 person-months

*Deliverables*

Task A report for Activity Period 5: 'Solar City Strategies: Summary'.

Volume 5 of the *Solar City Guide* (Fifth Task Report): 'Summary, Conclusions and Next Steps'.

Final report: 'Solar City Guide'.


## 6 Task B: Targets, baseline studies and scenarios

**Objectives** include the introduction of absolute greenhouse gas emissions targets aiming at 2050 or another agreed target year, and their translation into shorter-term milestones. The quantification of urban emissions is an equally important objective. This involves the assessment, development, application and main-tenance of city- and region-wide emissions inventories to gauge both current urban energy production and consumption performance. The contribution to a common reporting format is a third aim, allowing monitoring of progress across a number of cities. Comparable baselines will be required to gauge performance improvements over time and to evaluate future renewable energy technology policy and investment paths in terms of their energy and greenhouse gas emissions reduction benefits. This format document will also contain a glossary of terms used in the discussion of task issues so that non-experts can interpret task activities more easily.

The assessment and comparison of modelling and scenario-building tools – including strategic forecasting and the identification of incremental or intermediate steps – are also part of the package of objectives. Modelling extends to urban and regional transport policy choices. An overall outcome of this exercise will be to assist the continuing evolution of internationally comparable standards in urban emissions accounting for the purpose of crediting, trading and monitored policy implementation.

## B.1 Activity period 1: inventory, partnerships and approach advancement

### B.1.1 Inventory

Now the team is ready to study and evaluate selected approaches that are being taken in any partner cities embarked on a path to energy autonomy. This activity is designed to investigate each of these in detail: everything from the institutions affected to the data sets assembled and the scenario building planning models used. These findings will be discussed and used as means of building improved baseline and accounting approaches in partnership with the participating cities. An important focus will be understanding the experiences of other cities, as well as those promoted by relevant international and national programmes, including those of Cities for Climate Protection™, Clean Cities, Energy Cities and others.

### B.1.2 Partnerships

For this stage the embrace of suitable partnerships is envisioned, with communities and their government, civic, business, industry, environmental and other organisations involved in greenhouse strategies, model maintenance or accounting efforts.

### B.1.3 Approach development

Finally, in this activity period we will consider the options for adopting a common reporting format that may allow cross-referencing and monitoring of a number of cities on a path to energy autonomy. This will not replace the currently used approaches but permit the comparison of data across cities over relevant periods. Here we can also establish a means by which the community can usefully exchange lessons and insights with other cities and areas, in identifying, collecting, collating, analysing, and interpreting data and experiences.

### B.1.4 Reporting

It is envisioned that the remainder of this first activity period be dedicated to the assembly of the report. It is recommended that the overall Task B report be entitled 'Solar City Emissions Atlas: an Inventory of Urban Energy and Emissions Accounting Methods', and the Task B contribution to the overall Volume 1 of the 'Solar City Guide' assembled by the Task A leadership team. This Volume 1 might be entitled 'Solar City: Current Practice'.

*Duration*
Up to nine months. The initial three activities are expected to take six months, with another six months allocated to reporting and publication.

*Minimum time resource requirements*
Task leadership: 4.5 person-months
Task activity per country: 4.5 person-months

*Deliverable*
Task B report for Activity Period 1: 'Solar City Emissions Atlas: an Inventory of Urban Energy and Emissions Accounting Methods'.

## B.2 Activity period 2: practice analysis and strategy development

### B.2.1 Practice analysis

This activity is designed to provide information on the way in which other cities already on a path to energy autonomy go about applying baseline data, models and targets in their institutional arrangements, and make them an integral part of public information, policy development, decision support and community planning.

The analysis should focus on the strengths and weaknesses of current and emerging reporting and baseline reporting arrangements, evaluate the opportunities that exist and the threats that may militate against seizing such opportunities. This process is to be conducted after a careful evaluation of the work, in consultation with local and, as appropriate, with regional, state or national government staff, political leaders, community representatives as well as industry and business representatives.

### B.2.2 Strategy development

The development of a clear vision and statement on the expected outcomes, including targets, for the use in Task A is essential in the detailing of a strategy. The careful development of an approach, or the refinement of existing methods – such as the development and operationalisation of the Cities for

Climate Protection™ reporting and accounting system, as legitimate and appropriate – will take up the remainder of this stage.

The approach will include the setting of absolute targets aimed at a common finite sustainable horizon – the year 2050, for example – that are scientifically demonstrated as globally acceptable for climate stabilisation purposes. These targets could usefully be differentiated for UNFCCC Annex 1 and non-Annex 1 parties, to allow for equity in higher relative development trajectories for developing countries.

We will also begin to introduce unified or multiple modelling approaches and scenario building tools, as well as incremental action staging or retrospective path analytic methods, to assist during the Task A effort in innovating in decision-making and planning approaches.

### B.2.3 Reporting

As part of the second annual report a careful reporting and model practice analysis and strategy report is to be issued, in a form that is relevant to the local community as well as other interested cities. This report may be entitled 'Solar City Models: a Strategic Review'.

*Duration*
Up to six months. The two main activities of this stage are expected to take four months, with another two months dedicated to reporting and publication.

*Minimum time resource requirements*
Task leadership: 3 person-months
Task activity per country: 3 person-months

*Deliverable*
Task B report for Activity Period 2: 'Solar City Models: a Strategic Review'.

## B.3 Activity period 3: institutional innovation and implementation

### B.3.1 Activity description

The team will now focus on institutional reforms needed to be able to respond to climate change and the fossil fuel depletion challenge – to go beyond emergency responses and Band-Aid solutions. Two important paradigmatic shifts are being brought into alignment. One consists of changes in organisational thought that have permeated public and private administrations over the past two decades. And the other is the massive economic, cultural and environmental change affecting cities that is the outcome of climate change, and will be the result of fossil fuel production peaks. Both new paradigms have been with us for some time, but have not yet been incorporated into policy and practice innovations in most of the public administrational units charged with the governance, development policy and management of cities and other urban communities.

What are the organisational skills and tools needed to transform urban development, the strategic planning and urban design processes needed to introduce renewable energy technologies on a city-wide scale, in the context of wider efficiency strategies? Some cities have developed advanced ways of developing energy targets and emissions baseline data, and of applying them to their corporate practice, or even to their energy policies and programmes. Yet to-date none has embarked on a path that fully integrates quantitative data, models and targets in the overall decision-making apparatus of their urban community, city or city-region, encompassing all relevant aspects of urban policy and practice. However, it is increasingly important to design and implement broader change in the manner in which institutions of public governance relate to one another, and enact change to promote focused decision-making and implementation. At the outset, this is useful to help identify the barriers against the adoption of new planning methods, or even intelligence gathering and modelling efforts.

A key aim is to lend local institutional expression to an all-encompassing response to the highly interactive, uncertain yet increasingly destructive forces of climate change in both mitigation and adaptation measures. For example: evaporation of water resources leads to industrial and residential supply problems, and a diminished conventional power generation capacity. This in turn prompts increasingly desperate measures to capture new water sources, such as coal or nuclear powered desalination plants, while the overall efficiency of the generation system plummets. This is a physical problem exacerbated by rising ambient temperatures: the productivity of power plants declines in hot climates. Conventional institutional silos are not only incapable of coping with this problem: they lie at the very heart of the dilemma. Conventional responses are being rolled out without rectification of underlying supply or demand management problems.

The fundamental institutional challenge is to create an environment of *urban climate innovation* – the organisational capability to respond to an unprecedented, multifaceted crisis. This can only be done through processes of institutional structural adjustment (see especially Chapter 3 above for more guidance).

### B.3.2 Reporting

An institutional innovation and implementation report is to be issued in a form that is relevant to the local urban community, and meaningful and useful to other cities. It is suggested that the report be entitled 'Practical Approaches to Urban Energy Modelling'.

*Duration*

Up to nine months. The main two activities of this stage are expected to take four months, with another two devoted to reporting and publication.

*Minimum time resource requirements*
Task leadership: 4.5 person-months
Task activity per country: 4.5 person-months

*Deliverable*
Task B report for Activity Period 3: 'Practical Approaches to Urban Energy Modelling'.

### B.4 Activity period 4: monitoring, evaluation and feedback

### B.4.1 Activity description

In the fourth stage we will structure a careful monitoring programme while the model application and development efforts continue. Monitoring will be ongoing. A well-structured evaluation method will be applied that is useful in the local context as well as of meaning to the international application of the findings. This is also the key year for providing feedback and reflection in the institutions involved, to enable broad learning from own, other national as well as international failures and successes.

### B.4.2 Reporting

A detailed institutional evaluation and learning report is to be prepared, entitled 'Learning from Solar City's Target, Baseline and Model Applications'.

*Duration*

Up to six months. The main activities of this stage are expected to take four months, with another two months dedicated to reporting and publication.

*Minimum time resource requirements*
Task leadership: 3 person-months
Task activity per country: 6 person-months

*Deliverable*
Task B report for Activity Period 4: 'Learning from Solar City's Target, Baseline and Model Applications'.

## B.5 Activity period 5: refinement and final reporting

### B.5.1 Activity description
In the final stage we will refine the overall findings, including insights into the barriers against the broad application of quantitative tools and implementation of targets in local decision-making processes while the implementation of programmes and their institutionalisation are being concluded.

### B.5.2 Reporting
A detailed final report is to be issued, in a form that is relevant to the local community and meaningful and useful to the cities involved, combining the fourth and fifth activity period. A synopsis of these and the overall Task experience and results will be produced by the Task B team and entitled 'Solar City Strategies: Summary, Conclusions and Next Steps'. This is to be digested into main findings, new knowledge areas, policy recommendations and instructions, and a report that may be entitled 'Solar City Guide'.

*Duration*
Up to six months. The main activities of this stage are expected to two months, with the entire period dedicated to reporting and publication.

*Minimum time resource requirements*
Task leadership: 3 person-months
Task activity per country: 3 person-months

*Deliverable*
Task B report for Activity Period 5: 'Solar City's Target, Baseline and Model Applications: Summary, Conclusions and Next Steps'.

## 7 Task C: Urban renewable energy systems, business and industry development

The **objective** of this task is to work towards the advancement of renewable energy technologies and systems, and to help promote the renewable energy industry, in a way that can serve the future employment base of the city and function as a model for the rest of the national and even wider urban system. The emphasis is on investigations into and development of market-led approaches to urban technology systems development and deployment, through pricing, investment and purchasing policies; and information dissemination, exemplary action and other means.

Alternative strategies are to be developed, evaluated and implemented that are suitable for a broad introduction of renewable energy technologies as a comprehensive community portfolio, for use by city government agencies, municipal utilities, businesses, industries and households. Special emphasis will be on micro-generation and distributed energy production in buildings, facilities and urban systems. Current, emerging and potentially competing renewable energy technologies, systems and related urban services are to be assessed for their city-wide and systematic adaptation in ways that are meaningful to cities' development agendas – transportation and physical planning, sustainability objectives, administration, services – and their pursuit of targeted emissions reductions.

The focus will also be on what city governments can do in collaboration with industry and constituent urban communities to understand the urban potential and advance the use of renewable fuels for industry and transport; the generation of electricity in quantity, such as solar power stations, wind, biomass, geothermal and sustainable hydropower schemes; with special emphasis on the development and deployment of technology development strategies in industrial and residential consumer-oriented applications, such as stand-alone renewable power generators and cogeneration facilities, heat pumps, photovoltaic power, solar-thermal power, solar heating and cooling, and energy networking: the development of an e-web.

## C.1 Activity period 1: inventory, partnerships and approach refinement

### C.1.1 Inventory

This activity is designed to help record and characterise the urban energy supply base, with a primary emphasis on the municipal system – demonstrating the great gains in employment and industrial innovation to be achieved over coal, oil, gas or nuclear powered supply. Second, it will help document that part of the regional economy that offers focused renewable energy introduction opportunities, such as newly developed or emerging industrial and employment areas, or, even more significantly, the opportunities in revitalising peri-urban agricultural land for renewable energy production, such as the harvesting and processing of bio-fuel crops. An aim will be to guarantee the energy autonomy of new release areas for suburban housing. And it will encourage the city to target brown-field development areas, inner-city infill sites, as well as to examine building stock likely to undergo rehabilitation and upgrading.

We will further document city, state or industry led solar and other renewable energy technology introduction programmes that impact on the business and industry community more broadly, in a beneficial way. Finally, we will account for the role of the building industry as a supply and material chain in contributing to the energy use and greenhouse gas emissions profile of the city. Current industry programmes aimed at the broad introduction of solar and other renewable energy technologies for residential, commercial and industrial applications will also be documented.

## C.1.2 Partnerships
We will also complete in this stage the selection of suitable partnership communities and their government, civic and other organisations involved in renewable energy systems, business and industry development.

## C.1.3 Approach development
Finally, in this activity period we will develop a renewable energy business base accounting framework – a uniform method for understanding the role of the renewable energy and efficiency industry, and down-stream innovations, services and suppliers, in the investment and employment base of city and region.

## C.1.4 Reporting
The remainder of this first activity period is dedicated to the assembly of the report, the overall Task C report. It is best entitled 'Solar City: an Inventory of Approaches to Urban Renewable Energy Systems, Industry and Business'.

*Duration*
Up to nine months. The initial three activities are expected to take six months, with another six months dedicated to reporting and publication.

*Minimum time resource requirements*
Task leadership: 4.5 person-months
Task activity per country: 9 person-months

*Deliverable*
Task B report for Activity Period 1: 'Solar City: an Inventory of Approaches to Urban Renewable Energy Systems, Industry and Business'.

## C.2 Activity period 2: practice analysis and strategy development

### C.2.1 Practice analysis

Here the important task is to analyse and evaluate the manner in which the city and its relevant communities approach the transformation of the city's business and industry base. The analysis will examine the strengths and weaknesses of the current and/or emerging reform arrangements, evaluate the opportunities that exist and the threats that may militate against seizing such opportunities. This process is to be conducted after a careful evaluation of the work, in consultation with local and, as appropriate, with regional, state or national government staff, political leaders, community as well as industry and business representatives.

### C.2.2 Strategy development

The development of a clear vision and statement on the expected outcomes, including targets, for use in Task A is essential in the detailing of a strategy. The careful development of an approach, or the refinement of existing methods – such as the advancement and operationalisation of any current industry mobilisation methods – will take up the remainder of this stage.

### C.2.3 Reporting

As part of the second annual report a careful renewable energy systems, business and industry practice analysis and strategy report is to be issued, in a form that is relevant to other cities in the country and elsewhere. This report is to be entitled 'Solar City® Systems, Business and Industry: a Strategic Review'.

*Duration*
Up to six months. The main two activities of this stage are expected to take four months, with another two months dedicated to reporting and publication.

*Minimum time resource requirements*
Task leadership: 3 person-months
Task activity per country: 6 person-months

*Deliverable*
Task B report for Activity Period 2: 'Solar City® Systems, Business and Industry: a Strategic Review'.

## C.3 Activity period 3: institutional innovation and implementation

### C.3.1 Activity description
This activity will focus on the organisational, skills and tools requirements necessary to transform urban development, strategic planning and urban design provisions, procedures and processes to maximise the opportunities for renewable energy technologies and efficiency measures on a city-wide scale, providing input into the work and findings of Task A.

### C.3.2 Reporting
A concise institutional innovation and implementation report is to be issued in a form that is accessible to government, the general public and business communities but also meaningful to other cities. The report will be best entitled 'Practical Approaches to Urban Energy Business and Industry Development'.

*Duration*
Up to nine months. The two main activities of this stage are expected to take four months, with another two months dedicated to reporting and publication.

*Minimum time resource requirements*
Task leadership: 4.5 person-months
Task activity per country: 9 person-months

*Deliverable*
Task B report for Activity Period 3: 'Practical Approaches to Urban Energy Business and Industry Development'.

## C.4 Activity period 4: monitoring, evaluation and feedback

### C.4.1 Activity description
Here we will structure a careful monitoring programme while support for the industry and business development activities programme continues. Monitoring will be ongoing. A well-conceived and simple evaluation method will be developed and applied that is useful in the local context but also internationally. This is also the key year for providing feedback and reflection in the institutions involved, to enable broad learning from local, other national as well as international problems and successes.

### C.4.2 Reporting

As part of the third annual report a detailed institutional evaluation and learning report is to be issued for local communities: 'Learning from Solar City's Business and Industry Community'.

*Duration*

Up to six months. The main activities of this stage are expected to take four months, with another two months dedicated to reporting and publication.

*Minimum time resource requirements*
Task leadership: person-months
Task activity per country: 6 person-months

*Deliverable*
Task C report for Activity Period 4: 'Learning from Solar City's Business and Industry Community'.

## C.5 Activity period 5: refinement and final reporting

### C.5.1 Activity description

In the final stage we will refine the overall findings including insight into the barriers against the implementation of accelerated solar and other renewable energy commercialisation programmes that would benefit business and industry.

### C.5.2 Reporting

A final report, combining the work of the fourth and fifth activity periods, is to be issued to all local communities, but it should also be useful to other interested cities. It is to be entitled: 'Solar City Systems, Industry and Business: Summary, Conclusions and Next Steps'.

*Duration*

Up to six months. The main activities of this stage are expected to take two months while the entire six month period will be dedicated to reporting and publication.

*Minimum time resource requirements*
Task leadership: 3 person-months
Task activity per country: 6 person-months

*Deliverable*
Task C report for Activity Period 5: 'Solar City Systems, Industry and Business: Summary, Conclusions and Next Steps'.

# 8 Communications

The following elements are expected to form a useful part of any information and communication strategy for a comprehensive Solar City programme.

## Website

A dedicated website is likely to form a helpful communication, information and publishing base. It can be linked to master sites such as solarcity.org, wcre.org, ises.org, iclei.org and a number of other appropriate locations.

## Workshops and conferences

It will be useful to hold workshops throughout the year dedicated to specific task themes as well as to the entire programme. In addition, national and international conferences with other cities involved in similar initiatives can be held at which the results of the project stages can be discussed in the context of the global urban energy and renewable energy agenda.

## Annual reports and publishing

Each year is expected to produce in one volume of the final published product: the Solar City Guide. The Task A leader should work through the overall coordinator in producing annual reports and evaluations, assembling all three task documents into a single volume in each consecutive year.

## Summary of reports

**Task A reports** by Task A leader:
   Activity Period 1: 'Solar City strategies'.
   Activity Period 2: 'Solar City Planning Practice and Strategic Options'.
   Activity Period 3: 'How to Build a Solar City – a Handbook for Local Governments'.
   Activity Period 4: 'Learning from Solar City Planning'.
   Activity Period 5: 'Solar City Strategies: Summary, Conclusions and Next Steps'.

**Task B reports** by Task B leader:

Activity Period 1: 'Solar City Atlas: an Inventory of Urban Energy and Emissions Accounting methods'.

Activity Period 2: 'Solar City Models: a Strategic Review'.

Activity Period 3: 'Practical Approaches to Urban Energy Modelling'.

Activity Period 4: 'Learning from Solar City's Target, Baseline and Model Applications'.

Activity Period 5: 'Solar City's Target, Baseline and Model Applications: Summary, Conclusions and Next Steps'.

**Task C reports** by Task C leader:

Activity Period 1: 'Solar City: an Inventory of Approaches to Urban Renewable Energy Systems, Industry and Business'.

Activity Period 2: 'Solar City Systems, Business and Industry: a Strategic Review'.

Activity Period 3: 'Practical Approaches to Urban Energy Business and Industry Development'.

Activity Period 4: 'Learning from Solar City's Business and Industry Community'.

Activity Period 5: 'Solar City Systems, Industry and Business: Summary, Conclusions and Next Steps'.

**Summary of overall programme reports:** the *Solar City Guide*

Volume 1 of the Solar City Guide (1st programme report): 'Solar City: Current Practice'.

Volume 2 of the Solar City Guide (2nd programme report): 'Solar City: Understanding Practice – Developing Strategies'.

Volume 3 of the Solar City Guide (3rd programme report): 'Solar City: Implementing Institutional Innovations'.

Volume 4 of the Solar City Guide (4th programme report): 'Learning from Solar City'.

Volume 5 of the Solar City Guide (5th programme report): 'Conclusions and Next Steps'.

**Final report:** 'Solar City Guide' (refined compilation of all volumes).

These reports are to be issued as stand-alone documents and form the basis for either a set of publications, or a combined report and guide to be published by the city or community itself, or by commercial publishers.

# 9 Milestones: sample schedule

| | |
|---|---|
| Program start | 1 January 2007 |
| Stage 1 complete | 1 October 2007 |
| Stage 2 complete | 1 April 2008 |
| Stage 3 complete | 1 January 2009 |
| Stage 4 complete | 1 July 2009 |
| Stage 5 complete | 1 January 2010 |
| Final report due | 1 July 2010 |

(adapted from *Solar City*, 1999–2006)

## 6.2 THE RENEWABLE CITY™ RATING FRAMEWORK

This framework is developed to help evaluate progress and performance of cities and communities. The urban rating tool consists of 10 renewable performance dimensions, quantitative and qualitative, ranging from cultural to technological and institutional criteria, using a globally comparable points system. It draws from international practice and is compatible with other accredited programmes and performance measures.

Each area, numbered from 1 to 10 below, is valued at 10 per cent of the overall score, with each criterion making up an equal fraction – adding up to a possible 100 points. Detailed, quantified, professionally assessed and audited ratings can be arranged for cities, towns and other communities (Renewable City 2007).

### 1 Renewable culture

- Renewable energy generation and choice of freedom from fossil and nuclear power enshrined and safeguarded as a fundamental civil right.
- Renewable energy related public events, press articles and media features, as a percentage of total.
- Civil society engaged politically, with government agencies accountable to it.
- High degree of participation in energy and environmental interest groups.
- Sustained public information and professional education programmes.
- Voter determination expressed in electoral patterns.

- Broad organisational reform measures taken.
- Renewable City schools programmes active.
- Well-resourced, dedicated organisations in place.

## 2 Greenhouse gas emissions reduction targeting, planning and tracking

- Long-range emissions reduction plan targeted, monitored and adequately resourced, with tangible outcomes present.
- City-wide consumption-based greenhouse accounting method per capita in place.
- Carbon accounting by sector, source, geographical unit, household or business unit.
- Renewable energy technology introduction targets set; progress monitored.
- Municipal corporate emissions reductions leading the way.
- Individual and household reduction and verification.
- Industry and business involvement in reductions.
- Resourced organisations in place.

## 3 Renewable city finance

- Renewable power purchasing provisions as percentage of municipal electricity consumption.
- Total value of development support, as percentage of municipal budget.
- Renewable energy production support programmes in place.
- Commercialisation grant, loan and incentives programmes.
- Active municipal investments in renewable portfolio.
- Renewable energy market development measures.
- Renewable micro-finance available to the poor.
- Renewable energy feed-in provisions.

## 4 Renewable energy technology development and proliferation policies

- Green power purchasing offers, incentives or requirements in place.
- District heating or cooling systems city operated or contracted.

- Regional and urban wind power city operated or contracted.
- Regional biofuel development city-operated or contracted.
- Other renewable assets city-operated or contracted (hydro, solar-thermal etc).
- City-integrated photovoltaic programme in place.
- Partnerships with universities and industries.
- Resourced organisations in place.

## 5 Renewable institutions

- Municipal or municipal-controlled energy planning and policy agencies, utilities, power companies, generators and/or controlling providers.
- Municipal renewable power generation increasing annually, either operated or contracted, or both.
- Acquisition of urban and regional energy providers in the absence of existing utilities.
- Institutional renewable energy accountabilities established.
- Institutional change agencies resourced and empowered.

## 6 Renewable city design

- Renewable or sustainable building rating systems established as part of planning administration, development control or design review.
- Green roof and cool roof programmes, or equivalent urban thermal management programmes in place.
- Carbon or energy-sensitive land use and infrastructure models, policies and planning methods.
- Municipal land use planning integrated with regional transport planning, energy sensitive.
- Urban agriculture, wilds, parks, gardens incorporated in renewable city planning.
- Physical renewable city capacity and planning procedures in place.
- Land use and transport integration measures active.
- Transport emissions reduction policies in place.
- Transport greenhouse policy model in place.
- Solar ordinances in place for all sectors.
- Resourced organisations in place.

## 7 Longevity and success factor: Renewable City learning

- Overall monitoring programme in place; improvements registered and verified by recognised, established or future urban performance frameworks.
- Institutional feedback and learning mechanisms in place.
- Resourced organisations in place.

## 8 Climate change adaptation through mitigation

- Institutional reform agenda embraced to prioritise climate change response.
- Climate change mitigation measures integrated as central to adaptation.
- Local sensitivities mapped in social, economic and physical terms.
- Dynamic local climate models in place.
- Scenario building models in active use.
- Well-resourced organisations in place.

## 9 Business development and employment generation

- State government and national renewable energy laws with implementation programmes enacted; tangible market establishment frameworks in place.
- Public–private partnerships embraced.
- Well-resourced organisations in place.

## 10 Think locally, act globally

- Regional, national and international city networks and programmes engaged.
- Institutional linkages to international research and policy organisations.
- Participation in global action and research programmes.
- Well-resourced network organisations in place.

## Current best practice in Portland, Oregon

Tens of thousands of cities around the world pursue greater efficiency in their building stock, transport systems and energy infrastructures; and thousands have embraced renewable energy implementation strategies. Scores are nervous about climate change and develop adaptation strategies. Hundreds are serious about establishing greenhouse emissions targets for their municipal installations and fleets, and dozens have committed themselves to establishing and reaching such targets for their cities as a whole, and in a sustained manner. Only a few pursue all of these aims as a serious and core concern and as a matter of whole-of-city development priority. But all have learned that while there may be a clear longterm goal – renewable energy autonomy – there is no single path to the Renewable City. And while there may be clear strategic planning frameworks such as the International Council for Local Environmental Initiatives' Cities for Climate Protection™ (ICLEI CCP) framework, or self-guided tools such as the Solar City® programme presented above, each approach is arrived at via a discrete, individually charted path.

Because of the great variety of cities involved, their different levels of development, cultural setting, size and political systems, it is impossible to create a meaningful template or best-practice framework that fits all. This book is set out to provide a larger framework, informed in part by many city programmes in place around the world, changing daily. Using the best possible decision frameworks, each city pursues its own destiny with its staff, communities, advisors and local, state, national and international organisations. Therefore, instead of a single practice template for all, let us celebrate one of these advanced cities, as ranking high in the terms of this book, as the 'Renewable City 2007', so to speak, not as a literal model, but rather to provide an informal story of its path as a guide and inspiration, both ordinary and extraordinary. It is a snapshot of a state in flux, of institutional change, after more than a dozen years of persistent effort, and a tale of broad community participation as well as enlightened political advocacy. As early as 1993 Portland had been one of 12 municipal participants in ICLEI's Urban $CO_2$ Reduction Project, precursor to its CCP campaign. Captured at this particular moment in history, on the verge of a massive revolution, it will serve here as a time capsule in which to look back at important yet comparably humble beginnings.

Portland has always attracted people interested in the surrounding wilds, in the idea of nature – it is small enough to sustain a sense of community and direction, yet large enough to be a major city. The Willamette, lazily snaking through the city, hosting houseboat colonies steeped in loggers' traditions, reminds local folk of their home, their responsibilities and why they are here. This historical wood-felling outpost has become finely attuned to the call of nature in distress. It is little wonder the city's community was open to many means of achieving better urban performance, especially in energy practice.

Specific information about Portland's experience and success, and a range of other cities on the way to renewability, can be accessed on or via the Renewable City website, http://www.renewablecity.org (RC 2007). There, the story is offered through the Climate Group's voice (Climate Group 2006) and through current announcements and past archives of the City of Portland's Office of Sustainable Development (Portland 1993, 2001, 2005, 2006).

**A renewable city celebration in the 1950s**
Pat Thornson was elected as freshly elected 'Sun Goddess' in Phoenix, Arizona, to celebrate the first world symposium on applied solar energy. It was staged in the winter resort area November 1–5, 1955 – manifesting the long link between renewable energy technology, local communities and civic pride.

# Glossary

**Alternative energy**: The term is not usually used as being synonymous with renewable energy; it can denote a wide range of non-fossil power forms and sources, from nuclear to municipal waste combustion, including what are defined as renewable systems.

**City**: any urbanised area managed and represented by one or several local governments, culturally and communally understood as a city, with specific administrative and political boundaries.

**City region**: a city region is the general urbanised, ecological and economic area comprising and surrounding one or several urban nuclei, all or any of which may be defined as city.

**Climate-stable practice**: the working definition of a city's climate-stable practice is a practical commitment to lower greenhouse gas emissions by a given target year – for example, the year 2050 – to a level that is proportionally in keeping with a globally sustainable level of emissions.

**$CO_2$-e**: carbon-dioxide-equivalent; expresses the presence of all effective greenhouse gases as an amount that would be required in $CO_2$ to achieve the same effect.

**Clean energy**: See also **Green energy** – the term is used in similar ways to denote a wide range of applications, but is generally applied to higher-efficiency, lower-polluting forms of fossil fuel power, and even to nuclear power.

**Cogeneration**: denotes the combined production of electricity and heat in power plants that can supply a single building or an entire neighbourhood, business park, hospital or university. Cogeneration can be based on any fuel: traditionally natural gas, coal or wood. It can be powered by solar-thermal steam, biofuel, biogas and through renewable-energy fed hydrogen fuel cells. Cogeneration supports distributed or stand-alone generation and, given adequate management and supply conditions, can be more affordable than grid power.

**Differentiated globalisation**: the deployment of renewable energy technologies on a large scale has the potential to support a time of *differentiated globalisation* (Droege 1999, 2004), broadly distinguishing between locally sourced food and basic goods, and the comparably more global, footloose trade in financial and other advanced services.

**Embodied energy**: the total energy content of any product or service that led to its making or delivery: the energy required to produce concrete, make hamburgers, grow wheat, finish construction timber or cut hair, produce a TV show or run a cruise line. The total embodied energy of a service or product includes all power inputs required in the final good or service as purchased or consumed: in mining, administration, transport, salaries, insurance or entertainment, for example. Most significant – and implied in this definition – is the amount of embodied fossil, nuclear and other non-renewable energy involved in the entire process.

**Energy web or e-web**: an expression newly coined for this book, to denote the intelligent networking of dispersed energy producers, consumers and prosumers into an overall urban or regional area network. This concept is related to that of the city as **virtual power plant**: a city of distributed sources simulating a single large plant by virtue of the combined functioning of numerous small suppliers.

**Green energy**: This term is often used to express an aspiration of environmental friendliness in energy management. It is applied to all forms of renewable energy but often encompasses also non-renewable or unsustainable sources such as domestic waste incineration. It can also denote energy efficiency measures, high-efficiency natural gas devices, or even lower-carbon versions of coal power – somewhat 'greener' and 'cleaner' than the burning of high-sulphur coal, for example.

**Greenhouse gas (GHG)**: human activity effected gases that trigger global warming are carbon dioxide ($CO_2$), methane ($CH_4$), nitrous oxide ($N_2O$) and chlorofluorocarbons, especially CFC–11, HCFC–22 and $CF_4$. The emission levels of the latter three groups are often combined with $CO_2$ and jointly expressed as $CO_2$-e, ie calculated into the equivalent potency of carbon dioxide. The list of *standardised anthropogenic* emissions used by the Intergovernmental Panel on Climate Change (IPCC) is $CO_2$, $CH_4$, $N_2O$, $NO_x$, CO, NMVOCs, $SO_2$, HFCs, PFCs and $SF_6$.

**Hybrid supply**: a source or system combining several renewable energy technologies to achieve a more reliable overall service output, sometimes in combination with fossil fuel plants or generators. This **multi-media** supply portfolio may involve solar, wind, water and biofuel in a concentrated, stand-alone or network-connected formation. The term may also denote a virtual hybrid system, whereby a building, urban area, city or region is endowed with a well balanced mix of renewable sources and storage systems, achieving steady supply levels.

**Less developed countries**: the countries of Africa; Asia without Japan; Latin America and the Caribbean; and the archipelagos of Melanesia, Micronesia and Polynesia (PRB 2005).

**Mega-city**: an urban area with a population of at least 10 million (PRB 2005).

**Metropolitan area**: a concentration of urban population of generally at least 100,000 people, including a city core of at least 50,000 inhabitants (PRB 2005).

**More developed countries**: included here are all countries in Europe, North America, Australia, New Zealand and Japan (PRB 2005).

**Multi-media**: see **hybrid supply**.

**New Energy**: This has been broadly used as a vague term to denote most 'new' energy forms, including waste incineration, sometimes synonymously with 'green energy'. It has also been appropriated by some proponents of speculative or theoretical energy or particle physics such as *cold fusion* or *low energy nuclear reactions* (LENR), *vacuum energy*, or *environmental energy* (IE 2006).

**Peak Oil**: defined as the point in time when global oil and natural gas supplies reach their total global production peak. Estimated by many to be soon: Colin Campbell's 2005 revision suggested 2010 (Campbell 2005).

**Prosumer**: an individual or organisation acting as both consumer and producer: for example, a family operating a rooftop solar power array or wind generator, feeding power into a municipal grid as well as powering their own home.

**Rankine cycle engines**: vapour – or steam – generators, relying on one of ten theoretical and practical thermodynamic cycles to generate mechanical energy. The Rankine cycle involves, in sequence: heating water at a constant pressure, evaporating it, heating the saturated vapour to gas, expanding, exhausting and condensing it. Organic Rankine Cycle (ORC) engines use organic compounds instead of water vapour, reducing mechanical and material wear and increasing efficiency. The engines are used in cogeneration and solar-thermal plants. The

Rankine cycle is named after its developer, the Scottish engineer WJM Rankine (1820–70).

**Renewability**: a neologism created for this book, to denote the theoretical or practical capacity of a city, urban area or economy to rely exclusively on renewable energy.

**Renewable energy**: forms of renewable energy range from good building design – also termed, inadequately, 'passive solar' – to water, wave, wind, solar thermal, photovoltaic, biofuel and heat-pump power. Generally subsumed under 'renewables' are also other, related forms of benign and virtually inexhaustible non-solar power generation. *Lunar power* is harnessed by generators working with tidal movements. *Terrestrial power* is harvested by tapping into geothermal energy, derived from shallow or deep underground energy reservoirs fed by the heat emanating from the earth's molten core. The definitions of renewable, sustainable, green or alternative energy vary, and further the confusion. For example, landfill gas and waste incineration are frequently subsumed under renewable or sustainable energy categories: but these are not renewable because they depend on the finite supply of resources embodied in such urban *cradle-to-cremation* material streams. And in encouraging more waste and contributing to environmental pollution, many of these pseudo-renewable sources are not environmentally sustainable either.

**Sterling engine**: patented in 1816 by the Scottish minister Robert Sterling (1790–1878) as 'Heat Economiser', this highly efficient, quiet, non-combustion based mechanism generates mechanical energy from temperature differentials as small as 4 or 5 degrees Celsius, harnessing the differential pressure exerted by gas in a sealed chamber. Sterling engines have a wide range of specialised applications requiring continuous operation, such as pumps, propulsion or solar-thermal energy devices.

**Solar** (energy): 'solar' in its widest definition connotes all aspects of energy sources that can be traced to the action of the sun. These include the more narrowly defined systems of solar thermal, photovoltaic and 'passive' technologies and other 'renewables' – biomass, bio energy, wind and wave energy. Strictly speaking, fossil fuel is solar energy, too, but in this book we refer to 'solar and other renewable' energy to describe all sustainable sources of power that neither create greenhouse gas emissions nor non-degradable and/or toxic waste.

**Solar City**®: a programme defining urban communities tangibly committed to embracing a path of integrating a range of renewable energy technologies as well as efficiency measures into a broad, community-wide planning strategy aimed at climate-stable greenhouse-gas emissions levels by 2050 – or another target date of a community's choosing.

**Solar habitat**: describes any form of human settlement or community that derives the entirety of its energy requirements from renewable power sources: sun, wind, water and biofuel.

**Urban**: countries differ in the way they classify population as 'urban' or 'rural'. A settled community with a population of 2,000 or more is defined as urban. National definitions are listed in the United Nations Demographic Yearbook (PRB 2005).

**Urban agglomeration**: defined as areas of one million inhabitants or more, within contiguous territory and inhabited at urban levels of residential density, without regard to administrative boundaries (PRB 2005).

**Urbanisation**: growth in the proportion of a population living in urban areas (PRB 2005).

**Virtual power plant**: see *Energy web or e-web*.

# References and Webography

AAG – American Association of Geographers GCLP Research Group 2003, *Global Change and Local Places: Estimating, Understanding and Reducing Greenhouse Gases*. Cambridge: Cambridge University Press

Abercrombie, Sir P 1945, *Greater London Plan 1944*. London: HMSO

Adelaide, City of 2005, *Sustainable Business Directory*. Retrieved on 27 November 2005 from http://www.adelaidegreencity.com/sbdsa

AGO – Australian Greenhouse Office 2003, *Renewable Energy Commercialisation in Australia*. Canberra: Australian Greenhouse Office. Retrieved on 26 February 2006 from http://greenhouse.gov.au/renewable/recp/pubs/booklet.pdf

—— 2004, *Solar Cities: Statement of Challenges and Opportunities*. Retrieved on 26 February 2006 from http://www.greenhouse.gov.au

Akagawa, H 2002, 'Photovoltaic Capacity of Greater Sydney Roof Scapes.' Unpublished research paper, University of Sydney and Obayashi Technical Research Institute

—— 2003, 'Greening Buildings in Japan.' Unpublished best-practice presentation, University of Sydney and Obayashi Technical Research Institute

Aleklett, K 2004, 'The IEA accepts Peak Oil.' Uppsala Hydrocarbon Depletion Study Group, Uppsala University/Association for the Study for Peak Oil and Gas (ASPO). Retrieved on 26 February 2006 from http://www.peakoil.net/uhdsg/weo2004/TheUppsalaCode.html

Allen – Allen Consulting Group 2005, 'Climate Change Risk and Vulnerability – promoting an efficient adaptation response for Australia.' Report to the Australian Greenhouse Office. Retrieved on 27 November

2005 from http://www.greenhouse.gov.au/impacts/publications/pubs/risk-vulnerability.pdf

Alpensolar 2006, Retrieved on 9 July 2006 from http://www.alpensolar.de

Alt, F 2005a, 'Kraftwerk verwandelt Gras in Energie.' *News von der Sonnenseite*. Retrieved on 27 November 2005 from http://www.sonnenseite.com/index.php?pageID=7&article:oid=a562&template=article_detail.html

—— 2005b, 'Mit Gülle und 130 Sachen über die Schiene.' *News von der Sonnenseite*. Retrieved on 27 November 2005 from http://www.sonnenseite.com/index.php?pageID=6&news:oid=n3240&template=news_detail.html

—— 2005c, 'Der Ölwechsel für München: vom Erdöl zum Bioöl.' *News von der Sonnenseite*. Retrieved on 27 November 2005 from http://www.sonnenseite.com/index.php?pageID=6&news:oid=n4190&flash=true

—— 2005d, 'Rottenburg am Neckar siegt im Solarwettbewerb.' *News von der Sonnenseite*. Retrieved on 6 March 2006 from http://www.sonnenseite.com/index.php?pageID=6&news:oid=n4256

—— 2005e, 'Davos wird erste Gemeinde mit vollständiger $CO_2$-Bilanz.' *News von der Sonnenseite*. Retrieved on 16 December 2005 from http://www.sonnenseite.com/index.php?pageID=6&news:oid=n4263

ALTER – Le Groupe de Bellevue 1978, 'A Study of a Long-Term Energy Future for France based on 100% Renewable Energies' Paris. In *The Yearbook of Renewable Energies 1997/96*. London 1996, pp 104 ff

Annex 31, International Energy Agency (IEA), Committee on Energy Research and Technology (CERT) 2006, *Energy Related Environmental Impact of Building*. Retrieved on 26 February 2006 from http://www.iisbe.org/annex31/index.html

Appenzeller, T 2004, *The End of Cheap Oil*, National Geographic Magazine, June 2004, Washington DC: The National Geographic Society

Archer, CL and Mark Z Jacobson 2005, 'Evaluation of global wind power.' Unpublished typescript, Stanford University, 3 February

Ardila, A and G Menckhoff 2002, *Transportation Policies in Bogotá: Building a Transportation System for the People*. Washington, DC: Massachusetts Institute of Technology and World Bank

Arias, C 2002, 'The Trolley Bus System of the City of Quito, Ecuador.' Paper presented at a brainstorming session on Non-Technology Options for Stimulating Modal Shifts in City Transport Systems held in Nairobi, Kenya. March. STAP/GEF, Washington, DC

Arlinghoff, R, Michael Geyer and Frederick H Morse c 2004, *The Concentrating Solar Power Global Market Initiative*. Neumühle, Germany: ESTIA/Aguadulce, Spain: IEA SolarPACES/Washington, DC: SEIA

Arnold, JA 2005, 'The Urban Heat Island.' Retrieved on 27 November 2005 from http://weather.msfc.nasa.gov/urban/urban_heat_island.html

Arrhenius, S 1896, 'On the Influence of Carbonic Acid in the Air upon the Temperature of the Ground', *Philosophical Magazine* 41: 237–76

—— 1922, *Die Chemie und das moderne Leben*. Leipzig. Quoted in H Scheer 2005, *Energieautonomie*. Berlin: Antje Kunstmann, pp 112ff

AS – Standards Australia 2004, *Australian Standard AS4360: Risk*. Sydney: Standards Australia International

Ashton, TS 1998, *The Industrial Revolution, 1860–1930*. New York: Oxford University Press

ASIT – Asociación Solar de la Industria Termica 2005, 'Spain: Market Development and Perspectives'. Presentation at the Second European Solar Thermal Energy Conference, 22 June. Freiburg, Germany

Aubrey, C et al (eds) 2005, *Wind Force 12. A Blueprint to Achieve 12% of the World's Electricity from Wind Power by 2020*. GWEC/EWEA/Greenpeace

Barcelona [City of] 2000, 'Barcelona Ordinance on application of solar-thermal energy systems into the buildings.' Text and information supplied courtesy of Dr Josep Puig, former Barcelona Sustainable City Councillor 1995–9, Professor at the Autonomous University of Barcelona and consultant with Ecofys. Full ordinance downloadable from http://www.renewablecity.org

BASIX – Building Sustainability Index 2006, http://www.basix.nsw.gov.au. Retrieved on 26 February 2006 from http://www.basix.nsw.gov.au/ information/common/pdf/pn_basix_regscheme.pdf

BBC 2006, 'Ukraine "stealing Europe's gas".' London: BBC News. Monday, 2 January. Retrieved on 16 May 2006 from http://news.bbc.co.uk/1/hi/world/europe/4574630.stm

Bennello, CG et al 1989, Building Sustainable Communities: Tools and Concepts for Self-Reliant Economic Change, Ward Morehouse, Editor, New York: The Bootstrap Press, 1989

BLM – Bureau of Lands Management 2004, 'Instruction Memorandum No. 2005–006.' 20 October. Expires 09/30/2006. Retrieved on 3 March 2006 from http://www.blm.gov/nhp/efoia/wo/fy05/im2005-006.htm

Boyle, G (ed) 2004, *Renewable Energy*. Oxford/Milton Keynes: Oxford University Press/Open University

BRE – Building Research and Consultancy 2005, *BREEAM – the BRE Environmental Assessment Method*. Retrieved on 27 November 2005 from http://www.breeam.org

Broehl, J 2005a, 'Renewable energy legislation in Washington State.' 10 May. Retrieved on 27 November 2005 from RenewableEnergyAccess.com

—— 2005b, 'Wal-Mart Deploys Solar, Wind, Sustainable Design.' RenewableEnergyAccess.com, 22 July 2005. Retrieved on 27 November 2005 from www.renewableenergyaccess.com/rea/news/story?id=34647

Brown, MA, Frank Southworth and Therese K Stovall 2005, *Towards a Climate-Friendly Built Environment*. Arlington, VA: Pew Center on Global Climate Change

Bush, GW 2005, 'Energy Security for the 21st Century – Reliable, Affordable, Environmentally-Sound Energy.' Retrieved on 27 November 2005 from http://www.whitehouse.gov/infocus/energy

Butera, F 2004, *Dalla caverna alla casa ecologica – Storia del comfort e dell'energia*. Milan: Edizioni Ambiente srl

Byrne, J, Young-Doo Wang, Hoesung Lee and Jong-dall Kim 1998, 'An equity- and sustainability-based policy response to global climate change'. *Energy Policy* 26 (4): 335–43

—— and Leigh Glover 2000, 'Climate Shopping: Putting the Atmosphere Up for Sale.' *TELA*: Environment, Economy and Society Series: 28 pp. Melbourne, Australia: Australian Conservation Foundation

——, Leigh Glover, Vernese Inniss, Jiyoti Kulkarni, Yu-Mi Mun, Noah Toly and Young-Doo Wang 2002, 'Greenhouse Justice – Moving beyond Kyoto.' Position paper prepared for UNFCC COP–8, New Delhi, India, 23 October–1 November. University of Delaware: Center for Energy & Environmental Policy

——, Leigh Glover et al 2004, 'Reclaiming the Atmospheric Commons: Beyond Kyoto.' In V Grover (ed), *Climate Change: Five Years after Kyoto*. Enfield, New Hampshire: Science Publishers, pp 429–52

Calthorpe, P 1993, *The Next American Metropolis: Ecology, Community, and the American Dream*. New York: Princeton Architectural Press

Campbell, CJ 1998, *The End of Cheap Oil*. Geneva: PetroConsultants SA

—— 2003, *The Essence of Oil and Gas Depletion*. Brentwood, Essex: Multi-Science Publishing and Geneva: PetroConsultants SA

—— 2004, *The Coming Oil Crisis*. Brentwood, Essex: Multi-Science Publishing

—— 2005, 'Revision of the Depletion Model.' Association for the Study of Peak Oil and Gas (ASPO) – Article 624, Newsletter No 58, October. Retrieved on 27 November 2005 from http://www.peakoil.ie/downloads/newsletters/newsletter58_200510.pdf

Campbell, CJ and Jean H Laherrere 1995, *The World's Oil Supply 1930–2050*. Geneva: PetroConsultants SA

Capello, R, Peter Nijkamp and Peter Pepping 1999, *Sustainable Cities and Energy Policies*. Berlin: Springer

Carlowitz, Hans Carl von 1713/2000, *Sylvicultura oeconomica: Anweisung zur wilden Baum-Zucht*. Edited by Klaus Irmer and Angela Kießling. Freiberg: TU Bergakademie/Akademische Buchhandlung

Castells, M 2000, *The Rise of the Network Society*. Oxford, UK and Malden, MA: Blackwell

CCP – Cities for Climate Protection 2005, 'International Council for Local Environmental Initiatives (ICLEI).' Retrieved on 27 November 2005 from http://www.iclei.org/index.php?id=800

Cerda – Institut Cerda et al 2001, *Solar City Guide – New Solutions in Energy Supply*. Madrid: Institut Cerda. Supported by the European Commission Fifth Framework Programme and the Swiss Federal Office for Education and Science. Retrieved on 6 March 2006 from http://pvcityguide.energyprojects.net

CERES – California Environmental Resources Evaluation System 2006, *The Solar Rights Act of 1978*. Retrieved on 6 March 2006 from http://ceres.ca.gov/planning/preemption/Part2e.html

Cervero, R 1998, *The Transit Metropolis*. New York: Island Press

Chandigarh 2006, 'Genesis of the City.' Official website of Chandigarh Administration. Retrieved on 6 March 2006 from http://sampark.chd.nic.in/pls/esampark_web/city_history

Chapman, C 2005, 'Sun-starved Alpine villages "see the light" with the help of solar mirrors.' London: *Telegraph*, 16 January. http://news.telegraph.co.uk/news/main.jhtml?xml=/news/2005/01/16/walp16.xml

Cifuentes, L, Victor H Borja-Aburto, Nelson Gouveia, George Thurston and Devra Lee Davis 2001, 'Hidden Health Benefits of Greenhouse Gas Mitigation.' *Science* (17 August): Vol. 293 no. 5533, pp 1257–9

Clark, D 1996, *Urban World/Global City*. London/New York: Routledge

CLC – Cape Light Compact 2006, http://www.capelightcompact.org

Climate Group, 2006, Retrieved on 30 October 2005 from http://www.theclimategroup.org/index.php?pid=567

Cocks, D, Franzi Poldy and Barney Foran 2000, *A Comprehensive Simulation Model of Material and Energy Transformations and Transfers in the Australian Economy*. National Futures Group Working Document 00–11. Canberra: CSIRO. Retrieved on 30 October 2005 from http://www.cse.csiro.au/publications

Coghlan, A 2003, ' "Too little" oil for global warming.' Breaking News, *New Scientist* 5 October. Retrieved on 30 October 2005 from http://www.newscientist.com/article.ns?id=dn4216

Costanza, R and C Folke 1997, 'Valuing ecosystem services with efficiency, fairness and sustainability as goals.' In GC Daily (ed), *Nature's Services: Societal Dependence on Natural Ecosystems*. Island Press, Washington, DC, pp 49–67

Crotogino, F, Klaus-Uwe Mohmeyer and Roland Scharf 2001, 'Huntorf CAES: More than 20 Years of Successful Operation.' Paper presented at 15–18 April 2001 Compresssed Air Energy Storage (CAES) Meeting in Orlando, Florida. University of Saarland. Retrieved on 30 October 2005 from http://www.uni-saarland.de/fak7/fze/AKE_Archiv/AKE2003H/AKE2003H _ Vortraege / AKE2003H03c _ Crotogino _ ea  HuntorfCAES _ CompressedAirEnergyStorage.pdf

Dakal, S 2004, *Urban Energy Use and Greenhouse Gas Emissions in Asian Mega-Cities. Policies for a Sustainable Future*. Kitakyushu: Institute for Global Environment Strategies (IGES)

DCA – Davos Climate Alliance 2005, http://www.davosclimatealliance.org

Deffeyes, KS 2003, *Hubbert's Peak: The Impending World Oil Shortage*. Princeton, NJ: Princeton University Press

De Graaf, J, David Wann and Thomas H Naylor 2005, *Affluenza: The All-Consuming Epidemic*. Berrett-Koehler Publishers; San Francisco

dena – Deutsche Energie-Agentur 2005, *Planning of the Grid Integration of Wind Energy in Germany Onshore and Offshore up to the Year 2020 (dena grid study)*. Berlin: Deutsche Energie-Agentur GmbH

DEUS – Department of Energy, Utilities and Sustainability 2006, 'NABERS – The National Australian Built Environment Rating System.' Retrieved on 30 January 2006 from http://www.nabers.com.au/nabers

Diamond, J 2005, *Collapse – How Societies Choose to Fail or Survive*. London: Penguin, p 507

Docklands Authority 2002, *Melbourne Docklands ESD Guide*. Melbourne: Docklands Authority

DoE – US Department of Energy 2001, '4 Times Square.' Retrieved on 30 December 2005 from http://www.eere.energy.gov/buildings/info/documents/pdfs/29940.pdf

—— 2006a, *US Department of Energy/Energy Efficiency and Renewable Energy – High-performance Buildings Database.* Retrieved on 10 March 2006 from http://www.eere.energy.gov/buildings/database/index.cfm/. Content last updated: 31 October 2004

DoE, 2006 – United States Department of Energy, Energy Efficiency and Renewable Energy (EERE), 2006a, *Clean Cities.* Retrieved on 30 January 2006 from http://www.eere.energy.gov/cleancities

DoE – United States Department of Energy, Energy Efficiency and Renewable Energy (EERE) 2006a, *Clean Cities.* Retrieved on 30 January 2006 from http://www.eere.energy.gov/cleancites

Downing, AJ 1974, *Rural Essays*, ed George William Curtis. New York: Da Capo Press

Doxiades, KA and JG Papaioannou 1974, *Ecumenopolis: The Inevitable City of the Future.* Athens: Athens Center of Ekistics

DPWS – NSW Department of Public Works and Services 2006, 'LCAid – computer modelling for environmental design.' http://www.projectweb.gov.com.au/dataweb/lcaid

Drexler, KE 1986, *Engines of Creation.* New York: Anchor

Droege, P 1992, 'To Live in Harmony With the Sea – an Envelopment Strategy for the Next Three Generations.' *Coastal Management* 20 (1) (January–March): 73–88. Washington/Philadelphia/London: Taylor & Francis

—— 1999a, *Solar City.* http://www.solarcity.org

—— 1999b, 'Post-globalisation: cities in the age of climate change and fossil fuel depletion.' Retrieved on 30 January 2006 from http://www.solarcity.org

—— 2001, 'International Energy Agency Solar Heating and Cooling Implementing Agreement – Task 30 Solar City Work Program.' For a full list of experts developing this programme see Final Draft, 3 June 2001. Retrieved on 30 January 2006 from http://www.solarcity.org

—— 2004, 'Renewable Energy and the City.' In C Cleveland (ed), *Encyclopaedia of Energy.* London: Academic Press

—— 2005, 'Research infrastructure priorities – submission to the National Committee on Research Infrastructure.' Submitted by the Chair, Renewable and Sustainable ROUNDTABLE, 28 November 2005. Melbourne

—— 2006, 'Postsuburban Sydney: community between global commodity and local autonomy.' *Proceedings of the Postsuburban Sydney Conference*, November. Sydney: University of Western Sydney, Centre for Cultural Research

Droege, P (ed) 1997, *Intelligent Environments.* Amsterdam: Elsevier Science Publishers

DSIRE – Database of State Incentives for Renewable Energy 2006, http://www.dsireusa.org

Dunster, B 2005, '*The impossible dream – come true!*' Retrieved on 1 April 2006 from http://www.opendemocracy.net/debates/article-6-129-2470.jsp

Dürrschmidt, W, G Zimmermann and Alexandra Liebling 2004, *Renewable Energies – Innovation for the Future*. Berlin: Federal Ministry for the Environment, Nature Conservation and Nuclear Safety (BMU)

Easterling, WE, Brian H Hurd and Joe B Smith 2004, 'Coping with Global Climate Change – The Role of Adaptation in the United States.' Arlington, VA: Pew Center on Global Climate Change. Retrieved on 30 January 2006 from http://www.pewclimate.org/docUploads/Adaptation%2Epdf

E-C – Energie-Cités 2005, http://www.energie-cites.org

Ecofys 2005, *GreenPrices Extra Edition*. 3 August. Retrieved on 1 April 2006 from http://www.greenprices.com/eu/newsletter/NewsletterArchive/GPBE050802.asp

EGCN – European Green Cities Network 2005, http://www.europeangreencities.com

EIA – Energy Information Administration, United States Department of Energy 1995, 'Measuring Energy Efficiency in the United States' Economy: a Beginning.' October 1995. Retrieved on 1 April 2006 from http://www.eia.doe.gov/emeu/efficiency/ee_report_html.htm

—— 2006, 'Greenhouse Gases, Climate Change, and Energy'. EIA Brochures. Washington DC: US DoE. Retrieved on 1 April 2006 from http://www.eia.doe.gov/oiaf/1605/ggccebro/chapter1.html

Emanuel, K 2005, 'Increasing destructiveness of tropical cyclones over the past 30 years.' *Nature*. Posted on-line 4 August 2005. Retrieved on 1 April 2006 from http://www.doi.10.1038:nature3906

Energiestadt 2005, http://www.energiestadt.ch

EnviroMission 2005, http://www.enviromission.com.au. 'Move to High Capacity Solar Tower Power Option.' Press release 20 September 2005. Retrieved on 21 September 2005 from http://www.enviromission.com.au/financial/EVM%20CA207.pdf

EPA – US Environmental Protection Agency 2006a, *Heat Island Effect*. Retrieved on 1 April 2006 from www.epa.gov/heatisland/index.html. For cool roofs see also the Cool Roofs Rating Council http://www.coolroofs.org

—— 2006b, Retrieved on 1 April 2006 from http://www.energystar.gov

—— 2006c, *EPA's Personal Greenhouse Gas Calculator*. Retrieved on 1 April 2006 from http://yosemite.epa.gov/oar/globalwarming.nsf/content/ResourceCenterToolsGHGCalculator.html

EPA VIC – Environmental Protection Agency Victoria 2005, *The Australian Greenhouse Calculator*. Retrieved on 1 April 2006 from http://www.epa.vic.gov.au/GreenhouseCalculator/calculator/default.asp

ESCI – European Solar Cities Initiative. International Solar Energy Society (ISES) 2005. Retrieved on 1 April 2006 from http://www.eu-solarcities.org

Etherington, D 2005, 'Kokonut Pacific – empowering and bringing hope.' Retrieved on 1 April 2006 from http://www.kokonutpacific.com.au

Eurosolar 2005 [1992], *Der Weg zum Solarzeitalter – Bildungsmaterialien: Gründe und Möglichkeiten der Nutzung erneuerbarer Energien*. Bonn/Bad Godesberg: Eurosolar eV

——— 2006, 'Preisträger der Europäischen Solarpreise 2005:Bioenergiedorf Jühnde (Deutschland).' Retrieved on 13 May 2006 from http://www.eurosolar.org/ new/de/DSP_ESP_2006.html

Farrell, AE, Richard J Plevin, Brian T Turner, Andrew D Jones, Michael O'Hare and Daniel M Kammen 2006, 'Ethanol Can Contribute to Energy and Environmental Goals.' *Science* 311 (27 January): 506–8. Retrieved on 21 May 2006 from http://rael.berkeley.edu/EBAMM

FC – Fast Company 2005, 'The Wal-Mart You Don't Know.' Retrieved on 1 February 2006 from http://www.fastcompany.com/magazine/77/walmart.html

FEMA – Federal Emergency Management Agency 1980, *Dispersed, Decentralised and Renewable Energy Sources: Alternatives to National Vulnerability and War*. Washington, DC: FEMA

Fialka, JJ 2005, 'Energy Initiatives Gain Power in Some States.' New York: *Wall Street Journal*, 8 June, p A4

Finn, P 2006, 'Russia Cuts Off Gas to Ukraine in Controversy Over Pricing.' Washington, DC: *Washington Post Foreign Service*. Monday, 2 January 2006, p A07. Retrieved on 16 May 2006 from http://www.washingtonpost.com/wp-dyn/content/article/2006/01/01/AR2006010100401.html?nav=rss_world

Fischedick, M and Joachim Nitsch 2004, 'Die Rolle von Wasserstoff in der zukünftigen Energieversorgung.' Paper prepared for Eurosolar. Wuppertal Institut für Klima, Umwelt und Energie; and DLR-Institut für Technische Thermodynamik, Stuttgart

Fletcher, R 1996, *The Limits of Settlement Growth*. Cambridge: Cambridge University Press

Florida, RL 2002, *The Rise of the Creative Class – and How It's Transforming Work, Leisure, Community and Everyday Life*. New York: Basic Books

Foran, B, David Crane, Franzi Poldy, Simon Phipp and Malcolm Slesser 1998, 'The OzEcco Embodied Energy Model of Australia's Physical Function: Model Description and Calibration.' National Futures Group Working Document 98–06. Canberra: CSIRO. Retrieved on 1 March 2006 from http://www.cse.csiro.au/publications/reports.htm

———, Manfred Lenzen and Christopher Dey 2005. *Balancing Act – a Triple Bottom Line Analysis of the Australian Economy*. Canberra: CSIRO and Sydney: University of Sydney. Retrieved on 1 March 2006 from http://www.cse.csiro.au/publications/2005/balancingact1.pdf

Foster and Partners 2005, 'Foster and Partners.' Retrieved on 1 December 2005 from http://www.fosterandpartners.com

Freitas, RA Jr 2001, *The Grey Goo Problem*. Permanently published on KurzweilAI.net http://www.kurzweilai.net/meme/frame.html?main=/articles/art0142.html/ Originally published April 2000 as 'Some Limits to Global Ecophagy by Biovorous Nanoreplicators, with Public Policy Recommendations.' Excerpted version published on KurzweilAI.net 20 March 2001

Friedmann, J 2001, 'Intercity Networks in a Globalizing Era.' In AJ Scott (ed), *Global City Regions – Trends, Theory, Policy*. Oxford: Oxford University Press, pp 119–360

Friedmann, J and Robert Wulff 1976, *The Urban Transition: Comparative Studies of Newly Industrializing Societies*. London: Edward Arnold

Fuller, RB 1965, 'The Case for a Domed City.' First published in a special supplement, *St. Louis Dispatch*, 26 September 1965, pp 39–41. Retrieved on 1 June 2006 from http://www.waltlockley.com/manhattandome/domeappendix.htm

Fulton, L 2004, *Reducing Oil Consumption in Transport: Combining Three Approaches*. Paris: Organisation for Economic Co-operation and Development (OECD)/International Energy Agency (IEA). Retrieved on 1 March 2006 from http://www.iea.org/textbase/papers/2004/transporthree.pdf

Fwa, TF 2002, 'Transportation Planning and Management for Sustainable Development – Singapore's Experience.' Paper presented at a brainstorming session on Non-Technology Options for Stimulating Modal Shifts in City Transport Systems held in Nairobi, Kenya. STAP/GEF, Washington DC

Gartner, J 2004, 'Solar to Keep the Army on the Go.' Wired News, 26 June 2004. *Wired* magazine. Retrieved on 1 March 2006 from http://www.wired.com/news/technology/0,1282,64021,00.html

Gayoom, MA 1987, 'Address by His Excellency Mr. Maumoon Abdul Gayoom, President of the Republic of Maldives, before the 42nd session of the United Nations General Assembly on the Special Debate on Environment and Development, 19 October 1987.' http://users.rcn.com/jtitus/Maldives/Gayoom_speech.html

GBC – United States Green Building Council 2006. Retrieved on 1 March 2006 from http://www.usgbc.org

GC – Government of Canada 2006, 'The Greenhouse Gas (GHG) Calculator.' Retrieved on 1 March 2006 from http://www.climatechange.gc.ca/onetonne/calculator/english

Geller, H 2002, *Energy Revolution: Policies for a Sustainable Future*. Washington, DC: Island Press

Gideon, S 1948, *Mechanization Takes Command: A Contribution to Anonymous History*. New York: Oxford University Press

Glantz, M and Societal Impacts Group, National Center for Atmospheric Research, Boulder, CO 2005, 'Why good climates go bad? Creeping environmental change.' In Report of the Joint IPCC WG II & III Expert meeting on the integration of Adaptation, Mitigation and Sustainable Development into the 4th IPCC Assessment Report. St Denis, Reunion Island, France, 16–18 February 2005

Gleick, PH 1994, 'Water and Energy.' *Annual Review of Energy and Environment* 19: 267–99

—— 1998, 'Water in Crisis: Paths to Sustainable Water Use.' *Ecological Applications* 8(3): 571–9

—— 2000, *Global Water: Threats and Challenges Facing the United States. U.S. Policy and the Global Environment: Memos to the President*. D. Kennedy and J.A. Riggs Eds. Aspen, Colorado, Aspen Institute

GM – General Manager 2004, '2005 Budget Letter to Board of Directors.' Sacramento Municipal Utility District (SMUD), 3 November

Goodstein, David 2004, *Out of Gas: The End of the Age of Oil*. New York: WW Norton

Göteborg, Energi AB 1998, 'Göteborg, Energy Systems – A Project to Develop Long- and Short-term Energy Supplies and Use in the Municipality of Göteborg.' November 1998. Göteborg: Profu AB

Graham-Harrison, E 2005, 'China Mulls Raising Renewable Energy Commitment.' Planet Ark 6 September 2005. Retrieved on 1 March 2006 from http://www.planetark.com/avantgo/dailynewsstory.cfm?newsid=32360

Green, J 2005, *Nuclear Power – No Solution to Climate Change*. Report for the Australian Conservation Foundation, Greenpeace Australia Pacific, the Medical Association for the Prevention of War, the Public Health Association of Australia and the Climate Action Network of Australia. Melbourne: Friends of the Earth (Australia). Retrieved on 1 March 2006 from http://www.melbourne.foe.org.au/documents.htm

Green City 2005. Retrieved on 1 March 2006 from http://www.greencity-energy.de

Green Guide 2005, *America's Top 10 Green Cities*. Retrieved on 1 March 2006 from http://www.thegreenguide.com/doc.mhtml?i=107&s=cities

Grunwald, M and Susan B Glasser 2005, 'The Slow Drowning of New Orleans.' *Washington Post*. 9 October 2005. A01. Retrieved on 1 March 2006 from http://www.washingtonpost.com/wp-dyn/content/article/2005/10/08/AR2005100801458_pf.html

GSHP – Ground Source Heat Pump Club 2005, *What Are Ground Source Heat Pumps?* Milton Keynes: National Energy Foundation. Retrieved on 1 March 2006 from http://www.nef.org.uk

GVEP – Global Village Energy Partnership 2005. Retrieved on 1 December 2005 from http://www.gvep.org

Hall, PG 1977, *The World Cities*. London: Weidenfeld & Nicolson

—— 1998, *Cities in Civilization: Culture, Innovation and Urban Order*. London: Weidenfeld & Nicolson

Hamilton, C. and Richard Dennis 2005, *Affluenza: when too much is never enough*, Melbourne, Allen & Unwin

Hardin, G 1968, 'The Tragedy of the Commons.' *Science* 162: 1243–8

Hartung, WD 2005, 'The Hidden Cost of War.' The Fourth Freedom Forum. Retrieved on 1 December 2005 from http://www.fourthfreedom.org/pdf/Hartung_report.pdf

Hayter, S, Paul Torcellini and M Deru 2002, 'Photovoltaics for Buildings: New Applications and Lessons Learned.' Golden, Colorado: National Renewable Energy Laboratory (NREL). Prepared for the American Council for an Energy-Efficient Economy (ACEEE) Summer Study on Energy Efficiency in Buildings, Pacific Grove, CA, 18–23 August 2002. Retrieved on 1 December 2005 from http://www.eere.energy.gov/buildings/ highperformance/research_reports.html#2002

Heinberg, R 2003, *The Party's Over: Oil, War and the Fate of Industrial Societies*. Gabriol Island, Canada: New Society Publishers

Hensher, DA 2003, 'Integrated Transport Models for Environmental Assessment.' in DA Hensher and Kenneth J Button, *Transport and the Environment.* Handbooks in Transport Vol 4. Oxford: Elsevier, pp 787–804

Hensher, DA and Kenneth J Button (eds) 2003, *Transport and the Environment.* Handbooks in Transport Vol 4. Oxford: Elsevier

Hochschild, David et al 2002, 'Big Energy vs. Solar', *Los Angeles Times*, 11 August 2002. Retrieved on 30 October 2005 from http://www.commondreams.org/views02/0811-04.htm

Hook, W and L Wright 2002, 'Reducing GHG Emission by Shifting Passenger Trips to Less Polluting Modes.' Background paper for the brainstorming session on Non-Technology Options for Stimulating Modal Shifts in City Transport Systems. Nairobi, Kenya. March 2002. STAP/GEF, Washington, DC

Howard, E 1902, *Garden Cities of Tomorrow.* London: Swan Sonnenschein

Hubbert, MK 1956, *Nuclear Energy and the Fossil Fuels.* Publication No 95, June 1956. Houston: Shell Development Company. Retrieved on 7 March 2006 from http://www.hubbertpeak.com/hubbert/1956/1956.pdf

Ichinose, T 2005, *Recent counteractions for heat island for regional autonomies in Japan.* Tsukuba: National Institute for Environmental Studies (NIES)

Ichinose, T and Y Bai 2005, 'Mitigation of thermal stress by a large restoration of inner-city river (Cheong-Gye Stream in Seoul)', The Fourth Japanese-German Meeting on Urban Climatology, Tsukuba. Abstracts

ICLEI – International Council on Local Environmental Initiatives 2005a. Retrieved on 1 December 2005 from http://www.iclei.org

—— 2005b, 'Strategies and Policy Mechanisms to Promote Solar.' Retrieved on 31 December 2005 from http://www.greenpowergovs.org/Solar2 strategies.html

IE – Infinite Energy 2006, 'Frequently Asked Questions About New Energy Science and Technology.' Retrieved on 21 June 2006 from http://www.infinite-energy.com/resources/faq.html

IEA – International Energy Agency 2002, *Renewable Energy Almanac.* Paris: IEA

—— 2004, *World Energy Outlook.* Paris: IEA

—— 2005, *Saving Oil in a Hurry – Demand Restraint in the Transport Sector.* Paris: Organisation for Economic Co-operation and Development (OECD)

IEA PVPS – International Energy Agency Photovoltaic Power Systems Programme 2003, '1 MW decentralized and building integrated PV system in a new housing area of Amersfoort.' Last updated: 20 April 2003. Retrieved on 5 March 2006 from www.oja-services.nl/iea-pvps/cases/index.htm

IEE – Institution of Electrical Engineers 2005, 'The Energy White Paper, Two Years On – Challenges for the UK Energy Policy.' London, February 2005

IPCC – Intergovernmental Panel on Climate Change 1996, *The IPCC Second Assessment Synthesis of Scientific-Technical Information Relevant to Interpreting Article 2 of the United Nations Framework Convention on Climate Change.* New York: United Nations Environment Programme

—— 2001a. Retrieved on 1 May 2006 from http://www.ipcc.ch/present/graphics.htm. 6-2 and TS22

—— 2001b. *Climate Change 2001: Impacts, Adaptation and Vulnerability*. Geneva: IPCC. Retrieved on 30 June 2006 from http://www.grida.no/climate/ipcc_tar/wg2/001.htm

ISES – International Solar Energy Society 2005a, 'Solar Cities Congress 2006 Announcement.' Retrieved on 30 December 2005 from http://www.ises.org/ises.nsf!Open

—— 2005b, 'Renewable Energy Strategies for European Towns (RESETnet)' and 'Brundtland City Energy Network (BCEN).' Retrieved on 30 December 2005 from http://sc.ises.org/cgi-bin/sc/sc.py?shownetwork&16642/and http://sc.ises.org/cgi-bin/sc/sc.py?shownetwork&16629

Jacobs, J 1985, *Cities and the Wealth of Nations: Principles of Economic Life*. London: Viking

Jacques, M 2005, 'Integration of Intermittent Renewable Energy Sources into the Electricity Grid.' Paper delivered at the November 2005 World Wind Energy Conference, Melbourne, Australia

Jank, R 2000, *Advanced Local Energy Planning (ALEP) – A Guidebook*. IEA Annex 33/Energy Conservation in Buildings and Community Systems Program. Bietigheim-Bissingen, Germany: Fachinstitut Gebäude Klima eV(FGK)

Jansson, AM 1978, *Energy, Economic and Ecological Relationships for Gotland Sweden – A Regional Systems Study*. Stockholm: Swedish Natural Science Research Council

Johansson, B 2003, 'Transport Fuels – a System Perspective.' In DA Hensher and Kenneth J Button (eds), *Handbook of Transport and the Environment*. Amsterdam and Boston: Elsevier

JSP – 'Joint Staff Proposal To Implement A California Solar Initiative, June 14, 2005, www.cpuc.ca.gov.' See also Revised Joint Staff Proposal to Implement a California Solar Initiative, 13 December 2005. Retrieved on 30 June 2006 from http://www.environmentcalifornia.org/energy/million-solar-roofs

Kammen, DM, Kamal Kapadia and Mathias Fripp 2004, *Putting Renewables to Work: How Many Jobs Can the Clean Energy Industry Generate?* Renewable and Appropriate Energy Laboratory (RAEL) Report. Berkeley: University of California. Retrieved on 30 June 2006 from http://socrates.berkeley.edu/~rael/papers.html

Kates, RW, Michael W Mayfield, Ralph D Torrie and Brian Witcher 1998, 'Methods for Estimating Greenhouse Gases from Local Places.' *Local Environment* 3 (3). Carfax Publishing, London

Kenworthy, J 2001, 'Transport and Urban Planning for the Post-Petroleum Era.' Commonwealth Science Industry and Research Organisation (CSIRO) Sustainability Newsletter 15 April 2003. Glen Osmond, South Australia: CSIRO Waite Laboratories. Retrieved on 10 July 2006 from http://www.bml.cisro.au/susnetnl/netwl25E.pdf

Kim, J 2005, 'Building a Solar Cities Movement from Daegu.' In J Kim (ed), *Solar Cities for a Sustainable World. Proceedings of the International Solar Cities Congress 2004*. Daegu, South Korea: Research Institute for Energy, Environment and Economy, Kyungpook National University

Klare, MT 2002, *Resource Wars: The New Landscape of Global Conflict*. New York: Owl Books

Knutson, TR and Robert E 2004, 'Impact of $CO_2$-Induced Warming on Simulated Hurricane Intensity and Precipitation: Sensitivity to the Choice of Climate Model and Convective Parameterization.' *Journal of Climate* 17(18) (15 Sept): 3477–95

Kofoed-Wiuff, A, Kaare Sandholt and Catarina Marcus-Møller 2006, 'Renewable Energy Technology Deployment (RETD) – Barriers, Challenges and Opportunities.' 1 March 2006 draft report for the IEA RETD Implementing Agreement. Paris: International Energy Agency (IEA)

Langen, C 2005, 'The German Solar Experience – Lessons Learned for Application in Australia.' Conergy Pty Ltd presentation at the Business Council for Sustainable Energy Conference 2005. Melbourne, 27–29 April 2005

Latham, R and Saskia Sassen (eds) 2005, *Digital Formations: IT and New Architectures in the Global Realm*. Princeton, NJ: Princeton University Press

Le Corbusier 1929/1947, *The City of Tomorrow and its Planning (Urbanisme)*. London: Architectural Press

—— 1981, *The Ideas of Le Corbusier on Architecture and Urban Planning. Texts Edited and Presented by Jacques Guiton*, trans Margaret Guiton. New York: G. Braziller

Lehmann, H 2003, *Energy-rich Japan*. Aachen: Institute for Sustainable Solutions and Innovation (ISUSI)

Lenzen, M 1997, 'Energy and greenhouse gas costs of living for Australia during 1993/4.' *Energy* 23 (6): 487–586. Pergamon

Lenzen, M, Christopher Dey and Clive Hamilton 2003, 'Climate Change.' In DA Hensher, and Kenneth J Button (eds), *Handbook of Transport and the Environment*. Amsterdam and Boston: Elsevier

Lerner, J 2000, 'Curitiba Mass Transit System: A Challenge in Creativity.' *City Development Strategies Journal* 2 (spring 2000):

Little, AG 2005, 'Solar Derby.' *Grist* magazine, 23 June 2005. Retrieved on 30 June 2006 from http://www.grist.org/news/muck/2005/06/23/little-solar

Lovins, AB 2003, *Twenty Hydrogen Myths*. Boulder, CO: Rocky Mountain Institute

Lovins, AB and David R Cramer 2004, 'Hypercars®, hydrogen and the automotive transition.' *International Journal of Vehicle Design* 35 (1/2): 50–85. Retrieved on 30 June 2006 from http://www.rmi.org/images/other/Trans/T04-01_HypercarH2AutoTrans.pdf

Luce, B (ed) 2006, 'Renewable Energy and Energy Efficiency Incentives, both Federal and New Mexico.' New Mexico Coalition for Clean Affordable Energy (NMCCAE.org). Retrieved on 30 June 2006 from http://www.cfcae.org/Downloads/Incentives.pdf/. See also http://www.cfcae.org/Incentives_Laws/index.htm

Lynch, K 1981, *A Theory of Good City Form*. Cambridge, MA: MIT Press

—— 1990. *Wasting Away*. San Francisco: Sierra Club Books

McDonough, W and Michael Braungart 2002, *Cradle to Cradle: Remaking the Way We Make Things*. New York: North Point Press

McEvoy D, DC Gibbs and JWS Longhurst 1998, 'Urban sustainability: Problems facing the "local" approach to carbon reduction strategies.' *Environment and Planning C: Government and Policy* 16: 423–32

—— 2000, 'The employment implications of a low carbon economy.' *Sustainable Development* 8 (1): 27–38

McGee, T 1991, 'The Emergence of Desakota Regions in Asia: Expanding a Hypothesis.' In T Ginsburg, B Koppel and TG McGee (eds), *The Extended Metropolis: Settlement Transition in Asia.* Honolulu: University of Hawaii Press, pp 3–25

McGranahan, G, J Songsore and M Kjellen 1999, 'Sustainability, poverty and urban environmental transitions.' In D Satterthwaite (ed), Sustainable Cities, London: Earthscan, pp 107–30

Mandelbrot, BB 1982, *The Fractal Geometry of Nature.* San Francisco: WH Freeman

Manning, R 2004, 'The Oil We Eat – Following the Food Chain Back to Iraq.' *Harpers*, February

Martinot, E 2005, 'Renewable Energy in China.' Retrieved on 30 June 2006 from http://www.martinot.info/china.htm

—— 2006, 'Solar City Case Study: Portland (OR), USA.' Retrieved on 6 April 2006 from http://www.martinot.info/solarcities/portland.htm

Mazza, L 1988, *World Cities and the Future of the Metropoles.* Milan: Electa

Meadows, D, Donella Meadows, Erich Zahn and Peter Milling 1972, *The Limits to Growth, Report for the Club of Rome.* New York: Universe Books

Meadows, DH, Dennis L Meadows and Jørgen Randers 2004, *Limits to Growth: The 30-Year Update.* London: Earthscan

Melbourne, City of 2005, 'Sustainable Business Directory.' Retrieved on 30 June 2006 from http://www.melbourne.vic.gov.au

Mellaart, J 1967, *Çatal Hüyük: A Neolithic Town in Anatolia (New Aspects of Archaeology).* New York: McGraw-Hill

Menckhoff, G 1999, 'Curitiba Story.' Slides presented at the PIARC Conference in Kuala Lumpur, Malaysia, November 1999. World Bank, Washington, DC

Meyer, A 2000, *Contraction and Convergence – the Global Solution to Climate Change.* Schumacher Briefings. Deven: Green Books

Meyer, U 2006, 'Vertikaler Perlfluß.' Baunetz.de. 4 April 2006. Retrieved on 21 June 2006 from http://www.baunetz.de/db/news/?news_id=81850

Mills, D 2005, 'Solar Thermal Central Generation Option for Cities.' Paper presented at the November 2004 International Solar Cities Congress, Daegu, Korea

Mills, E 2005, 'Insurance in a Climate of Change.' *Science* 309 (5737) (12 Aug): 1040–4

Monroe, L 2005, 'Rocky Mountain Institute: Approach to Energy.' Buildings. com. Retrieved on 9 March 2006 from http://www.buildings.com/Articles/detail.asp?ArticleID=661

Moore, A and Harvey Rosenfield 2001, 'Energy Crisis: Who Can Keep California Turned On?' *San Francisco Chronicle*, 13 May 2001. Retrieved on 9 March 2006 from www.reason.org/commentaries/moore_20010513.shtml

Morris, D 1982, *Self-reliant Cities: Energy and the Transformation of Urban America*. Washington, DC: Institute for Local Self-Reliance

Morse, FH 2004, 'The Global Market Initiative (GMI) for Concentrating Solar Power (CSP).' Washington, DC: Morse Associates, Inc. American Solar Energy Society (ASES) Conference presentation, Portland, Oregon, 13 July 2004

MSR – Million Solar Roofs 2006. Retrieved on 30 June 2006 from http://www.millionsolarroofs.org

Mumford, L 1961, *The City in History: Its Origins, Its Transformations, and Its Prospects*. Harmondsworth: Penguin

Murphy, D 2002, 'For Solar Power, Foggy City Maps Its Bright Spots.' *New York Times*, 24 November. Retrieved on 30 September 2005 from http://www.votesolar.org/press_nyt_20021124.html

Nakicenovij, N and Rob Svart (eds) 2001, *Special Report on Emissions Scenarios*. Chapter 5.6 'Regional Distribution and Gridding.' Zürich: Intergovernmental Panel on Climate Change (IPCC). Retrieved on 30 June 2006 from http://www.grida.no/climate/ipcc/emission/128.htm

NASA 2005, 'Sunshine Mapping from Space Means Brighter Solar Energy Future.' Media Alert 29 June 2005. Retrieved on 30 November 2005 from http://eobglossary.gsfc.nasa.gov///Newsroom/MediaAlerts/2005/2005062919407.html

NCMSR – North Carolina Million Solar Roofs Partnership 2006. Retrieved on 30 June 2006 from http://www.ncsolar.net

NCSolar – North Carolina Millions Solar Roofs Partnership 2006, 'Solar Resources Toolkit for Local NC Governments.' Retrieved on 30 November 2005 from http://www.ncsolar.net

Newman, PWG and Jeffrey R Kenworthy 1987, *Gasoline Consumption and Cities: a Comparison of U.S. Cities with a Global Survey and Some Implications*. Murdoch, WA: Murdoch University

—— 1992, *Winning Back the Cities*. ACA/Pluto Press London

—— 1999. *Sustainability and Cities: Overcoming Automobile Dependence*. Washington, DC: Island Press

NRC – National Research Council, Committee on Abrupt Climate Change (Chair Richard B Alley) 2002, *Abrupt Climate Change – Inevitable Surprises*. Washington, DC: National Academy Press

NREL – National Renewable Energy Laboratory of the United States Department of Energy 2005a 'Dynamic Maps and GIS Data.' Retrieved on 30 November 2005 from http://www.nrel.gov/gis/. US Solar Atlas retrieved on 30 November 2005 from http://mapserve1.nrel.gov/website/L48NEWPVWATTS/viewer.htm

—— 2005b. Renewable Resource Data Center. Retrieved on 30 June 2006 from http://rredc.nrel.gov. Solar Radiation Resource Information retrieved on 30 November 2005 from http://rredc.nrel.gov/solar. Wind Energy Resource Information retrieved on 30 November 2005 from http://rredc.nrel.gov/wind

—— 2005c. Retrieved on 30 June 2006 from http://www.nrel.gov

Obayashi Corporation 2005, *Obayashi Environmental Report 2005*. Tokyo: Obayashi Corporation. Retrieved on 30 November 2005 from http://www.obayashi.co.jp/english/environment/pdf/eco_report2005.pdf

ODPM – Office of the Deputy Prime Minister 2004. *Planning Policy Statement 22 (PPS 22) – Renewable Energy*. August 2004. London: United Kingdom Stationary Office

Odum, HT 1971, *Environment, Power and Society*. New York: Wiley Interscience

OECD – Organisation for Economic Co-operation and Development 1995, *Urban Energy Handbook*. Paris: Organisation for Economic Co-operation and Development (OECD)

Okonski, K (ed) 2004, *Adapt or Die – The Science, Politics and Economics of Climate Change*. London Profile Business and International Policy Network (IPN)

ORER – Office of the Renewable Energy Regulator 2006. Retrieved on 30 June 2006 from http://www.orer.gov.au

Orr, DW 2002, *The Nature of Design: Ecology, Culture, and Human Intention*. New York: Oxford University Press

Patz, JA, Diarmid Campbell-Lendrum, Tracey Holloway and Jonathan A Foley 2005, 'Impact of regional climate change on human health.' *Nature* 438 (17 November 2005): 310–17

Peatling, S 2006, 'Nuclear question looms large at climate change talks.' *Sydney Morning Herald*, national section article, 12 January

Peatling, S and W Frew 2006, 'Greenhouse battle handed to industry.' *Sydney Morning Herald*, national section article, 13 January

Perlman, J 2005, 'ENVIRONMENT: Rethinking the Grid: Distributed Generation and Urban Development.' *Urban/Rural Edge* 8(April). New Haven, CT: The Next American City. Retrieved on 30 November 2005 from http://www.americancity.org/article.php?id_article=117

Peter, S and Harry Lehmann 2004, *Das deutsche Ausbaupotential erneuerbarer Energien im Stromsektor*. Aachen: Institute for Sustainable Solutions and Innovations (ISUSI). Eurosolar study

Pimentel, D, G Rodrigues, T Wang, R Abrams, K Goldberg, H Staecker, E Ma, L Brueckner, L Trovato, C Chow, U Govindarajulu and S Boerke 1994, 'Renewable Energy: Economic and Environmental Issues.' *BioScience* 44 (8) (Sept): 536–47. Washington DC: American Academy of Biological Sciences

PNM – Power New Mexico 2006, 'Customer Solar PV Program.' Retrieved on 30 March 2006 from http://www.pnm.com

Pontenagel, I (ed) 2001, *The City – a Solar Power Station: the State of the Art of Solar Building and Ecological Urban Planning*. Proceedings, 6th European Conference for Solar Energy in Architecture and Urban Planning. Bonn: Eurosolar

—— 2005, 'Keine Alternative – allein die Erneuerbaren Energien haben eine Zukunft.' *Frankfurter Allgemeine Zeitung*, 17 May

Popham, P 1985, *Tokyo: the City at the End of the World*. Tokyo: Kodansha International; New York: Harper & Row

Portland, City of 1993, 'Global Warming Reduction Strategy.' City of Portland. November 2003. Retrieved on 1 January 2006 from http://www.sustainableportland.org/GW%20Reduction%20Strategy.pdf

—— 2001, *Local Action Plan on Global Warming. City of Portland and Multnomah County.* Portland: Office of Sustainable Development. April 2001. Retrieved on 1 January 2006 from http://www.sustainableportland.org/Portland%20Global%20Warming%20Plan.pdf

—— 2005, *A Progress Report on the City of Portland and Multnomah County Local Action Plan on Global Warming.* Portland: Office of Sustainable Development. June 2005. Retrieved on 1 January 2006 from http://www.sustainableportland.org/osd_pubs_global_warming_report_6-2005.pdf

—— 2006, 'Climate Change.' Office of Sustainable Development. Retrieved on 1 January 2006 from http://www.sustainableportland.org/stp_glo_home.html

Potter, S 2003, 'Transport energy and emissions: urban public transport.' In DA Hensher, and Kenneth J Button (eds) 2003, *Handbook of Transport and the Environment.* Amsterdam and Boston: Elsevier

PRB – Population Reference Bureau 2005, 'Patterns of World Urbanization.' Retrieved on 30 November 2005 from http://www.prb.org/Content/NavigationMenu / PRB / Educators / Human _ Population / Urbanization2 / Patterns of World_Urbanization1.htm

ProColorado.org. 2006, 'City of Lamar and Prowers County Profile.' Retrieved on 21 May 2006 from http://www.procolorado.org/Prowers_Profile.PDF

RE – Renewable City 2006, 'Renewable City™.' http://www.renewablecity.org

RECS – Renewable Energy Certificate System 2006. Retrieved on 1 January 2006 from http://www.recs.org

Rees, W and M Wackernagel 1996, 'Urban ecology footprints: why cities cannot be sustainable – and why they are a key to sustainablility.' *Environmental Impact Assessment Review* 16: 223–48

REGIOprojekt eV 2005, 'REGIOenergie – Arbeitspapier für ein Regionalgeld auf der Basis erneuerbarer Energien aus der Region (Working paper for a regional currency based on regionally generated renewable energy).' Weimar: REGIOprojekt eV. Draft, July 2005

REN21 – Renewable Energy Policy Network 2005, *Renewables 2005 Global Status Report. Washington*, DC: Worldwatch Institute. Retrieved on 1 January 2006 from http://www.ren21.net/and http://www.martinot.info

Reuters 2005. 'Ex-PM: World's N-Waste to Outback.' Reuters report in CNN. 27 September 2005. Retrieved on 1 January 2006 from http://www.cnn.com/2005/WORLD/asiapcf/09/27/australia.nuclear.reut/index.html

Revkin, AC 2006, 'Climate Expert Says NASA Tried to Silence Him.' *New York Times*, Science Section, 29 January. Retrieved on 5 May 2006 from http://www.nytimes.com/2006/01/29/science/earth/29climate.html?ex=1296190800&en=28e236da0977ee7f&ei=5088&partner=rssnyt&emc=rss

Roaf, S and Rajat Gupta 2006, 'Developing the Oxford Route Map for Solar Cities.' Unpublished draft. Oxford: Oxford Brookes University and Oxford City Council

Roaf, S, David Crichton and Fergus Nicol 2005a, *Adapting Buildings and Cities for Climate Change*. London: Academic Press

Roaf, S, Manuel Fuentes and Rajat Gupta 2005b, 'Solar Cities: the Oxford Solar Initiative.' In M Jenks, and Nicole Dempsey, *Future Forms and Design for Sustainable Cities*. Oxford: Architectural Press

Roberts, P 2004, *The End of Oil: On the Edge of a Perilous New World*. Boston: Houghton Mifflin

Rossmanith, K 2006, 'Engineers harness the power of the sea.' *UniNews* 28(2) (10 March): 1 and 5. Sydney: University of Sydney

Ruck, N et al 2000, *Daylight in Buildings. A Sourcebook on Daylighting Systems and Components. A Report of IEA SHC Task 21/ECBCS Annex 29*. Berkeley, CA: Lawrence Berkeley National Laboratory

SA – Government of South Australia 2005, 'Adelaide to Host International Solar Cities Forum.' Press announcement by the Hon John Hill, Minister for Conservation and the Environment, 7 June. Retrieved on 1 January 2006 from http://www.environment.sa.gov.au/data/press/solar_cities.pdf

Saddler, H undated, 'Energy intensity trends in the Australian economy.' Retrieved on 1 January 2006 from http://www.ergo.ee.unsw.edu.au/EEWS_energyintensity.pdf

——, M Diesendorf and R Denniss 2004, 'A Clean Energy Future for Australia.' Sydney: Clean Energy Future Group. Retrieved on 1 January 2006 from http://www.wwf.org.au

Sartogo, F et al 1999, 'Saline Ostia Antica – Ecological Urban Plan with a 93% Integration of Renewable Energies.' *Ecology and Architecture*. Florence: Alinea International

Sassen, S 1991, *The Global City: New York, London, Tokyo*. Princeton, NJ: Princeton University Press

—— 1994, *Cities in a World Economy*. Thousand Oaks, CA: Pine Forge Press (2nd edn, 2000)

—— (ed) 2002, *Global Networks, Linked Cities*. London: Routledge

SAVE 2005, 'Charter of the Regional and Local Energy Management Agencies in Europe.' Brussels: European Commission SAVE Programme. Retrieved on 1 January 2006 from http://europa.eu.int/comm/energy/ en/pfs_save_en.html

SC – Smart Communities 2006, The New Mexico Solar Rights Act 1978. Retrieved on 1 January 2006 from http://www.smartcommunities.ncat.org/codes/nmsolar.shtml

SCB – Statistiska centralbyrån (Statistics Sweden) 2005, 'Energy intensity of the economy.' Retrieved on 1 January 2006 from http://www.scb.se/templates/tableOrChart___83924.asp

Scheer, H nd, 'Germany's 100,000 Roof Photovoltaic Programme.' Retrieved on 1 January 2006 from http://www.hermann-scheer.de/pdf/Hu-ta-e2.PDF

—— 2002, *The Solar Economy – Renewable Energy for a Sustainable Global Future*. London: Earthscan. (Original in German, 1999)

—— 2005, *Energieautonomie*. Berlin: Antje Kunstmann

Schneider, A 1996, 'Architektur und Entropie. Am Beispiel der Nationalgalerie.' In A Schneider and Focus Film, *Solar Architektur für Europa*. Basel: Birkhäuser, pp 19–23

Schwartz, P and Doug Randall, 'An Abrupt Climate Change Scenario and its Implication for United States Security', October 2003. Retrieved on 9 July 2006 from http://www.environmentaldefense.org/ documents/3566_AbruptClimateChange.pdf

SEA/RENUE – Sustainable Energy Action/Renewable Energy in the Urban Environment 2006. Retrieved on 1 January 2006 from http://www.sustainable-energy.org.uk

Sennett, R 1992, *The Fall of Public Man*. New York: W.W. Norton

Sklar, S 2005, 'Sleepers that are coming to light.' *Renewable Energy World*, 2 July. London: James & James

Sloterdijk, P 2005, *Im Weltinnenraum des Kapitals*. Frankfurt am Main: Suhrkamp, pp 349–64

Smil, V 1994, *Energy in World History*. Boulder, CO: Westview Press

—— 2003, *Energy at the Crossroads: Global Perspectives and Uncertainties*. Cambridge, MA: MIT Press

Smith, R 2004, 'States Take Lead in Widening Use of Green Energy.' *Wall Street Journal*, 22 September, p A8

SN – Solar Energy News Center. 2006, 'January 12, 2006/San Francisco, CA, USA: California Commission $3.2bn Solar Plan Approval Draws Standing Ovation.' Retrieved on 1 January 2006 from http://www.solarbuzz.com/news/NewsNAGO287.htm

Solarserver 2005, *Solarpark Bavaria: größte Photovoltaikanlage der Welt*. Retrieved on 30 December 2005 from http://www.solarserver.de/solarmagazin/anlageaugust2005.html

Solar Online 2006. SolarSizer™. Retrieved on www.solenergy.org/html/about/SolarSizer.html

SOM – Skidmore, Owings & Merrill 2005, 'Freedom Tower.' Retrieved on 1 January 2006 from http://www.som.com

Solar City®. 1999–2006. http://www.solarcity.org

Stanhill, G and S Cohen 2001, 'Global Dimming: A Review of the Evidence.' *Agricultural and Forest Meteorology* 107: 255–78

Stevenson, A 2005, 'Plan for ethanol without labelling for Aussie petrol.' *Sydney Morning Herald*, national section, 22 September. Sydney: Fairfax

Stockholm Partnerships for Sustainable Cities 2006, 'BedZed green water system.' Retrieved on 7 March 2006 from http://www.partnerships.stockholm.se/search_view.asp?Id=89

Strohalm Foundation 2006. http://www.strohalm.org

Tanaka, Y 2004, 'Japan – Photovoltaic technology status and prospects'. In Osamu Ikki, RTS Corporation Annual Report 2004. Retrieved on 1 January 2006 from http://www.oja-services.nl/iea-pvps/countries/japan/index.htm

Thoreau, HD 1997, *Walden*, ed S Fender. Oxford and New York: Oxford University Press

Titus, JG 1989, 'Policy Implications of Sea Level Rise: the Case of the Maldives.' In S Hussein (ed), *Proceedings of the Small States Conference on Sea Level Rise.* Malé, Republic of Maldives. 14–18 November. Retrieved on 1 January 2006 from http://users.rcn.com/jtitus/Maldives/Small_Island_States_3.html

—— 1991, 'Strategies for Adapting to the Greenhouse Effect.' American Planning Association (APA). Retrieved on 1 January 2006 from http://users.erols.com/jtitus/JAPA/adapt.html

Turnbull, Shann, 1975, *Democratising the Wealth of Nations*, Sydney: Company Directors' Association of Australia

—— 1992, 'The Invisible Structure of Ecological Cities.' Second International Eco-Cities Conference, Adelaide, Australia. Saturday, 18 April 1992. Retrieved on 1 January 2006 from http://papers.ssrn.com/sol3/papers.cfm?abstract_id=741945

UNDESA – United Nations Department of Economic and Social Affairs 2002, *World Urbanization Prospects: the 2001 Revision*. New York: Press release 21 March: United Nations Population Division. Retrieved on 1 January 2006 from http://www.un.org/esa

UNEP – United Nations Environment Program 2005. Solar and Wind Energy Resource Assessment (UNEP SWERA). Retrieved on 1 January 2006 from http://swera.unep.net/swera/index.php

USGS – United States Geological Survey 2005, Central Region Energy Resources Team: worldwide web information on United States Energy and World Energy Production and Consumption Statistics. Retrieved on 1 January 2006 from http://energy.cr.usgs.gov/energy/stats_ctry/Stat1.html#WProduction

van Dalm, R 2005, 'The city is a vanguard space.' Statement magazine on real estate no. 9, The Hague: ING Real Estate/Script Media

van Schaik, L 2003, *Ecocells – Landscapes & Masterplans by Hamzah and Yeang*. Chichester: Wiley-Academy

Vikkelsø, A (ed) 2003, *The Middelgrunden Offshore Wind Farm – A Popular Initiative*. Copenhagen: Copenhagen Environment and Energy Office (CEEO)

Virilio, P and Sylvere Lotringer 1997, *Pure War*. New York: Semiotext(e)

Vote Solar 2005, 'The San Francisco Story.' Retrieved on 1 January 2006 from http://www.votesolar.org/sf.html

Warren Centre 2005, 'The World's greenest commercial building in its most liveable city!' University of Sydney, The Warren Centre for Advanced Engineering. Retrieved on 1 January 2006 from http://www.warren.usyd.edu.au/bulletin/NO44/ed44art1.html

WCRE – World Council for Renewable Energy 2006. http://www.wcre.org

WDR – Westdeutscher Rundfunk 2005, 'America's new oil target.' Broadcast on 4 October 2005 at 20.30 on Special Broadcasting Service (SBS) *Cutting Edge* programme

Webster, P et al 2005, 'Changes in tropical cyclone number, duration, and intensity in a warming environment.' *Science* 309: 1844–6

WEC – World Energy Council 2005, 'Survey of Energy Resources 2001 – Solar Energy.' Retrieved on 14 March 2006 from http://www.worldenergy.org/wec-geis/publications/reports/ser/solar/solar.asp

WEF – World Economic Forum 2005. http://www.weforum.org

Wimmer, N and Dipal C Barua 2004, 'Micro-finance for Solar Energy in Rural Areas.' *Words Into Action* companion volume to the International Conference for Renewable Energies, Bonn, Germany, 1–4 June 2004, London: Faircount, pp 25–33

—— 2005, 'Less Is More.' *Renewable Energy World*, pp 170–8

Wiser, R., K. Porter R. Grace and R. Grace 2004, the basis for designing sustainable intensive buildings. 'Evaluating Experience with Renewables Portfolio Standards in the United States.' Berkeley, CA: Ernest Orlando Lawrence Berkeley National Laboratory. Retrieved on 1 January 2006 from http://eetd.lbl.gov/ea/EMP/reports/54439.pdf

Wong, THF 2005, 'Water sensitive urban design.' Presentation on the concepts and services. Prahran, Victoria: EcoEngineering Pty Ltd

Wong, THF and Peter F Breen 2002, 'Recent advances in Australian practice on the use of constructed wetlands for stormwater treatment.' *Proceedings of the 9th International Conference on Urban Drainage*. Portland, Oregon, 9–13 September 2002. Reston, VA: American Society of Civil Engineers (ASCE)

World Bank 2002, *Cities on the Move – A World Bank Urban Transport Strategy Review*. Private Sector Development and Infrastructure Department, Washington, DC

WRDC – World Radiation Data Centre 2005. http://wrdc-mgo.nrel.gov

Wright, FW 1932, *The Disappearing City*. New York: William Farquhar Payson

Yeang, K 1994, *Bioclimatic Skyscrapers*. London: Artemis

—— 1996, *The Skyscraper Bioclimatically Considered: A Design Primer*. London: Academy Editions

—— 1999, *The Green Skyscraper*. Munich: Prestel

—— 2002, *Reinventing the Skyscraper: A Vertical Theory of Urban Design*. Chichester: Wiley-Academy

—— 2004, *Designing for Survival: Architecture and Ecological Design*. New York/Chichester: Wiley

—— 2006, *Ecodesign*. Chichester: Wiley-Academy

## Additional worldwide web based resources

### 1 Renewable cities and urban areas programmes and sources

http://www.adelaidegreencity.com

Adelaide Green City programme

http://www.americancity.org/article.php?id_article=117

Distributed Generation and Urban Development

http://www.austinenergy.com/Energy%20Efficiency/Programs/Green%20Choice/index.htm

GreenChoice® Austin Energy's Renewable Energy Program, United States
http://brundtlandnet.esbensen.dk
Brundtland City Energy Network
http://www.cabe.org.uk
Commission for Architecture and the Built Environment, UK
http://www.capelightcompact.org
The Cape Light Compact – Regional aggregated renewable energy supply in
  Massachusetts
http://www.citiesnet.uwe.ac.uk
European Sustainable Cities
http://www.energie-cites.org
Energie-Cités Association: Promoting sustainable energy policy through local
  action
http://www.energie-cites.org/db/hanover_566_en.pdf
Hannover, Germany Case Study
http://www.energiestadt.ch
Swiss national energy programme
http://www.europeangreencities.com
European Green Cities Network (EGCN)
http://www.global-vision.org/city/aalborg.html
The European Sustainable Cities and Towns Campaign
http://www.greencity.dk
Green City Denmark – Forside
http://www.greenpowergovs.org
Information on local government policies and programmes in the United States
http://www.iclei.org/co2
Cities for Climate Protection™ (CCP)/International Council for Local Environmental Initiatives
http://www.iges.or.jp/en/index.html
Asian sustainable cities resource – Institute for Global Environmental Strategies
http://www.ladwp.com/ladwp/cms/ladwp001220.jsp
Los Angeles Department of Water and Power (LADWP) – Renewable Energy
  Sources
http://www.lipower.org/solar
Long Island Power Authority's Solar Pioneers programme
http://www.pbs.org/frontlineworld/fellows/brazil1203
PBS Program 'Frontline' story on Brazil's Curitiba Urban Experiment
http://www.seattle.gov/light/Green/greenPower/greenup.asp
Seattle City Light Green Up Renewable Energy Program, United States
http://www.sierraclub.org/globalwarming/coolcities/renewable.asp
Cool Cities – Renewable Energy Solutions
http://www.siliconvalleypower.com/res/?doc=renewable
Silicon Valley Power City of Santa Clara Renewable Energy Program, United
  States
http://www.smud.org/green/index.html
Sacramento Municipal Utility District renewable energy programs,
  California, USA

http://www.sustainable.org
Sustainable Communities Network (SCN)
http://www.sustainability.org.uk
Environ – Local environmental initiative, UK
http://www.sustainable-cities.org.uk
European Sustainable Cities Project, Campaign Interactive
http://www.sustainableportland.org
City of Portland – Office of Sustainable Development
http://www.theclimategroup.org
The Climate Group – Advancing business and government leadership on
    climate change
http://www.unchs.org/scp
Sustainable Cities Programme of the United Nations Centre for Human
    Settlements
http://www.votesolar.org
The Vote Solar Initiative promoting the implementation of solar projects by city
    governments in California, USA
http://web.mit.edu/urbanupgrading
Upgrading Urban Communities – A Resource for Practitioners


## 2 Sustainable building guidance tools, and solar design research

http://www.basix.nsw.gov.au
BASIX – Building Sustainability Index
http://www.iea-shc.org
International Energy Agency – Solar Heating and Cooling Programme
http://www.oja-services.nl/iea-pvps
IEA Photovoltaic Power Systems Programme
http://pvcityguide.energyprojects.net
PV City Guide project supported by the European Commissions


## 3 Renewable energy, energy efficiency, greenhouse

http://www.climatenetwork.org
Climate Action Network (CAN)
http://www.climnet.org
Climate Action Network Europe (CNE)
http://www.dsireusa.org
Database of State Incentives for Renewable Energy, United States
http://www.eere.energy.gov/de/electric_utility_regulation.html
U.S. Department of Energy – Energy Efficiency and Renewable Energy 'Distrib-
    uted Energy Program Deployment'
http://www.eere.energy.gov/RE/solar-intl.html
U.S Department of Energy – Energy Efficiency and Renewable Energy 'Interna-
    tional Organisations'
http://www.erec-renewables.org

EREC – European Renewable Energy Council
http://www.eurosolar.org
EUROSOLAR – The European Association for Renewable Energy
http://www.greenhouse.gov.au/renewable/index.html
Renewable Energy in Australia – Australian Greenhouse Office, Department of
   the Environment and Heritage
http://www.greenprices.com
GreenPrices – Market for green energy in Europe
http://www.inforse.org
International Network for Sustainable Energy
http://www.ises.org
ISES – The International Solar Energy Society
http://www.nef.org.uk
The National Energy Foundation, UK
http://www.nrglink.com
Green Energy News – Renewable Energy Technology, Issues, Policy and
   Business
http://www.resetters.org
RESET – Renewable Energy Strategies For European Towns
http://www.wcre.org
World Council for Renewable Energy
http://www.whitepaper.ises.org
ISES Whitepaper Transitioning to a Renewable Energy Future
http://www.wrenuk.co.uk
WREC/WREN – World Renewable Energy Congress/ Network


## 4 Renewable energy, efficiency and sustainability of buildings and urban areas

http://www.bundesbaugesellschaft.de/en/index1.htm
Bundesbaugesellschaft Berlin MBH
http://www.eere.energy.gov/buildings/database/index.cfm
US Department of Energy – Energy Efficiency and Renewable Program
Buildings Database
http://www.egbf.org/index.htm
EGBF – European Green Building Forum
http://greenbuilding.ca/iisbe/gbpn
Green Building Policies Network (GBpN), Netherlands
http://www.gbcaus.org
Green Building Council of Australia
http://www.greenhouse.gov.au/renewable/recp/pv/fifteen.html
Queen Victoria Markets urban integrated photovoltaics, Victoria, Australia
http://www.millionsolarroofs.org
U.S. Department of Energy partnership program
http://www.nrel.gov
A national laboratory of the US Department of Energy Office of Energy Efficiency
   & Renewable Energy

http://www.rmi.org/sitepages/pid208.php
Rocky Mountain Institute – International Netherlands Group (ING) Bank, Amsterdam, Netherlands
http://www.seav.vic.gov.au/buildings/etf/projects/current_projects.asp
Sustainability Victoria, Australia
http://www.solarbau.de/english_version/index.htm
Energy Optimized Building - SolarBau
http://www.solarintegration.de/index.php?id=1
Information on building with photovoltaics, Germany
http://www.task23.com
IEA Task 23 – Optimisation of solar energy use in large buildings
http://www.toolbase.org
ToolBase Services – The Home Building Industry's Technical Information Resource, United States


## 5 New Urbanism and transit-oriented development

http://www.apta.com/research/info/briefings/briefing_8.cfm
American Public Transportation Association: Transit Resource Guide
http://www.congresswest.com.au/TOD
Congress for the New Urbanism
http://www.cnu.org
Congress for the New Urbanism
http://www.eurocities.org
Eurocities, Car Free Cities (CFC)
http://www.metrokc.gov/kcdot/transit/tod
King County Department of Transportation, 'Transit-oriented development'
http://www.newurbanism.org/pages/532105
Centre for Transit Oriented Development: New Urbanism
http://www.reconnectingamerica.org/html/TOD
Reconnecting America: The Center for Transit-Oriented Development
http://www.rtd-denver.com/Projects/TOD
The Regional Transportation District, Denver – Transit Oriented Development
http://www.todadvocate.com
Transit Oriented Development Advocate
http://transitorienteddevelopment.dot.ca.gov
California Transit Oriented Development Database
http://www.vtpi.org/tdm/tdm45.htm
Online TDM Encyclopedia – Transit Oriented Development


## 6 Sustainable development in general

http://www.care2.com/channels/ecoinfo/sustainable_development
EcoInfo> Sustainable development links
http://www.ecnc.nl/bep/infor/links/dirorg.html
Directory of Organisations on Sustainable Development Organisations (Brabant European Partnership)

http://www.ecosustainable.com.au/links.htm
Ecosustainable Links – Eco Sustainable Gateway & Resources
http://www2.gtz.de/urbanet
Network for Regionalisation, Decentralisation and Municipal Development
http://www.mfe.govt.nz/publications/urban/urban-sustainability-worldwide-nov03/html
Urban Sustainability Worldwide: An Information Resource for Urban Practitioners, Ministry for the Environment, NZ
http://www.peakoil.net
ASPO – The Association for the Study of Peak Oil and Gas
http://www.peakoil.org
Peak Oil – The end of cheap energy
http://www.rmi.org
Rocky Mountain Institute
http://www.unchs.org
UN-HABITAT – United Nations Human Settlements Programme
http://www.worldenergy.org
World Energy Council – Energy for sustainable development

## 7 Ecosystem assessment
http://www.greenfacts.org
GreenFacts – Facts on Health and the Environment
http://www.millenniumassessment.org
Millennium Ecosystem Assessment

## 8 Micro-finance and sustainable development
http://www.grameen-info.org
Grameen Bank microfinance foundation
http://www.grameen-info.org/grameen/gshakti
Grameen's renewable energy based income generation programme
http://www.gvep.org
Global Village Energy Partnership
http://www.strohalm.org
Strohalm Complementary Currency Systems – New Money Systems for a Sustainable Economy

## 9 Specific urban technology product references
http://www.cleanenergy.de/related2.html
Portal for clean energy related sites
http://www.greenandgoldenergy.com.au
SunBall solar concentrators

## 10 Renewable energy portals; conference portals
http://www.cabinet.nsw.gov.au/greenhouse

The New South Wales Greenhouse Office
http://www.greenpowerconferences.com
Green Power Conferences – Renewable Energy and Energy Efficiency Exhibitions and Conferences
http://www.renewableenergyaccess.com
Renewable Energy Access – Renewable energy news and information network
http://www.solarpaces.org
Concentrating Solar Power / solar-thermal technology


## 11 Mapping resources and resource mapping

http://swera.unep.net/swera/index.php
United Nations Environment Program Solar and Wind Energy Resource Assessment (UNEP SWERA)
http://www.energyatlas.org
Renewable Energy Atlas of the West, United States


## 12 Solar City advice, assessment, rating, strategic guidance and design

http://www.epolis.com.au
Epolis – Strategic services in urban design and development, climate change and sustainability
http://www.hermann-scheer.de
Dr Hermann Scheer – Member of the Bundestag, Member of the German House of Parliament, President of EUROSOLAR, General Chairman of the World Council for Renewable Energy
http://www.solarcity.org
Solar City™ program resources

CURE – Centre for Urban and Regional Ecology 2004, 'Adaptation Strategies for Climate Change in the Urban Environment (ASCCUE).' University of Manchester: School of Planning and Landscape; Newsletter 1 and 2, http://www.sed.manchester.ac.wc/research/are/projects/current/Asccue.htm

Karekezi, S, L Majoro and T Johnson 2003, 'Climate Change Mitigation Strategies from the Transport Sector – Priorities for the World Bank.' AFREPREN and World Bank, New York: Institute for Transport and Development Policy (ITDP). Retrieved on 9 July 2006 from http://www.itdp.org/read/Karakzei%20and%20Johnson%20GEF%20Africa.pdf

Keiner, M and Arley Kim 2006, 'Transnational City Networks for Sustainability.' Draft version dated 23 February 2006. Institute for Spatial and Landscape Planning, ETH Zürich, Switzerland. Forthcoming as article in *European Planning Studies* Retrieved on 10 July 2006 from http://www.bml.csiro.au/susnetnl/netwl2SE.pdf

# Index

*Note*: Figures in italics indicate captions; those in bold type indicate Glossary terms.